Networked Humanities

NEW MEDIA THEORY
Series Editor, Byron Hawk

The New Media Theory series investigates both media and new media as complex rhetorical ecologies. The merger of media and new media creates a global public sphere that is changing the ways we work, play, write, teach, think, and connect. Because these ecologies operate through evolving arrangements, theories of new media have yet to establish a rhetorical and theoretical paradigm that fully articulates this emerging digital life.

The series includes books that deploy rhetorical, social, cultural, political, textual, aesthetic, and material theories in order to articulate moments of mediation that compose these contemporary media ecologies. Such works typically bring rhetorical and critical theories to bear on media and new media in ways that elaborate on a burgeoning post-disciplinary "material turn" as one further development of the linguistic and social turns that have already influenced scholarly work across the humanities.

BOOKS IN THE SERIES

NETWORKED HUMANITIES

WITHIN AND WITHOUT THE UNIVERSITY

Edited by Jeff Rice and Brian McNely

Parlor Press
Anderson, South Carolina
www.parlorpress.com

Parlor Press LLC, Anderson, South Carolina, USA
© 2018 by Parlor Press
All rights reserved.
Printed in the United States of America on acid-free paper.

S A N: 2 5 4 - 8 8 7 9

Library of Congress Cataloging-in-Publication Data on File

978-1-64317-017-6 (paperback)
978-1-64317-018-3 (hardcover)
978-1-64317-019-0 (PDF)
978-1-64317-020-6 (ePub)

1 2 3 4 5

New Media Theory
Series Editor: Byron Hawk

Cover image: Photo by Brian McNely. Used by permission
Copyeditor: Jared Jameson.
Cover design: David Blakesley

Parlor Press, LLC is an independent publisher of scholarly and trade titles
in print and multimedia formats. This book is available in paper, cloth and
eBook formats from Parlor Press on the World Wide Web at http://www.
parlorpress.com or through online and brick-and-mortar bookstores. For
submission information or to find out about Parlor Press publications, write
to Parlor Press, 3015 Brackenberry Drive, Anderson, South Carolina, 29621,
or email editor@parlorpress.com.

Contents

Networked Humanities

1 Introduction: Networked Humanities

Jeff Rice and Brian McNely

In our contemporary environment of decimated state funding, administrative and bureaucratic entropy, attacks on the Humanities from local and national legislative bodies, and the concomitant burgeoning of the digital humanities, scholarly responses struggle to respond. There are endless defenses of the Humanities, and such defenses are even more exigent in the wake of the 2016 presidential election. Such responses focus on traditional Humanities outcomes: critical thinking, questioning, interpretation, language usage, understanding different perspectives, and the ability to form an argument. These outcomes are, no doubt, goals of a Humanities-based education. On their own, however, they do not address what might be called the networked humanities, humanities-based work that does not reside in one space or object of study but in the interactions—the network—of multiple sites of learning.

To ask what a networked humanities *is* or might *be* is to both shape and deconstruct a view of the world, and a way of living and working within it. It begs new research questions, new objects of scholarly study, new attention to the nature of the humanities in general. As the notion of a digital humanities takes shape and congeals, the authors in this collection explore the humanities and networks, and in some cases, the humanities *as* network. The approach of *Networked Humanities* is therefore both aligned with and potentially orthogonal to work in the digital humanities. This is because networks are both digital and not, just as humanistic pursuits are both digital and not. These questions currently exist at the periphery of digital humanities scholarship; this collection makes such questions central to our work as humanists, within and without the university. To that end, *Networked Humanities* is an intervention into the questions and ideas traditionally posed by the Humanities, but it does so at the level of the network.

Generally, digital humanities scholarship has focused on the computational, particularly regarding the study of literature or artistic practices. The computational, in turn, has offered the digital humanities alternative approaches to interpretation. *Networked humanities*, on the other hand, offer more open and inclusive terms for humanistic inquiry, ones not bound to interpretation or specific disciplinary focuses. Despite the presence of "network" in this volume's title, the networked humanities, we contend, is not dependent on the computational. Instead, this volume is an intervention in digital humanities work as it proposes other objects and methods of study left out of traditional digital humanities conversations. As Clay Spinuzzi summarizes Bruno Latour's work: "differences in quality are no longer what we're investigating" ("Symmetry as a Methodological Move" 35). What is or is not the digital humanities (i.e., the degree of quality at stake when a body of study is incorporated into an approach) is not the focus of this volume; instead, the focus is on the networked spaces of inquiry, research, and pedagogy among a variety of digital humanities spaces and interactions.

For the past decade, as the digital humanities has gained prominence in English departments, information science, and library science, it has held to a strict, or narrow, disciplinary category instead of a more open network for the humanities—one that often fails to account for digital moments outside of that narrow scope. Pedagogy is one such moment. In 2012, for example, academic publications shared no shortage of the humanities' declarations of concern over the rise of MOOCs (Massive Online Open Courses). Stanford professors Sebastian Thrun and Peter Norvig's course "Artificial Intelligence"—with 160,000 students enrolled—had sparked widespread interest and critique regarding the usage of digital environments for large-scale teaching. While digital education was not new to the humanities and other areas of study, digital education on such a massive scale represented either liberation or oppression for many humanists as they responded to the influx of MOOC attention. Historian William Thomas commented on the evocation of "unrestrained hyperbole about the 'reinvention' of higher education" found in MOOCs. Andrew Delblanco's lament for the supposed loss of face-to-face interactions in MOOCs was sarcastically titled "The MOOCs of Hazard." Writing in the *MIT Technology Review*, Nicholas Carr took no position on the matter, but titled his piece as a foreshadowed disaster in waiting: "The Crisis in Higher Education." Beyond the general fears of inferior education, a loss of face-to-face interaction, and increasing efforts to limit the size of the tenure line professoriate that MOOCs raised for the humanities, the digital humanities remained fairly silent, and few commentaries emerged from digital humanists. Its most prominent voices, beyond Duke's Cathy Davidson, offered little interest in the MOOC phenomenon and kept their focus, instead, on non-pedagogical or institutional disruptions such as data mining, the preservation of media artifacts, and textual archiving.

Indeed, the overall question of pedagogy—online or face to face—has not been a major issue for the digital humanities since its initial appearance, often traced to the publication of John Unsworth and Ray Siemen's 2004 *A Companion to Digital Humanities.* That text, it might be noted, only features five occurrences of the word "pedagogy." Matthew Kirschenbaum's canonical "What is the Digital Humanities, and What is it Doing in English Departments?" notes that "Whatever else it might be then, the digital humanities today is about a scholarship (and a pedagogy) that is publicly visible in ways to which we are generally unaccustomed" but offers little regarding what that pedagogy might entail beyond hermeneutical readings of texts in digital contexts (6). While the HASTAC (Humanities, Arts, Science, and Technology Alliance) website features graduate students discussing—to some extent—issues of pedagogy, and while *The Chronicle of Higher Education* ran a January 2013 piece on digital humanities teaching at UCLA,[1] pedagogy is mostly absent from journals associated with the digital humanities or recent publications in this area of scholarly interest. Burdick et al.'s collaborative *Digital Humanities* offers no discussion of the digital spaces that support humanities teaching. Contributors to David Berry's collection *Understanding Digital Humanities* are silent on the issue. With all the attention to texts and new media

---

1. See http://chronicle.com/article/How-the-Humanities-Compute-in/143809/

present in the digital humanities, one wonders why teaching is absent from the majority of conversations?

Still, we do not begin this volume on networked humanities with a critique of this lack of interest in digital or online teaching. Many areas of scholarly interest ignore the pedagogical, and what we call network humanities is not obligated to be pedagogical either. Instead, the digital humanities' lack of pedagogical attentiveness, even as its literature often calls for inclusiveness, serves as an exigence for a larger issue regarding what is or what is not classified as belonging within the digital humanities or its overall network of self-declared inclusion. Digital humanists obviously teach even if they divorce teaching from a great deal of their scholarship. The lack of pedagogy, though, indicates that the "big tent" of the digital humanities may not be as inclusive as claimed. The lack of such an important aspect of higher education points to the larger issue of why the digital humanities lacks a networked perspective regarding the influence of the digital on humanities based work.

The notion of a "big tent" digital humanities is a metaphor often heralded by scholars as what William Pannapaker calls "the comprehensive activist project that uses technology to respond to the interconnected cultural and structural problems of academe."[2] This use of "interconnected," however, excludes, among other things, the most basic aspect of higher education: pedagogy. Even Patrik Svenson's effort to move away from the popular "big tent" metaphor, captured in the collection *Debates in the Digital Humanities*, leaves him with the limited observation that "the interrelation between the humanities and the digital can be discussed in terms of different modes of engagement: the digital or technology as tool, study object, medium, laboratory, and activist venue" (41). Once again, pedagogy remains outside of the tent. By ignoring this aspect of university and humanities work—the basic area of teaching—digital humanities scholarship demonstrates a limited network of influence and research. Thus, one might question, overall, the network the digital humanities recognizes as part of its own taxonomic status. Indeed, we can ask: Are the terms *network* and *big tent* both part of the same category? Do both approaches exemplify the digital humanities in its supposedly interconnected status? Does a big tent provide the same kind of connectivity a network does? If the

---

2. See Stanford University's 2011 "Big Tent Digital Humanities" conference and William Pannapacker's coverage of the event http://chronicle.com/article/Big-Tent-Digital-Humanities/128434/

"computational turn" facilitates "disciplinary hybridity that leads to a post-disciplinary university," as David Berry argues (13), there would appear to be little room for the network or networks the humanities finds itself within (and within itself). In that sense, we can inquire whether the digital humanities is actually part of a larger network of thought that should not include pedagogy but should emphasize specific areas of academic and non-academic interest. Such a question asks how the digital humanities envisions its own network of influence and activity across academic and non-academic venues. Network, it often seems, does not appear as a keyword vital for digital humanities work. Even when Berry calls for a post-digital humanities as response to current digital humanities scholarship, that focus seems to be something other than networked, asking only that scholarship "critically analyze the way in which cadences of the computational are made and materialized" ("Post-Digital Humanities"). Critique may be in the network, but it is not the network itself, as Berry suggests. And the network, as we've noted, is not always computational.

Network is an often-used term, or keyword, in digital studies, if not the digital humanities. Steven Shaviro, Manuel Castells, Alex Galloway, John Law, Bruno Latour and others have used the term to describe a variety of political, economic, philosophical, spatial, and textual phenomena that exist in a culture that, in the words of Marshall McLuhan, resembles the global village. Castells's specific understanding is partly based on the concept of

> two fundamental attributes of the network: its *connectedness*, that is, its structural ability to facilitate noise-free communication between its components; and its *consistency*, that is, the extent to which there is a sharing of interest between the network's goals and the goals of its components. (171)

Like Deleuze, and to a large extent, Castells as well, Alexander Galloway and Eugene Thacker view networks through the lens of structural ability as well, particularly that of a given structure's relationship to control:

> Human subjects thrive on network interaction (kin groups, clans, the social), yet the moments when the network logic takes over—in the mob or the swarm, in contagion or infection—are the moments that are the most disorienting, the most threatening to the integrity of the human ego. (5)

For Barry Wellman and Lee Raine, issues of control are left aside as the authors detail how we live in a networked social operating system where networked individualism predominates; networked individualism allows people to "function more as connected individuals and less as embedded group members" (12). Their focus shifts attention away from structural issues (the state, the institution, the group) and proposes the individual (person or subject) as what connects. Proposing new controls in digital humanities scholarship, Nathan Johnson argues for influence over the individual, offering a practice of factor mapping, a networked examination of "unconsidered factors significantly influencing how institutions, geography, friendship links, or a number of other factors shape texts" (106). Within the category of network, as this brief overview attests, we find another keyword: connected. One would assume that connected spaces, such as networked individualism or connected influence, extend from the individual to the discipline, the concept, the ideology, and the humanities as a whole. If people (individuals) are networked beings and not only groups embody the network, one would assume that so are objects of study and their accompanying ideologies.

Even if that point were the case, seldom is the term *network* used to describe the specific situations and issues faced by the loosely bounded group of individual objects of study we call the humanities. The humanities, with all its interlinking and contradictory parts, too, is a network, whether its individual bodies recognize that point or not. Indeed, the humanities has always been a network. Bruno Latour, in particular, taught that nothing is ever outside of a network. "Network is a concept, not a thing out there," Latour writes (*Reassembling* 131). By that point, Latour means that a network is not necessarily a physical object you point to—such as a department or university—but the various connections that make up a belief, body, subject, action, and so on. The best way to understand the network, Latour teaches, is to follow the connections or traces connections produce. A network is the "trace left behind by some moving agent" (*Reassembling* 132). While telephone, computer, railroad, and other communication/transportation hubs are popular objects of study for network analysis (exemplified in the few examples mentioned here) because of both their physical and conceptual construction, a network need not be reduced to such obvious items. "The consequence," Latour argues regarding tracing network activity in any number of areas (what is also called

actor–network theory), "is that you can provide an actor–network account of a symphony, a piece of legislation, a rock from the moon, an
engraving" (*Reassembling* 131). Thus, any engagement of actors produces traces—expressions, ideas, beliefs, failures, success, objects of
study, etc.—and these traces show the network in play. One would
think that an area of interest explicitly called *digital* humanities would
have taken up discussion and research of its own occupied networks,
from within and without the university, but it hasn't. Pedagogy is but
one example of that lack. Others, no doubt, exist.

Ours is not solely a project of reading. Instead of focusing on its
own ever-changing networks, digital humanities scholarship studies
tools for textual and cultural reading, studies textual reading overall,
and studies the identification of patterns among that reading in order
to foster complex interpretative strategies supposedly absent in nondigital forms. That is not to say that all digital humanities projects are
based on reading, but many remain as such. This reading presumably
allows for better interpretative practices that are essential to the humanities in general. As Stephen Ramsey writes of his own algorithmic
criticism (whose focus is textual reading), "the hermeneutic proposed
by algorithmic criticism does not oppose the practice of conventional
critical reading, but instead attempts to reenvision its logics in extreme
and self-conscious forms" (32). These forms can be traced throughout
digital humanities scholarship in order to reveal a network of reading
and interpretive practices.

While that tracing would reveal a network (the various actors who
assemble a given moment of reading), it would not reveal the larger
network of digital studies scholarship relevant to the humanities that
this volume presents. A networked humanities would obviously include reading practices, but it must—to be a network—include much
more. When "Networked Humanities: From Within and Without
the University," took place on February 14–15, 2013 at the University of Kentucky, the rationale for the event was to situate broader
networked tracings of scholarship relevant to humanities work, tracings that were not limited to reading or interpretive practices only.
Attendees from a variety of disciplines and from various universities
and colleges presented networked approaches to problems and issues
relevant to humanities scholarship and the overall question of what a
networked humanities is or might be. Journal dissemination, reading
practices, pedagogy, disciplinary evolution, database logics, geographi-

cal approaches, and other issues dominated the two-day event. This volume is our attempt to provide a portion of the event to a broad readership in order to further the conversation, to extend network studies into the realm of the university itself. This volume, in other words, offers a semblance of a networked tracing of two days at the University of Kentucky, whose own tracings were of a variety of humanities related items, moments, beliefs, and events. This Introduction frames the event as a continuing response to the digital humanities and networked perspectives.

Because networked tracings are difficult and never complete, it is not possible to accurately situate all possible understandings of the conversation regarding networked humanities work that took place at the University of Kentucky. No volume could capture all of the networks within networks in which participants, discussions, moments after the event, and moments shared online participated. Even Latour, whose networked accounts are canonical in this area of study, admits to never being able to fully trace any given network. As his fictional character Norbert declares in *Aramis*: "the farther we go, the more crowded [this investigation] is. Every part of the system is as complicated as the systems as a whole. Every plate we unfold is itself made up of plates to be unfolded!" (*Aramis* 243). Instead of that type of totalizing attempt, we offer in this volume connections and disconnections, provocations, collated and juxtaposed fragments, patterns, and other items relevant to network thinking. We offer no grand narrative or totalizing "big tent" figuration of what a networked humanities is or might be. Big tents are fine, but no tent, as Norbert learned, could be big enough; instead, we offer tracings and trails through disparate areas of thought. Sometimes these tracings move through the tent, but sometimes they do not.

Rather than think of tents, we want to think in terms of connections. In that sense, one might think of this collection as a set, or network, of ideas and approaches that shape a position regarding the networked humanities. Raymond Williams understood that keywords—terms and positions—shape institutional behavior and ideology. Even though he never used the term network, Williams' breakdown of keywords functions as a type of tracing of networked language. Culture, one of Williams' most famous keywords, is "one of the two or three most complicated words in the English language," Williams writes, "mainly because it has now come to be used for important concepts in several distinct intellectual disciplines and in several distinct and incompatible systems of thought" (87). Digital humanists and humanists in general, we believe, might suggest the same logic regarding the term network. But to assume network as a keyword, it is also useful to note its own incorporation of other keywords into itself—its nodes within its own network. We want to consider for a moment key terms that speak to a *networked humanities* so that the distinct and incompatible is viewed as belonging within the same sphere of influence and being. If it is possible to clarify *what* a *networked humanities is*, it might be possible to do so via some of its key terms: aggregation, node, juxtaposition, fragment, weave, and splice. These, we can surmise, are keywords shaping a networked humanities. These are the parts of a larger networked keyword we refer to as the humanities. These are parts that provide a departure point for the collection much in the way Williams' work with keywords provided a departure point for cultural studies.

Networks, after all, are made up of a variety of actors as well, actors that include the key terms and words used to define and inform. Theories such as object-oriented ontology borrow from Latour the notion that non-human actors affect thought as much as humans do. As Ian Bogost writes,

> The objects of object-oriented thought mean to encompass *anything whatsoever*, from physical matter (a Slurpee frozen beverage) to properties (frozenness) to marketplaces (the convenience store industry) to symbols (the Slurpee brand name) to ideas (a best guess about where to find a 7–11). The density of being makes it *promiscuous*. Anything is thing enough to party. (23–24)

A keyword, as one such non-human actor, plays a significant role in how networked humanities might form or be traced because of the ideological and theoretical shaping it might perform. We can consider these offered keywords as a set of some of those actors whose interaction with humans and nonhumans generates a version of a networked humanities. Version itself might be a keyword as well since, following Latour, if one swaps out one part of the network (i.e., substitutes a keyword), another network (version) forms. Thus, ours is but one version of a networked humanities. As readers make their way through this collection, we ask that they consider these terms as influential regarding *Networked Humanities* and *the ideas it proposes*. The network humanities, as proposed in this collection, is not an opposition to the digital humanities but another iteration of the digital humanities concept circulating throughout the humanities.

Aggregation

RSS (Really Simple Syndication) popularized aggregation for web-browser reading by placing website feeds in one location; this meant that information was bundled and delivered to individuals, replacing the need to visit websites separately for new updates. Even with the closure of Google's popular RSS reader, aggregation continues: as a logic of assemblage (parts of thinking consolidating into one space) and feeds (delivering images, news, ideas, short movie clips, status updates) into one space. More broadly, information consumption has become naturalized as feeds. Short, continuously updated excerpts or fragmented pieces of knowledge (or knowledge potential) are delivered into our digital and physical spaces—syndicated. We base interpretations, arguments, and information acquisition on these feeds. While we still cling to totalizing narratives within the humanities as tools for explaining various phenomena, we also have to recognize the importance of feed logic. The feed does not simply provide information; instead, it provides a *wider breadth* of information that is of the moment, information that is placed, by default, in juxtaposition with other incoming items, often serendipitously. Contributions to a discussion on the networked humanities, in turn, can be thought of as feeds—streams of potential aggregation.

Node

The principal point of connection in a network is a node. "Each of us is part of a larger cluster," Albert-László Barabási writes (18). In those clusters, we discover nodes connecting to other nodes. "It require[s] only one link per node to stay connected" (*Linked* 18). Too often, we concentrate on obvious nodes such as a text connecting to another text (intertextuality) and leave aside the supposedly less important nodes (a computer, a time of day, a song, a room, a person, a moment, a belief) that gather in a given cluster. Thomas Rickert's theory of ambient rhetoric potentially alters our view of nodes and clusters, and more important, what kinds of ambiguous, nuanced, and everyday nodes influence work in the humanities. Material environments, accompanying sounds, and nonhuman objects abound in a networked humanities; the key difference, however, is that in a networked humanities we may attend to and trace node formations and connections through and beyond texts alone. Nodes may be affective, sensory, or largely nonhuman. In a networked humanities, the roster of potential agents broadens, and nodes may thus emerge in unexpected ways. Rickert argues that "the things of the world take on real agency; we do not gather things but are rather gathered across them" (15). How might a networked humanities function as one such gathering?

Juxtaposition

When unlikely items brush against each other, Marshall McLuhan famously noted, the results are startling and effective. From the remix to sampling to the CNN website, information is constantly being juxtaposed with unlikely items. Juxtaposition can be trivialized as a form of digital expression (LOL Cat memes as juxtaposed cat photographs with misspelled text) or can be valorized as a form of social critique (remixes of John Pike pepper-spraying Occupy Wall Street protestors at the University of California Davis in November, 2011). Unlike Fredric Jameson's canonical critique of pastiche (a type of juxtaposition) as anti-historical (the joining of temporal reference points in *American Graffiti*, Jameson claims, ignores Civil Rights issues), the combinatory acts of juxtaposition need not be reduced to a politics or ideology. Instead, we might consider, particularly from the vantage point of humanities scholarship, what the startling and effective results of disciplinary joinings might entail or are fostering. Within any given humanities network, unlike material is brushing against other unlike material. Which startling and effective results occur in the assemblage?

Fragment

Lester Faigley's *Fragments of Rationality*, an exploration of the postmodern subject and the teaching and theory of composition studies, attempted to reconcile traditional humanist concerns such as the "humane values" of the Declaration of Independence to the nuanced situatedness of lived experience (46). To argue that humane values are heterogeneous and local—rather than homogenous and global—is to introduce fissures into the bedrock of foundational principles and cherished notions. Valuing fragments and fragmented experience, in other words, changes not only perspectives on values and traditions, but on objects of study and ways of doing scholarship. Fragmentation is cha-otic on the surface (16). Yet, as Steven Shaviro has argued, networks may be shaped like fractals (12). Such network structures are self-sim-ilar; what seems fragmented and chaotic may in fact be patterned and regular. The logic of fragments reveals how a networked humanities embraces a both–and moment: fragments are situated and nuanced, and embracing new fragments may yield new forms of scholarship and new research questions. At the same time, certain patterns may emerge and persist. In the aggregate, the logic of fragmentation is *both* chaotic *and* patterned. What fragments emerge, therefore, in a networked hu-manities, and what do network tracings and new digital tools mean for a humanities open to exploring them and their potentiality?

Weave and Splice

Clay Spinuzzi's 2008 book *Network* explores the conflation, develop-ment, and interpenetration of networks in both material and symbolic forms. Spinuzzi places cultural-historical activity theory into dialogue with actor–network theory throughout the book, not simply to dis-cern which approach is more effective for understanding networks, but in order to explore what each approach contributes to studies of networks. In other words, Spinuzzi explores the complex phenomena of networks with a complex methodology—one that productively bal-ances the tensions between two very different conceptualizations of networks. In activity theory, with its roots in Lev Vygotsky's studies of childhood learning and development, networks are *woven* together from linked systems of activity. In everyday life, these systems some-times overlap and become entangled, but the logic and structure of underlying activity systems may still be discerned. In activity theory, therefore, a strong emphasis is placed on human intentionality, agency, and labor, where the relationship between humans and nonhumans is asymmetrical. In contrast, the actor–networks of actor–network theo-ry encompass both humans and nonhumans in associational, rhizom-atic, symmetric assemblages. ANT is an ontology rather than a theory of human development (*Network* 62); for ANT, networks are *spliced* together from both human and nonhuman actants.

Spinuzzi shows how the logic of the weave and the logic of the splice substantively shape theories of networks. By tracing the hetero-geneous people, practices, and texts that move through one organiza-tion—itself enmeshed in and a provider of both material and symbolic networks—Spinuzzi demonstrates how both logics are often operative simultaneously. In other words, our networks are *both* woven *and* spliced. Sometimes we may trace the clearly woven development of a particular network; at other times we capitalize on opportunities to splice networks together into new, hybrid formations. Network aggregates weave and develop over time, while network fragments are periodically spliced together, creating new nodes from previously unaligned juxtapositions. As Latour has argued, our networks grow and transform by lengthening enrollments, by incorporating ever more fragments, and by aligning humans and nonhumans in wider, stronger associations (*Science*).

Networked Humanities: Arguments and Provocations

The various logics and affordances embedded in the conceptual frameworks and keywords discussed above help bring a networked humanities into relief. In a networked humanities, the weave and the splice continually oscillate. We ask readers to acknowledge this volume's contributions as a series of woven and spliced nodes in a juxtaposed space of aggregated ideas, fragments whose meaning is found within the network itself. We ask from readers, therefore, to consider the potential networks that the humanities belong within and to network with this volume's specific approaches that weave the digital through the humanities. In some ways, the humanities have always been networked, even when they have not been digital. Our work juxtaposes fragments, coalesces and massages aggregates into nodes, weaves and splices public ideas, university teaching, and archival recovery. That this work is now substantively digital, and that it is accomplished in new ways, is no small matter. But from a networked perspective, it may be no large matter either. Instead, when the humanities is explored via the logics of networks, the digital and the nondigital, the human and the nonhuman, the archival and the ephemeral, and the political and the banal are symmetrically engaged and considered anew. This volume presents an array of such engagements.

This volume contains two kinds of contributions: individual chapters that extend arguments originally made at the Networked Humanities conference and shorter, invited provocations from scholars whose work emerges from or intersects with the humanities. In chapter 3,

"A Natural History of Networks," Jeff Pruchnic takes us back to the thirteenth century as a starting point for exploring the techno-cultural networks that have shaped humanities research and practice in the West. Pruchnic's argument looks forward, however, to imagine possible futures for a digital and networked humanities. Pruchnic helps us see that the historical development of network as a notion encompasses significantly more than what is typically understood in contemporary usage of the term. Networks are too often reduced to "network computing," while historical notions of networks incorporated nuanced perspectives on space and time. Most important, he argues that the humanities has, in the past, adapted slowly to changes in previous cultural conceptions of networks; by yoking work in the humanities to work in the social and natural sciences, however, an adaptive and networked humanities may better respond to the rapid advance of network computing and digital media.

Pruchnic's argument thus establishes the groundwork for the provocative networked reading of Jillian Sayre and James Brown, Jr. In chapter 4, "Reading in Slow Motion: Thinking with the Network," Sayre and Brown describe an undergraduate course designed to blur the boundaries between the network and the classroom. Drawing on a Latourian notion of networks, they encouraged their students to become "network administrators, attending to reading and writing as an experience of navigating a text's inter and intranets." In this way, they fostered a pedagogy of thinking and writing *with* the network, where the central text, *Moby Dick*, is but one node among many. Their arguments are made from data collected during the course, primarily student writing and aggregation in the Tumblr blogging platform. Ultimately, Sayre and Brown reimagine the notion of distraction in a networked humanities. In this sense, distraction is a mode of attunement to network possibilities across both deep and hyper forms of attention.

Chapters 8 and 12 offer important perspectives on new materialisms and network infrastructures. Laurie Gries, Jenny Bay, Derek Mueller, and Nathaniel Rivers, like several other authors in this volume, begin by yoking work in the humanities to recent developments in the social sciences. In "New Materialisms, Networks, and Humanities Research," Gries, Bay, Mueller, and Rivers argue that network relations are foundational to new materialist theories that "privilege immanent and emergent relationality." Their chapter extends ideas that were, in Rickert's terms, ambient and enveloping during the Networked Humanities conference: nonhuman things matter, they have suasive and affective potential, and they participate in the networked relations and assemblages of humanities work. In "Homeless Infrastructure," Casey Boyle applies new materialist ideas to a specific case: the potentially exploitative use of unhoused residents of Austin, Texas as "homeless hotspots" during the 2012 South by Southwest conference. Boyle shows how our contemporary network infrastructures enable adaptive reconfigurations of humans and nonhumans, an environment fraught with significant ethical challenges.

Chapters 6, 15, and 19 explore broad institutional, disciplinary, and cultural problems encountered in a networked humanities. John Jones, in chapter 19, "Hacking the Humanities," explores some of the ways in which a networked humanities—and, more specifically, networked tools—will impact humanities research. He argues, in fact, that the humanities itself should be hacked according to contemporary networked logics, creating and sustaining new disciplinary nodes and practices by reshaping both digital and nondigital conceptions of humanities scholarship. In chapter 6, "Networked Asymmetry and Survivability in the Digital Humanities," Nate Kreuter argues for stronger disciplinary networks that connect well-funded digital humanities centers with humanities scholars in diverse institutions so that "the big tent" is not limited to specific sites of knowledge production. Moreover, he suggests that such relationships will foster greater public participation in the work of humanists. Finally, in chapter 15, "The Limitations of Choice: Toward a New Materialist Reading of 'Mommy War' Rhetorics," Naomi Clark traces rhetorics of motherhood through multiple networks as a way of exploring the material effects of globalization, particularly for how a media network institutionalizes ideology.

Chapters 17 and 20 bring this volume's connections to the social and natural sciences into greater relief, positioning a networked humanities as a vital node in epistemological and ontological concerns within and without the university. In chapter 17, Lars Söderlund considers the relationships between the field of psychology's elaboration likelihood model and an expansive theory of rhetoric. Söderlund explores the value of expanding rhetoric's networks to include statistical modeling in the study of persuasion. Söderlund's chapter brings quantitative reasoning to bear on the situational variables that condition rhetorical action. In chapter 20, "Three Theses for an Ontology of Networks," Levi Bryant argues for a materialist theory of networks by drawing from concepts in the physical and natural sciences. He sees social relations (and the networks that support or circumvent them) in entropic terms, focusing in particular on the material and symbolic means by and through which networks generate, maintain, and dissipate energy. Bryant's chapter focuses the attention of humanities scholars on the materiality of networks, and on the extradiscursive objects, relations, and intensities of a networked humanities.

In addition to these chapters, several scholars have contributed concise provocations that answer the question: What *is* a networked humanities, or what might a networked humanities *be*? These provocations are sometimes woven and sometimes spliced among the chapters detailed above, networking this volume itself through challenging juxtapositions and fragments and emergent argumentative nodes that, when seen in the aggregate, comprise a substantive and varied scholarly contribution to a *networked humanities*. As a whole, the scholars contributing to this volume—scholars in rhetoric, writing studies, literature, digital media, computer science, and film—push back, reimagine, contest, and reassemble our views of a networked humanities. Finally, the Afterword written by Byron Hawk explores a model of rhetorical situatedness derived from the control structures of computing languages. "If networks are movements and relations of operations," he argues, "then control structures make those relations work and operate in particular ways." His discussion of networks and rhetorical situatedness, through the example of computing languages and potential exploits, envisions a networked humanities as a way of considering digital and material networks together, as they emerge and co-constitute one another. Hawks's Afterword does not serve as a conclusion, per se, but as one more node within this larger network of connected thoughts, ideals, and actions.

WORKS CITED

Barabási, Albert-László. *Linked: The New Science of Networks*. Perseus, 2002.

Berry, David M. "Post-Digital Humanities: Computation and Cultural Critique in the Arts and Humanities" *Educause Review*, vol. 49, no. 3, May/June 2014, pp 22–26, www.educause.edu/ero/article/post-digital-humanities-computation-and-cultural-critique-arts-and-humanities. Accessed 30 Nov. 2016.

Bogost, Ian. *Alien Phenomonology, or What it's Like to be a Thing*. U of Minnesota P, 2012.

Carr, Nicholas. "The Crisis in Higher Education." *MIT Technology Review*, 27 Sept. 2012, www.technologyreview.com/featuredstory/429376/the-crisis-in-higher-education/. Accessed 30 Nov. 2016.

Castells, Manuel. *The Rise of the Network Society*. Wiley, 2009.

Faigley, Lester. *Fragments of Rationality: Postmodernity and the Subject of Composition*. U of Pittsburgh P, 1992.

Galloway, Alexander and Eugene Thacker. *The Exploit: A Theory of Networks*. U of Minnesota P, 2007.

Johnson, Nathan. "Modeling Rhetorical Disciplinary: Mapping the Digital Network." *Rhetoric and the Digital Humanities*, edited by Jim Ridolfo and William Hart-Davidson, U of Chicago P, 2015, pp. 96–107.

Kirschenbaum, Matthew. "What Is the Digital Humanities, and What Is It Doing in English Departments?" *ADE Bulletin*, no. 150, 2010, pp. 1–7.

Latour, Bruno. *Aramis, or the Love of Technology*. Harvard UP, 1996.

—. *Science in Action: How to Follow Engineers and Scientists Through Society*. Harvard UP, 1987.

Pannapaker, William. "Big-Tent Digital Humanities: A View From the Edge, Part 2." *The Chronicle of Higher Education*, 18 Sept. 2011, chronicle.com/article/Big-Tent-Digital-Humanities-a/129036/. Accessed 30 Nov. 2016.

Raine, Lee, and Barry Wellman. *Networked: The New Social Operating System*. MIT Press, 2012.

Rickert, Thomas. *Ambient Rhetoric: The Attunements of Rhetorical Being*. U of Pittsburgh P, 2013.

Ramsay, Stephen. *Reading Machines: Toward an Algorithmic Criticism*. University of Illinois P, 2011.

Shaviro, Steven. *Connected, or What it Means to Live in a Networked Society*. U of Minnesota P, 2003.

Spinuzzi, Clay. *Network: Theorizing knowledge work in telecommunications*. Cambridge UP, 2008.

—. "Symmetry as a Methodological Move." *Thinking with Bruno Latour in Rhetoric and Composition*, edited by Nathaniel Rivers and Paul Lynch. SIUP, 2015, pp. 23–37.

Svenson, Patrik. "Beyond the Big Tent." *Debates in the Digital Humanities*, edited by Matt Gold, U of Minnesota P, 2012, pp. 36–49.

Williams, Raymond. *Keywords: A Vocabulary of Culture and Society*. Oxford UP, 1976.

Williams, Thomas. "The MOOC Bubble: Where Do We Go From Here?" 28 Jan. 2013, railroads.unl.edu/blog/?p=967.

NETWORKED DISCIPLINARITY

2 Provocation: On the Question of What a Networked Humanities Might Be

Jeffrey T. Grabill

I have been asked to write some provocative words that address the question what is a networked humanities. The context for this provocation, as I understand it, is the continued development of the digital in relation to the humanities (if not, more narrowly, the "digital humanities").

I must admit that the more I think about the question, the less I understand it. I'm also not sure it's the right question, which means my answer might be "who cares?" Let me try to explain.

My lack of understanding begins with the varied ways we humanists use the term *network*. For some it is a material thing, for others it is a technology, and for many more network is a metaphor or a trope. There is much fondness for drawing network diagrams. Those of us who are interested in social network analysis produce different though visually similar representations of "networks." For the most part, we rarely provide our readers with sufficient context to understand how we are using the term. My confusion is often a function the fact that the network is too often a black box. More importantly, "the network" *per se* cannot be the point. What matters is the very human work of *networking*. Verbs matter more than nouns.

The "who cares" aspect of my response is shaped by the thought that perhaps this is the wrong question to ask. A few years ago, my colleagues Bill Hart-Davidson, Mike McLeod, and I wrote a short piece for a larger conversation essay in *Computers and Composition* in which we argued that robots would bring about changes in how writing is practiced and valued. We described these robots as a new class of little machines that might provide things like analytics, listening services, and the like, functions that would collect what people are doing and saying to one another across a variety of media and enable analytics that would make mundane tasks easier (in many cases) but perhaps also produce remarkable insights (in fewer cases).

Whether we were right or wrong about robots is immaterial to my provocation (but we were right). At the WIDE Research Center, we have long argued that we should be making things, and in that short piece that Bill, Mike and I wrote, we argued that we need to be making robots. Here is why making things is so essential for the humanities. The commitment to making things—software, services, analytics, robots—is a commitment to turning theory into objects that do work in the world. Turning theory into material things that do work is both a test of theory and a way to build new theory. But what has always surprised us about the move to make things is how powerfully it brings humans back into the humanities. Yes, there is no question that humans are often part of the networks constructed via various forms of network analysis (e.g., the Networked Materialism section of this book). But it is also true that humanists are just as likely to study objects as humans (see much of this book). It turns out that bringing humans into the humanities is a provocative idea.

Precisely at this moment in human history, issues of meaning, culture, and practice are heightened in importance and some of the most difficult problems we face require humanists to lead. In WIDE's efforts to make things, the most difficult problems were not technological. They were cultural. The most difficult problems required us to build relationships with others, make those relationships the center of our projects, and in doing so, listen and learn from other humans how the digital things we were making should look, act, and feel.

Put differently, if anyone is to make robots, it should be humanists.

So, I'm not sure I understand the question about a networked humanities, and if I did, I'm betting my answer would be "who cares" because I'm not that interested in either networks or the humanities. I

AM deeply interested in humans and the difficult problems we face to live caring and just lives. Those challenges will require the leadership of humanists. To lead, however, will require us to make some (very human) technologies that must be of use. Does it matter what we call it?

WORK CITED

Walker, Janice, Kristine Blair, Douglas Eyman, William Hart-Davidson, Michael McLeod, Jeffrey T. Grabill, Fred Kemp, Mike Palmquist, James Purdy, Madeleine Sorapure, Christine Tulley, and Victor Vitanza. "Computers and Composition 20/20: A Conversation Piece, or What Some Very Smart People Have to Say about the Future." *Computers and Composition*, vol. 28, 2011 pp. 28, 327–46.

3 A Natural History of Networks

Jeff Pruchnic

The title of this essay is borrowed from that of a relatively obscure talk given by the cybernetics researcher Gordon Pask in 1959 at an interdisciplinary conference on the topic of "self-organizing systems." Pask makes two interrelated arguments in his "The Natural History of Networks." The first is for a somewhat broader definition of what can count as a network. Whereas for Pask's audience the concept of network would be largely familiar only in reference to the material and transparent networks of machinery (circuits, prototypical computing technology) and physiology (the animal nervous system, emerging understandings of brain chemistry), Pask argues for a much broader understanding of how we might conceive of networks subsisting across a variety of domains: "I AM using the term network in a general sense, to imply any set of interconnected and measurably active physical entities. Naturally occurring networks are of interest because they have a self-organizing character, are, for example, a marsh, a colony of microorganisms, a research team, and a man" (232).

Concomitantly, Pask also argues that to accurately describe and engage such an expanded concept of networks, we will need to adopt a new kind of critical perspective, or perhaps more precisely a shifting one, an approach that borrows or moves back and forth between the sciences and the humanities. As signaled in his title, Pask suggests the discipline of natural history and the practice of the "nautral historian" as a reference point for such a perspective, "natural history" being a discipline that is both intrinsically invested in exploring the interconnections and relationships between categories of phenomena and also one that had its heyday during a time wherein the dividing lines between the sciences and the humanities were not quite as clear, and their methodologies not nearly as distinct. Pask leaves his own description of what this natural historian would look like and operate purposely undefined—"It's not so easy to say what I mean by a natural historian" (232)—suggesting instead that such a perspective must shift and reframe its disciplinary boundaries in a way similar to how Pask sees the same flexibility within the self-organizing networks that form their subject of study; as he writes in regards to the consideration of "man" as self-organizing system, "In conversation the system appears to be bounded at one moment by the anatomist's skin, and at the next moment, by its region of influence upon other men in society. Typically, a natural historian must change his viewpoint to suit a changeful system" (233).

There is much in Pask's brief, half-century old discussion of networks that might seem prescient for our own hyperconnected and overwhelmingly networked age; his interest in expanding network theories to encompass admixtures of humans, other natural phenomena, and material objects of various types seems to anticipate much of what we have come to know as actor-network theory, for instance, and his engagement with the question of what point the "natural historian" he sees investigating the social systems and the information technology of the time of his writing might risk becoming themselves an integral part of the network they are analyzing—a major theme of the latter part of Pask's "Natural History"—likewise might seem at home in more contemporary studies of scientific epistemology as well as the ethics and politics of humanities research.

However, in the following I want to leverage what might be taken as two relatively minor points of Pask's argument—that the types of networks possible at a given time might be productively used to define particular ages and that these networks also seem to designate the changing shape of the sciences and the humanities and their relationships with one another—to attempt something of my own, however brief, "natural history of networks." More specifically, in what follows I am going to suggest periodizing Western culture into three different schemas, each of which will be defined by its dominant network formation as identified by the distinctive way in which what we might broadly call technics—material processes and techniques as well as actual technologies—are combined with "media," used here to code dominant modes of representation, communication, and persuasion. Additionally, I will trace how each of these network formations has exerted its own unique pressure on the humanities to redefine itself and its missions. Finally, I will argue that producing such a natural history of networks here has much to teach us about our own time, one during which the *network* as concept and as material reality have become increasingly apparent and unavoidable in contemporary cultural life, and the role and work of the humanities during such a moment.

I. Pantometrics and the Division of the Sciences and Humanities

Luckily for our purpose here—that of condensing roughly 6,000 years of intellectual history into three broad constellations of the sciences and humanities—we can find an important precursor for at least the first step in this process in the work of historian Alfred W. Crosby. In his 1997 study *The Measure of Reality*, Crosby makes a compelling case for tying the rapid progress of Western European society during the late Middle Ages and early Renaissance—the position of that part of the continent at the epicenter of an earlier mode of globalization and at the forefront of breakthroughs in science, technology, and the arts—to the spread of a retrospectively simplistic process for associating phenomena across different categories and different cultures. Crosby uses a concept and term coeval with the timeframe under review—*pantometrics*—to describe this new process of "universal measurement" that came to prominence between 1250 and 1600 in Western Europe and across the globe. During this period, as Crosby details, large numbers of individuals become enculturated into the process of "visualizing the stuff of reality as aggregates of uniform units" and of treating "the universe in terms of quanta uniform in one of more characteristics, quanta that are often thought of as arranged in lines, squares, circles, and other symmetrical forms: music staffs, platoons, ledger columns, planetary orbits" (10–11). Through this fairly straightforward rearranging of human imagination and visual representation would come a significant number of revolutionary changes in a variety of disciplines, arts, and other cultural fields, from the development of mechanical "counting boards" for performing and representing arithmetical operations and the construction of public clocks in town spaces to establish and regulate shared time to the expansion of gold currency and accounting ledgers in international finance and from the refinement in uniform cartography to the introduction of geometrical perspectives into painting.

The emergence of pantometrics as a cultural dominant of this time served to anticipate at least prototypic, pre-digital versions of both of the contemporary meanings we tend to attribute to the so-called "network society" of the present: pantometrics both made highly complex and standardized modes of experience, organization, and affiliation possible between categories of phenomena (e.g., the value of material objects as represented in standard currency or speculative stock contracts or the conceptualization of collectives both inanimate and material as joined by their possibilities for connection) as well as greatly aiding the spread of communication and uniform calculation across nations and cultures (categories of quanta becoming the *lingua franca* of trading partners and international efforts in science and the arts). More specifically, and importantly for our purposes here, the emergence of pantometrics might also be connected to two other relationships that I will suggest are consistently aligned with historical changes in the dominant "network" mode of a culture: that between technics and media, broadly considered, and that between the sciences and the humanities.

Briefly stated, we might take pantometric culture to anticipate not only the connective and combinatory qualities of contemporary digital media, but also the mutating boundaries between technics and media, or between technology and representation, that have become a hallmark of considerations of what put the "new" into "new media" from its earliest theorizations. Technologies like counting boards and public clocks are notable for the ways in which they serve as both forms of representation as well as technologies for establishing relationships between individuals and items, functions through which they blurred the distinction between acts of (ostensibly immaterial) communication and material, physical functions of these devices in ways far more extreme than those of oral and visual discourse and earlier print technologies. For their part, even more recognizably static signifying media such as uniform musical notation and reliable cartographic projections were emblematic of an increasingly "executable" form of representational media, one in which its representational capacity was only useful insofar as it was operational for its users. In this sense then, we have a significant historical precursor to the now common conception of the growing indiscernibility between these two boundaries that has marked much discourse on contemporary digital culture, one in which, for instance, computer programming languages appear as the most literal and far-reaching example of a performative discourse, as, in the words of media theorist Alexander R. Galloway "the first language that actually does what it says" (166).

However, more notable, at least in regards to our primary topic here, is the ways in which the emergence of pantometrics as cultural dominant, and the moment of cultural confusion caused by the blending of technics and media in pantometric forms and devices described above, impacted the evolution of the sciences and humanities as formal disciplines. As Crosby argues in his analysis, the sea-change occasioned by the outbreak of pantometrics is perhaps only truly appreciated by contrasting the pantometric emphasis on *quantities* against the emphasis on *qualities* that dominated Western thought and culture from the Greeks up into the thirteenth-century (12–16). In this sense, while the ubiquity of pantometrics can be read as the natural progression of a variety of movements in academic disciplines and engineering processes, it is at the same time a relatively dramatic reversal of post-Platonic Western intellectual thought's dedication to the studying the tranhistorical qualities of concepts and things and its concomitant denigration of techniques and disciplines that focused on mechanical processes and the study of change in systems and phenomena (a division that has been handed down to us in the contrasting categories of being/becoming and *episteme/techne* amongst others).

While by the end of the sixteenth century the former (qualities) would tend to become associated with the humanities and the latter (quantities) with the natural sciences, intellectual history from the Greeks is marked by fierce debates over which of the two should dominate both of these (then, often only uneasily distinguished) categories. Indeed, Plato's prioritizing of the transhistorical and its concomitant hierarchy of knowledge domains would become formalized in Aristotle's more familiarly scientific approach to metaphysics and natural philosophy, one that would cast a long shadow on Western science well into the thirteenth century. Aristotle's prototypic work on taxonomical categories as fundamental structuring mechanisms of both the material world and human perception would similarly seek to separate the constitutive qualities of phenomena from the "differentia" or "contrarities" taken to be either an affection of human conception, or at least secondary to the defining characteristics of a living creature, mental concept, or inanimate object.[1] More generally, this focus on "being" would also inform Aristotle's more

---

1. See, for instance, Aristotle, Topics, VI.6.

detailed ordering of knowledge domains in accordance with their precision and priority in investigating the forces that structure "being" at the most basic level. Thus, for instance, in the *Metaphysics*, the question of whether theology or life science will serve as "first philosophy" is considered specifically along the lines of these two concerns:

> One might indeed raise the question whether first philosophy is universal, or deals with one genus, i.e., some one kind of being; for not even the mathematical sciences are all alike in this respect,—geometry and astronomy deal with a certain particular kind of thing, while universal mathematics applies alike to all. We answer that if there is no substance other than those which are formed by nature, natural science will be the first science; but if there is an immovable substance, the science of this must be first philosophy, and universal in this way, because it is first. And it will belong to this to consider being *qua* being—both what it is and the attributes which belong to it *qua* being. (*Metaphysics* VI.1, 1026a-24–32)

Setting aside the rather vexed question of to what degree theological concerns and commonplaces influenced natural philosophy in subsequent decades, the influence of Aristotle's emphasis on absolutes, qualities, and suggestion had on science lasted well into the Middle Ages, particularly in how the perceived priority of logical reasoning's role in making such determinations resulted in the retrospectively odd dismissal of the kind of physical experimentation that marks later empirical methods. Thus, despite its title, the *scientia demonstrativa* practiced in medieval universities applied not to physical demonstrations but an appropriation of Aristotle's style of logical demonstration using syllogisms and propositions.[2] While, as the historian A. C. Crombie suggests, one might detect instances of "proto-quantification" in the twelfth and early thirteenth centuries via the introduction of some geometric methods into fields such as optics, the vast majority of the scientific work of the time remained wedded to the Platonic-Aristotlean division between *episteme* and *techne* (145–48). Notwithstanding a series of important critiques of the Greek metaphysical tradition within late medieval science that lead thinking of this time to take on an increasingly analytical rather than speculative form, late medieval scientific epistemology continued to function, in the memorable phrase of historian John E. Murdoch, as

2. See, for instance, Kaye, Economy & Nature in the Fourteenth Century, 164.

largely a "natural philosophy without nature," an investigation into the natural order of things that prioritized mental abstraction and imaginative constructs over the observation of material reality.

The vast difference between these approaches and the modes of defining and dividing the humanities and sciences—their domains, methodologies, and social purposes—of more recent history is in many ways a testament to the immense impact of the progression and popularization of pantometrics in the late Middle-Ages and Renaissance eras. While into the late twentieth-century and the present (of which, more in a moment) there remains much heated debate over which of the modes we now associate with humanistic and scientific work have the greatest value within different contexts—as any number of references to the "two cultures" and subsequent skirmishes will testify—after the pantometric moment there were few who would disagree over the placement of these methodologies within said disciplinary divisions.

II. Prognometrics and the Critical Humanities

It may be tempting to jump directly from the avatars of contemporary network culture described above to the contemporary moment and the current question of the role of the (digital) humanities in the present; however, I want to hesitate a moment here over the time between what Crosby has designated as the moment of pantometrics and our own recognizable digital age. Doing so, I think, is necessary not only to keep an already ambitious periodizing schema from becoming overly hasty but also to unpack another shift in the relationship between the sciences and humanities—one much more familiar to us and one that we still find consistently invoked in debates over the role of the humanities in a time of ubiquitous information technology.[3]

We might follow Crosby's resurrection of the archaic "pantometric" by positing our own portmanteau word for the dominant mode of measurement, networking, and the convergence of media and technics that took place from the seventeenth century into the twentieth: "prognometrics" (for "prognosticate" or predict + "measurement"). As numerous historians of science have suggested, the really innovative change in scientific methodology, and particularly, in the spread of the social

---

3. The discussion of "prognometrics" below and of "parametrics" that follows is an extension of a more general attempt to periodize the history technics that can be found in Pruchnic, 60–99.

sciences, is the emergence of complex statistical mechanisms for both calculating probability and predicting future states of phenomena based on the gathering of data about its past.[4] If the pantometric moment was formed by the staggered emergence of such technologies as the counting board and such techniques as the use of perspective in painting, we might find a somewhat more singular starting point for a variety of prognometric technologies and techniques in the "co-discovery" of the calculus by Leibnitz and Newton around the turn of the seventeenth century and the subsequent variety of mathematical formula that would arise around calculating and predicting the present and future states of physical matter, social collectives, and patterns of growth and change. Similarly, if the network model of the pantometric era was the result of methods in the sciences and humanites for making connections between diverse phenomena across space, then the dominant network model of the prognometric era would be caused by those same forces being pressed into the service of making connections across time: linkages made between the (studied) present and the (forecasted) future.

Into this mode of measurement and connectivity we might place such period developments as the formation of actuarial tables for estimating the life-span of individuals based on genetics and behavior (a concern of political economy that quickly became one of pragmatic economics through the growth of insurance schemes); the large-scale mapping of the spread of disease and the formation of thresholds for the quarantine and evacuation of populations; the rise of international stock exchanges based on predictive models of return and of currency rates; modes of social control based on the probability or possibility of surveillance or punishment that Foucault famously designated as "disciplinary power"; and even architectural movements such as those baroque styles in which the appearances of structures were not static but, rather, mutated in real-time as the perspectives of the individuals moving through them changed. All such phenomena are defined not so much by the "translation" quality of reducing items and ideas into quanta as they are by the ability to dynamically connect the probable future state of something with its present position and function.

There are innumerable observations one might make about the effects of what we are coding "prognometrics" here on the earlier division

---

4. See, in particular Ian Hacking's The Emergence of Probability and The Taming of Chance, as well as the collection the The Empire of Chance (Gigerenzer, et al.,)

and relation of the humanities and sciences we associated with pantometrics, perhaps the most obvious being the birth of statistics as a recognizable discipline and the ways in which the methods of prognometrics
became prominent in the social sciences and influenced the traditional
humanities, in their own way, to also shift toward more of a predictive
or "future-focused" spirit of social intervention. However, as a bit of
ground-clearing here, I want to jump directly to the rearrangement of
the humanities and its self-fashioning in relation to other domains of
thought that became hugely influential near the end of prognometrics'
reign as a cultural dominant, particularly one that will likely be familiar
to anyone trained in humanistic disciplines over the past several decades.
If by the end of the pantometric moment we might depict, however vul-
garly, the humanities and natural sciences settling into their own terri-
tories around questions of quality and quanta, or being and becoming,
then the end of the prognometrics as a dominant mode of Western *men-
talité* left us with a somewhat more antagonistic relationship (at least insofar as we focus on what was "new" in the humanities at the moment).
I am thinking here of the humanist critique of science and positivist
methodologies that perhaps reached its fever pitch around the pre- and
post-war periods of the twentieth-century but that cast its shadow over
the decades to come, through the "big-theory" era of the humanities and
the so-called culture wars of the latter decades of the century. Indeed,
we might save ourselves some time here by recalling the critiques of this
type leveled by scholars on both sides of the war (in timing, but, depending on the way one reads Heidegger's vexed and complicated relationship to the Nazi Party, perhaps in partisanship as well). Famously, for
Heidegger, the rise of the "calculative" mode of thought that dominated
contemporary engineering and the prototypical computer science of cybernetics was rapidly undermining the possibilities for the "meditative"
mode of engagement with being and the world that was at least at some
point an ideal of the humanities.[5] Likewise, the immensely influential
post-war writings of Adorno and Horkheimer in *The Dialectic of Enlightenment*, to give just one more example, were also ones in which the
death knell of humanist ideals are shown to be eclipsed when the dominant modes of cultural valuation and judgment end up "confirming the
scientific system as the embodiment of truth" (6). Without too much

---

5. This is, of course, a motif of Heidegger's work of all periods, but I am thinking in particular of his early critique in Introduction to Metaphysics.

exaggeration, we can draw fairly straight lines between Heidegger's distaste for epistemologies driven by science and industry on the one hand, and Adorno and Horkheimer's denunciation of the "Culture Industry," on the other, and the emergence of "big theory" and of cultural studies in the subsequent decades, movements in which the humanities would often find their identity thorough the critique of the social and natural sciences and their material effects on contemporary culture. It is the decline of this identity of the humanities, I take it, that largely coincides with both the current craze for rethinking the humanities around the capacities of digital media and a new network model that we might see as overtaking that of prognometrics; it is to those two questions that we now turn.

III. Parametrics and the Future of the Digital Humanities

These all too-brief surveys of the proto-network societies of the past might position us well to understand the network society of the present as something different than just the mode of culture dominated by network computing or as just the moment in which the mere connection between individuals and forces of all stripes through the products of telecommunication and globalization seem to define the age. Rather I would suggest that what makes the present cultural moment distinct is the ways in which such networks combine the connecting of space and of time that was prominent in these earlier periods. In what we might call the current "parametric" mode of society—to borrow a term from computer-aided architecture in which changes to part of a planned structure are automatically adapted and accommodated across the entire design—the dominant network modes seem to be those that are designed not so much to reduce phenomena to quanta or to predict the future state of phenomena, but those systems that adapt in real-time to subtle changes in their area of coverage. Perhaps the most obvious and pervasive example of such a network formation can be found in the types of niche-production and marketing made possible by networked communication technologies and post-Fordist modes of production. If the kind of consumer conformity that Adorno and Horkheimer critiqued under the rubric of the culture industry, and that Heidegger bemoaned as the engine for our "thoughtless" consumption of the material world, is a primary output of Fordist production—one in which consumers must

be convinced they need or desire a good that is mass-produced in advance—then the current parametric mode of production is by contrast
one in which goods can be quickly made in rapid response to the extant
needs or desires of ever smaller segments of the population. While there
is certainly a degree of question-begging involved in declaring such needs
or desires "natural," as numerous social theorists have pointed out in the
last decade or so, they hardly leave the critical wing of the humanities
in the same position they were in decades past. While we might expand
such a parametric mode from production and marketing to a wide variety of other cultural realms here, I want to begin concluding this essay
and moving to the question of the humanities today by briefly reviewing
only three examples from contemporary life: (post-genomic) medicine,
speculative finance, and mass (new) media.

Medicine. At least up until a few years ago, the most consistent go-to
symbol of the effect of contemporary (information) technology on medical research, and thus in many ways also the constellation point for a
variety of fears about its "mechanizing" or dehumanizing effects, was,
of course, the Human Genome Project. The international attempt to
map the tens of thousands of protein-coding genes of humans was both
an impressive example of how contemporary technologies were changing the shape of medical research as well as an obvious and disturbing
symptom for those who worried that the paradigm of bioinformatics
was leading to reductionist conceptions of the human body, and/or that
gene sequencing technologies might open the door to everything from
the "gene-screening" of potential employees to the massive privatiza-
tion of genetic structures as proprietary intellectual property. If these
fears—though by no means inconsequential in the present—were particularly emblematic of concerns over the changes information technology had made to epistemological representational economies in science
and society, then perhaps the so-called "post-genomic" therapies emergent today emphasize the more recent parametric intersections of culture
and technique.

Concerns over the mapping of the human genome were based on the
idea that gene sequencing would end up presenting a single genetic "blue-
print" that might stand-in for all humans and new universal norms for
health and disease, but, strangely enough, the (currently largely speculative) applications of such a capacity have trended toward the inverse
scenario: the tailoring of therapies based on knowledge of a the specific
structure of an individual's genetic make-up. In place of the "one-size fits
all" approach to analysis and treatment that seemed to be implicit to map-

ping the human genome, we instead have the acknowledgment, as some proponents recently phrase it, that "each person's disease may be unique and therefore that person needs to be treated as an individual" (Ginzburg and McCarthy 492). Although the most impactful current applications of post-genomic techniques may be individualized diagnostics by medical institutions—post-op cancer patients who have the means and desire, for instance, can have their individual tumors genetically analyzed in the hopes that such specific information will help build more targeted therapies in the event of recurrence—the most striking phenomenon may be the number of "healthy" individuals having genetic analyses produced and, in some cases, the crowdsourcing of their genetic information for use by other parties.

Finance. While speculative capital of various types has been around for several centuries, I take it that the truly novel characteristics of finance today, the changes that people are actually trying to refer to when "speculation" or "connectivity" are discussed in this fashion, are the increases in the magnitude and variety of market relationships and the ways these phenomena are themselves parametrically or algorithmically connected in contemporary financial exchanges. We can see this characteristic formally in the ways that modern trading is based not so much on calculations of underlying value or even presumed future value, but instead on the present and future state of a vast variety of associations between commodities, prices, and currencies—ones largely defined by the mechanisms of formal exchange itself. For one, there is a vast expansion of the kinds of things one can "speculate" on, including, in many ways, others' (or your own) speculations on the value commodities; all investment trends toward being a virtual form of arbitrage, exchanges based on the relative values of different commodities and financial instruments.

As Daniel Buenza and David Stark write in their ethnographic study of an arbitrage firm, the modern-day trading room "is an engine for generating equivalences": "traders locate value by making associations between particular properties or qualities of one security and those of other previously unrelated or tenuously related securities" (373; 376). As they go on to argue, arbitrage follows a logic and methodology far different from the "momentum trading" of the go-go nineties, and in many ways the inverse of the corporate raiding strategies of the 1980s. While raiding strategies are based on carving up a company into assets and selling it piecemeal, arbitrageurs "carve up abstract qualities of a security":

> For example, they do not see Boeing Co. as a monolithic asset or property but as having several properties (traits, qualities) such as being a technology stock, an aviation stock, a consumer-travel stock, an American stock, a stock that is included in a given index, and so on. Even more abstractionist, they attempt to isolate such qualities as the volatility of a security, or its liquidity, it convertability, its indexability, and so on." (Buenza and Stark 376)

In other words, in the realm of arbitrage, it is not the ability to break down an asset into component parts that might somehow be more valuable than their sum, but the ability to identify and manipulate a wide variety of its connections and co-implications with other phenomena, the flexible management of associations rather than the efficient calculation of an underlying value.

Even more striking than the formal introduction of relational or processual principles into such trading is the very *real* introduction of algorithmic programming into the process. As numerous commentators have had reason to relate over the past few years, if modern finance has a founding document, a kind of Federalist Papers that relates the prehistory of a new and indelible era, it is the Nobel-prize winning papers on option theory by Black, Scholes, and Merton. The Black and Scholes equation for the theoretical determination of the market value of call options quickly became an operational algorithm, the Black-Scholes formula, precipitating a revolution in derivatives training as well as in the overall techniques and material technologies used in trading. In the early days, traders looking to benefit from the Black-Scholes formula could be seen on trading floors carrying elaborate fold-out copies of the equation on papers. In the last several decades, however, these so-called "sheet monkeys" have been replaced by traders packing much less onerous digital hand-held devices wherein both requisite information and the desired calculations are automatically transmitted. Even more recently, variations on Scholes-Black have been incorporated in automated algorithmic trading in which software "robots" can not only advise times to trade, but in some cases automatically initiated trading unless manually interrupted by human traders. The joint investigation of the US Commodity Futures Trading Commission and the US Securities and Exchange Commission into the so-called "Flash Crash" of the US market on May 10, 2010—in which the Dow Jones plunged six hundred points in nine minutes—identified both a series of feedback gestures between algorithmic trading, as well as the loss of liquidity caused when algorithmic trading automatically ceased, as root causes. If a number of Cold War-era cultural fears—and more than a few sci-fi thrillers of the time—revolved around the potential outbreak of international nuclear war caused by the triggering of game-theoretic scenarios and automatic "switches" on nuclear weapons, perhaps incidents like the "Flash Crash" are more demonstrative of the political economy of the present moment: one in which the spiraling recursion of trading robots threatens a total elimination of "value" that only exists in a virtual form, as opposed to the "actual" destruction of the material world.

(*Mass*) *Media.* The most visible impact of contemporary information technology and its attendant techniques on mass media, as a non-stop parade of "death of the newspaper" features have told us over the past several years, seems to have been one of displacement and fragmentation. If, as Jürgen Habermas amongst others has detailed, the progression of mass print media from the early 1800s onwards has been one of consolidation—local and parochial print organs being absorbed or bought by national, and then international, firms—and a resulting heterogeneity of content and distancing from their core audience, movements from the late twentieth-century onward might be seen as a total reversing of this trend (168–75). We have, on the one hand a disaggregation of the functions of centralized media like newspapers (whether in print or online) to a variety of new, typically localized or "local-centric" networked media— Craigslist takes over as the major avenue for classified ads, hyperlocal blogs take over local news coverage, social media feeds become our new go-to resources for breaking news and trend-spotting. On the other hand, we have an integration of the formally "passive" reader or viewer into the production or content of media itself; the carefully curated and relatively rare "letter to the editor" gives way to the infinity of unfiltered comments on online news and blog features, and by-now quaint features like having audience members report the temperature in their backyard or submit on-air questions for television news anchors to field are crowded out by the introduction of scrolling social media feeds and user-submitted video and audio of newsworthy events. Perhaps most notably, we have in many cases the total replacement of the professional journalist or commentator by the "citizen journalists" or the crowdsourced coverage of events.

These tendencies alone might be taken as appearances of what I have been calling the "parametric" in contemporary culture, given the ways in which they demonstrate how the managing of dynamic relationships

between the producers and receivers of mass media, with the hybrid categories in-between, has become a dominant concern. There are, however, a number of other related but less-commented upon trends that
could be taken to indicate an even more intense integration of algorithmic or parametric qualities into this domain. One is what we might
call an increased focus on *process* and *potentiality* in contemporary news
commentary. If access to news and the ability to distribute it has been
proletarianized to the extent that virtually anyone has the potential to report and offer opinion on current events, and at a faster speed than that
of "old media" organs, it makes sense that that traditional mass media
would be pushed into a another direction, in this case a forecasting of
"the future," or at least a wide variety of potential future events, their
likely consequences, and the actions individuals should take in response.

Indeed, Richard Grusin has suggested that the function of contemporary mass media is increasingly less based on the mediation of events
during or after they take place, and more rooted in what he calls "premediation": "the production of specific future scenarios and the creation
and maintenance of an affective orientation towards the future" (48).
Although it might be said that mass media news always had a predictive quality—the prediction of weather being an obvious if quotidian
example, with the common discussion of the likelihood of pivotal events
such as the outbreak of conflict or results of a campaign being perhaps
more significant ones—the contemporary shift has been one away from
analyzing the likelihood of discrete events based on precipitating causes,
and toward the presentation of a multitude of possible events, the chains
of sequences that might promote one or more of them as opposed to others, and the cascade of effects that might in turn be triggered by these
occurrences. Perhaps as a mirroring of a variety of other ways we tend
to understand contemporary phenomena via processes and "if-then" scenarios, mainstream news seems to be delivering not just the present but
also increasingly the future(s) back to us in a similar fashion.

Finally, it is worth remarking on how the parametric qualities of
niche-media have, perhaps paradoxically, been useful in maintaining
particular equilibriums of opinion and disposition despite the ostensibly huge increase in perspectives and arguments of all strips in the me-
diasphere. If the primary negative effects of the centralization of media
into large firms was that it tended to both restrict interaction between
its producers and consumers while also limiting the range of acceptable
positions or opinions to those that were unlikely to offend a large audi-

ence—the qualities that, for good or ill, made media *mass* media—then it would seem that the vast proliferation of media sites and opportunities for interactivity would correct these problems, and thus perhaps even help inaugurate a new and more ameliorative modality of civil society or the public sphere. However, you need go no further than the nearest comment thread on a controversial news story or partisan blog post to see that something like the opposite has been the case. Indeed, the unparalleled ability for audiences to search and access media created by individuals with which they already share political dispositions, as well as for aggregative technologies and media portals to "push" such media based on data collected about their users, has instead likely resulted in a decline in an individual's exposure to opposing viewpoints and of "rational-critical" communicative interaction between individuals with partisan divisions. Indeed, the realm of contemporary niche-media looks much less like a global village or universal agora, and much more like an ever more intense balkanization of our political or ideological landscape.

So where does this leave the humanities? While the humanistic disciplines found an identity in keeping up the focus on the qualities and (trans)historical essence of concepts and ideas that were being abandoned by the natural philosophy and precursors of today's highly divergent natural science disciplines during the era of pantometrics, and by acting, at times, as the loyal opposition to the sometimes brutal pragmatism of the sciences and engineering fields during the mode of prognometrics, no such easy distinctions or oppositions seem available in the present. On the one hand, as only a small number of "decline of the humanities" missives have failed to announce, at least some of the more traditional touchstones of humanistic study and training now seem out of step with both the media and the competencies that seem to dominate contemporary culture. On the other hand, as the above analysis has attempted to detail, these very same cultural changes seem to be ones in which the focus on media's communicative and persuasive techniques (always been the focal points of the humanities, despite other permutations), seem to be increasingly prominent, perhaps even constitutive, of the very same changes. As the all-too-hasty trip through several centuries of the humanities as seen from the vantage point of the dominant cultural networks of the time suggests, the resultant ambiguous state of the field should be expected, especially given the length of time—decades if not centuries—that it took the humanities to reform in relation to previous network regimes, and it is quite possible it will take us some time to determine the appropriate identity for this period—a question and charge that will be eventually worked out by gatherings and exchanges such as the one that occasioned the collection you are reading now.

However, by way of addressing the question for the demands of the present, I would like to conclude here by arguing that our most promising futures for the digital humanities will likely be those that see the current connections and cross-couplings of the humanities and the social and natural sciences now prominent in the age of ubiquitous communication and information media through the lens of earlier moments in world culture in which the traditional dividing lines between the fields were not so distinct. Similarly, it may turn out to be true that there is much work for humanists to do in theorizing digital culture through the modes and mechanisms that were available in such earlier moments and lost during the transition into these fields as we have known them the past several centuries, of engaging network culture through the lens provided by such lost hybridities. In short, we might still find value in such projects as attempting, for instance, a "natural history" of networks.

WORKS CITED

Adorno, Theodor W. "The Actuality of Philosophy." *Telos*, vol. 31, Spring 1977, pp. 121–33.

Aristotle. *Metaphysics*. Trans. W. D. Ross. *The Complete Works of Aristotle*, translated by W. D. Ross, edited by Jonathan Barnes, vol. 2, Princeton UP, 1984, pp. 1552–1728.

—. *Topics. The Complete Works of* Aristotle, Translated by W. A. Pickard-Cambridge, vol. 1., Princeton UP, 1984, pp. 166–277. Print.

Buenza, David, and David Stark. "Tools of the Trade: The Socio-Technology of Arbitrage in a Wall Street Trading Room." *Industrial and Corporate Change*, vol. 13, no. 2, April 2004, pp. 368–400.

Crombie, A. C. "Quantification in Medieval Physics." *Isis*, vol. 52, no. 2, 1961, pp. 143–60.

Crosby, Alfred W. *The Measure of Reality: Quantification and Western Society, 1250–1600*. Cambridge UP, 1997.

Galloway, Alexander R. *Protocol: How Control Exists After Decentralization*. MIT Press, 2004.

Ginsburg, Geoffrey S., and Jeanette J. McCarthy. "Personalized Medicine: Revolutionizing Drug Discovery and Patient Care." *Trends in Biotechnology*, vol. 19, no. 12, 2011, pp. 491–96.

Gigerenzer, Gerd, et al. *The Empire of Chance: How Probability Changed Science and Everyday Life. Ideas in Context*. Cambridge. Cambridge UP, 1989.

Grusin, Richard. *Premediation: Affect and Mediality After 9/11*. Palgrave, 2010.

Habermas, Jürgen. *The Structural Transformation of the Public Sphere: An Inquiry Into a Category of Bourgeois Society.* Translated by Thomas Burger with Frederick Lawrence. MIT Press, 1989.

Hacking, Ian. *The Emergence of Probability: A Philosophical Study of Early Ideas About Probability Induction and Statistical Inference.* 2nd ed, Cambridge UP, 2006.

—. *The Taming of Chance. Ideas in Context.* Cambridge, UP: 1990.

Heidegger, Martin. *Introduction to Metaphysics.* Translated by Gregory Fried and Richard Polt. *Note Bene* Series, Yale UP, 2000.

Kaye, Joel. *Economy and Nature in the Fourteenth Century: Money, Market Exchange, and the Emergence of Scientific Thought.* Cambridge UP, 2000.

Pask, Gordon. "The Natural History of Networks." *Self-Organizing Systems: Proceedings of an Interdisciplinary Conference*, edited by Marshall C. Yovits and Scott Cameron, vol. 2, Pergamon Press, 1960, pp. 232–63.

Pruchnic, Jeff. *Rhetoric and Ethics in the Cybernetic Age: The Transhuman Condition.* Routledge, 2013.

US Commodity Futures Trading Commission and US Securities & Exchange Commission. *Findings Regarding the Market Events of May 6, 2010.* US Commodity Futures Trading Commission and US Securities and Trade Commission, 2010, www.sec.gov/news/studies/2010/marketevents-report.pdf

4 Reading in Slow Motion: Thinking with the Network

Jillian J. Sayre and James J. Brown, Jr.

In 2010, Richard Miller, frustrated by the physical restrictions of scholarly publication, posted a PDF of his new article on digital pedagogy to his website. In the accompanying blog post, "So Much Depends on the Carriage Return," Miller decries a journal's refusal to keep his original formatting for the article "Reading in Slow Motion," insists on the importance of spatial arrangement as an element of composition, and bids adieu to academic publishing as a whole. The article itself addresses the tension between print text and electronic environments, and while Miller's blog post concerned forsaking the inherently limited and limiting venue of print publication in favor of the accessibility and unlimited potential of digital distribution, the article reinscribes the physical environment of the classroom and the text as separate from if not primary to the digital tools that distract us in our daily lives with their constant flow of buzzing and dinging ("Reading in Slow Motion" 3).

The title of Miller's article recalls (without citing) Reuben Brower's essay "Reading in Slow Motion," and indeed they are both locating a similar dilemma. As we read Brower's essay about the fate of reading in a world defined by a "flood of words and images" (5), it would be easy to place Brower in the category of those Miller represents through Nicholas Carr, who wonders if Google is "making us stupid," those who think the increasing availability of information lead us to "shallow" thinking. But this would be wrong for two reasons. For one, Brower's essay about "mounting lists of important books" and information overload appeared in 1962 (5), and although the first high-level computer language, FORTRAN, was five years old when Brower's essay was published, the Internet as we know it was far off. The buzzing, beeping, and dinging described by Miller is not equal to the rivers and floods of Brower's essay, but the relation between the object of the two texts reveals that the proliferation of information is not, as Carr would have it, a *digital* effect. Secondly, despite being more than forty years older than Carr's, Brower's argument is also surprisingly more progressive. In "Reading in Slow Motion," Brower promotes a course called "Literature X" that teaches "slow reading," a course realized as Harvard's Humanities 6 and made famous by Paul de Man's reference to Brower's course in his essay, "Return to Philology." Brower's course attends to the ways that reading a work of literature is both a "solitary" and "social" act (Brower was already embracing the text's inter- and intranets, as we will call it, whether he knew it or not) and embraces the mess and risk of reading as thinking. Brower was not interested in a course on the appreciation of literature nor was he aiming at a class that would ask students to report on the content that they had learned. Instead, he wanted to help students cultivate an attunement to language and textual relationships, and to experiment with the text:

> Reading a novel forcibly reminds us that literature is embedded in history, that the meaning of the work in itself changes when we view it in relation to other works and to the social situation in which it first appeared. Literature X will move on in its later phases to some experiments in historical interpretation, "historical" being used here to include the relation of a work to its time, especially to more or less contemporary works, and to literary tradition. (14)

Brower is already, to borrow from Jentery Sayers's more recent attempt at this kind of course, "networking the novel" in his attention to the relationality of the text and the work of reading.

Nearly fifty years after Brower, Richard Miller's "Reading in Slow Motion" reinvents the central interrogation to *account for* instead of ignore competition from informational technology. "How does one get students to use the Internet as a tool for thinking new thoughts?" Miller asks ("Reading in Slow Motion" 2). His answer, though, is surprisingly similar to Brower's: a technology-free classroom in which students read a single text over the course of a semester. Class meetings are cut off from technological resources in order to focus on the encounter with the "words on the page" ("Reading in Slow Motion" 6). Miller devises this restricted classroom as a drag on the fast-paced digital environment, "making time," as Miller says, "for students to have the embodied *experience* of learning" ("Reading in Slow Motion" 4). "The ability to focus, to follow a long argument, to know in depth are all on the table," Miller says ("Reading in Slow Motion" 4). Miller is no Luddite, and his students perform slow reading while also sharing supplementary discoveries on a social bookmarking site outside of the classroom. Nonetheless he sees these as distinct practices. Miller says: "I'll stipulate . . . that reading a book and reading on the Internet are different activities and that the books are less actively distracting than the Internet is" ("Reading in Slow Motion" 2). We would like to question the integrity of this division. *Reading in print and digital environments are not wholly different activities*; the two share important qualities and attending to that overlap may help us meet the central pedagogical challenges Miller identifies: cultivating curiosity, fostering attentiveness, encouraging inventiveness. This, as Miller argues, is how teachers "lay the foundation for the mind to have a life outside of the classroom" ("Reading in Slow Motion" 2).

Miller's positing of the difference between print and digital media mirrors the work of Katherine Hayles, who examines this difference in terms of an attention economy. For Hayles, digital media encourage hyper attention while print media call for deep attention:

> Deep attention, the cognitive style traditionally associated with the humanities, is characterized by concentrating on a single object for long periods (say, a novel by Dickens), ignoring outside stimuli while so engaged, preferring a single information stream, and having a high tolerance for long focus times. Hyper attention is characterized by switching focus rapidly among different tasks, preferring multiple information streams, seeking a high level of stimulation, and having a low tolerance for boredom. (187)

Hayles argues that we are amid a cognitive "generational shift" from deep to hyper attention and that the contemporary educational apparatus (particularly in the humanities, which often relies upon the operations of deep attention) must adapt to this shift. She suggests that educators look for ways to teach digital and print objects alongside one another and to do so by "starting with hyper attention and moving toward more traditional objects of study" (Hayles 196). One example would be teaching *The Education of Henry Adams* alongside a discussion of "strategies of self-presentation at the wildly popular Facebook" (Hayles 196). By starting with a more recognizable, hyper attentive space, one can ease into books that require deep attention.

However, by separating digital technologies (associated with hyper-attention) from print (associated with deep-attention), we run the risk of restricting particular cognitive modes to particular media, rather than seeking out, in Hayles words, "the frustrating, zesty, and intriguing ways in which the two cognitive modes interact" (198). While we would grant that digital and networked environments have shifted how we attend to texts and other objects, that they have reconfigured cognitive space, we would also like to suggest that deep and hyper attention are not necessarily the provenance of any particular media. Printed books can call for hyper-attention; certain videogames reward deep attention. There is no question that digital environments give us access to more information and more media channels, and those of us engaging digital media on a regular basis are perhaps more sensitive to the demands of hyper attention because we are being pulled in many directions by many different demands on our attention. But this situation is not purely created by digital media, and can be deployed productively in the study of print media as well.

The clearest evidence that hyper-attention is not a purely digital phenomenon is the similarity with which Miller and Brower describe the exigencies of their essays. Miller's "young modern reader" is inundated with "the buzz signaling the arrival of a text message; the ding of the ongoing chat session; status updates from one's friends on Facebook; emails announcing the latest hilarious YouTube video is just a click away; notification that it's your turn in virtual Scrabble; your on-demand queue with Netflix out there, just waiting" ("Reading in Slow Motion" 3). Brower's student faces a similar predicament, one that is also felt by her parents. However, this is a problem that is not produced by exposure to digital environments:

> But why a course in slow reading? The parent who has a son or daughter in college may well feel confused, since almost certainly he has at least one child with a reading difficulty, the most common complaint being that the child cannot read fast enough. As the parent himself watches the mounting lists of

important books, and as he scans the rivers of print in the daily paper, he may well feel that like Alice and the Red Queen, he and his children are going faster and faster but getting nowhere.

The difficulties of parent and child point to conditions that have led to the introduction of how-to-read courses in our colleges and universities. We might note first the sheer mass of printed material to which we are exposed—not to mention to flood of words and images pouring through radio and television. (5)

Brower seems to anticipate Miller's predicament and both seem to be gesturing toward the generational shift described by Hayles, albeit in drastically different generations. What this similarity demonstrates is the work of proliferating texts—print *and* digital—in producing the hyper-attentive subject, drawing attention in many directions at once, insisting on distraction.

These thinkers see the work of reading a novel as an activity that requires deep attention, and this activity conflicts with the subject of that work, the contemporary reader (the location of which is uncertain) who is accustomed to sifting through multiple information streams and paying attention to a "flood" of data. Brower offers us a solution of deep attention as pure restriction: "By a method that might be described as 'slow motion,' by slowing down the process of reading to observe what is happening in order to attend very closely to the words, their uses, and their meanings" ("Reading in Slow Motion" 4). Miller's course on "reading in slow motion" is an attempt to get students to do both, to cultivate both deep and hyper attention by moving between two distinct spaces: the classroom and the network. Much like Hayles's model of teaching social media alongside but separate from *Henry Adams* or videogames alongside but separate from novels, Miller requires a separation of the classroom from the "buzzing" and "dinging" of the network. However, what if this sensibility could be cultivated by blurring the lines between digital networks, embodied spaces (the classroom), and material artifacts (print texts). What if we could draw upon the overlap between, rather than insisting on the division between hyper and deep attention? How might we use digital technologies to make us more sensitive to the ways that the print text is *already* networked? We propose that the insistence that books are "less actively distracting" is a trace of the same reverence for material forms that gives rise to Carr's nostalgia. Instead, we offer an account of how distraction can be pedagogically productive, that distraction is not always something to be fought off or held to the side in the interest of interpretation or meaning, but rather that it *is* interpretation and meaning. In presenting this account, we argue, like Hayles, that networked technologies are formative cognitive environments, but we also argue that thinking *with* the network attunes us to certain modes of reading, writing, and understanding the world that are not exclusive to digital technology.

Like Miller, we hope to get students to use the Internet to think new thoughts, and our aim is to nudge them in this direction by blurring, instead of insisting on, the boundaries between the network and classroom. Drawing on the idea of the network as theorized by Bruno Latour in *Reassembling the Social*, we describe a classroom that encourages students to become something akin to network administrators, attending to reading and writing as an experience of navigating a text's inter and intranets. To do this, we use examples from a slow reading course on *Moby Dick*. The course asked students to mine the text as a site of invention, to explore it as a node in various networks, but thinking *with* the network requires *writing* with the network. We conclude by exploring a student multimedia project that shows how slow reading helps readers and writers create (in) networks.

THINKING WITH NETWORKS

In a course called "Caught in the Net(work): Reading Moby Dick in Slow Motion," students were asked to understand narrative as a network and to reimagine the work of reading and writing as the tracing of networks. The course was not just an investigation of an author or a text or a literary period or environment, but also— and more importantly—an investigation, through a prolonged engagement with a single text, of the act of reading itself. The course was explicitly modeled on the classroom Miller describes in "Reading in Slow Motion," but throughout the semester the class found itself increasingly sensitive to the hyperattentive qualities of the "words on the page."

Mirroring Miller's classroom, the class insisted on an austere and artificial isolation of the classroom experience, focusing solely on the novel, while outside of class students were asked to develop a network of knowledge that would enhance their understanding of the text. Their task was to consider the ways in which digital networks might contribute to their understanding of the novel *separate from* the limited experience of reading for and in class discussion. In class meetings, students maintained an aggressive attention on the text and the text alone. The environment cultivated in the classroom was important, and sometimes taxing for the students. As Miller warns, students become confused, lost, and even bored when so severely limited in terms of material and *amount* of material. But instead of refusing or ignoring or working to "correct" these negative experiences, students were encouraged to labor on with the text and to use those negative reactions as opportunities to ask questions: What is going on in the text that drives these reactions? How does the experience of reading provoke these feelings? How might the experience of reading contribute to meaning in the novel?

As Miller prescribes, students were required to work outside the classroom to build a sort of library of electronic resources to supplement and develop their readings. Miller used social bookmarking, but students in this class used the Tumblr blogging platform to build their networks throughout the semester. Tumblr's affordances for exploring relations are multiple, but one particularly interesting function is its mobile application. With its mobile capabilities, this tool allowed students to explore not only the possibilities offered by the Internet for thinking new thoughts about texts, but also their everyday lived experiences. Students were encouraged to reflect on how their experience in the classroom affects or calls on them to reinterpret how they move about in the world at large, bringing those extracurricular environments, digital or not, to bear upon the text. One student noted on his Tumblr that while he was walking home and listening to a new album, he recognized in the melody the narrative structure of his reading for that week:

> Around these moments Ishmael [sic] narration seems chaotic and dissonant, as if he is jumping from one set of opinions and outlooks as it suits his particular situation. Ishmael's viewpoints always are underscored by foreboding [sic] sense of what is to come, but like the phantoms that haunted him, they seem blurry and just out of reach. Likewise, The opening track of the album "Seven Steps" felt equally ominous and chaotic at points. As a listener I found [myself] lost in the noise, until out of it finally [there is] some sort of eerie, slow, yet determinable melody. For me in that moment the song seemed to encapsulated [sic] all that I had read up until that moment in Moby-Dick.

This student builds a network that reaches out from the text and connects to the world in which he lives, an inter-net(work) of a distinct type, and in so doing he accomplishes what Miller identifies as the goal of such work: to use the connectivity of electronic environments to think new thoughts about the text, to encourage "the mind to have a life outside of the classroom" ("Reading in Slow Motion" 2).

But during the "Reading in Slow Motion" course, a focus on the work of "networking the novel," made it more and more obvious that the practice of slow reading also exposes us to the network *of* the novel: no matter how ascetic the environment, we were always being called, being "distracted" by the work of the text itself, the ways in which it exposes itself as already multiple, multi-directional, connected. The class started to attend to those ways that the networked sensibilities we had previously exorcised from the classroom could help us *read* in new ways, even without the technical apparatus that is thought inextricable from the concept of the network. On the instructor Tumblr, Jillian began to explore the way allusion in the text mapped onto a consideration of remix and how, in a text like *Moby Dick*, a text that weaves—or looms, as Ishmael would say—its narrative through interactions with other texts, a structure of citationality highlights the work of relation as both a theme in and a mode of the text. In short, the practice of slow reading allowed both instructor and students to engage in rather than eschew distraction because we became more sensitive to the ways that the print text already calls for and upon the kind of connectivity highlighted by electronic environments and digital epistemologies.

Attending to *Moby Dick* as a network meant changing the way that we *composed* networks as well, not just creating edges between existing nodes (through social bookmarking or Tumblr), but also constructing "risky accounts" of the novel's various relational flows (Latour 122). What do we mean when we call *Moby Dick* a network, and what are we asking students to do when asking them to create their own networks? We use the term *network* here much the way that Bruno Latour does when he uses it to describe good writing:

> The network does not designate a thing out there that would have roughly the shape of interconnected points, much like a telephone, a freeway, or a sewage "network." It is nothing more than *an indicator of the quality of a text* about the topics at hand. It qualifies its objectivity, that is, the ability of each actor to *make* other actors *do* unexpected things. A good text elicits

> networks of actors when it allows the writer to trace a set of relations defined as so many translations. (129)

Latour and others have discussed the problems with the term network. It is slippery and too often tidies up that which we hope remains a messy web of connections. For instance, in *Protocol: How Control Exists After Decentralization*, Alexander Galloway uses the term to describe material technological arrangements; Clay Spinuzzi's *Network* also uses the term, but his focus is on understanding complex webs of activity. The term introduces numerous problems, and even Latour recognizes this: "The word network is so ambiguous that we should have abandoned it long ago." (129). But Latour doesn't abandon the term, and he still finds some use for it. We too recognize these problems, and we also grant that the term can too often slip into a celebration of connectivity and rhizomatic flow. Our aim is to avoid this uncritical approach to networks while also using it to note how reading in slow motion allows different modes of attention to intersect and overlap.

However, a detailed account of the literature on networks is outside the scope of this essay, and for now we want to focus on how Latour uses the term to describe writing that "traces a network," and that is willing to take risks. For Latour, a textual account can fail just as an experiment can. This risk of failure emerges from attempts to account for various causal factors (in the terms of his actor-network theory, actors) rather than a few important "chosen" ones (130). A network, in Latour's sense, is a piece of writing that "can easily fail—it does fail most of the time— since it *can put aside neither the complete artificiality of the enterprise nor its claim to accuracy and truthfulness*" (133, emphasis in original). We must live in this uncomfortable zone, between recognizing that we are making a network and understanding that our network is only helpful if others find it persuasive or useful. This kind of work is not separate from the essay, the traditional product of the literary studies classroom, but an essay could only be a network if we allowed it to be messy, to explore multiple possibilities, and to refuse the traditional thesis-driven writing that insists that we choose one path at the expense of others. A network does not choose a single actor as the "key" to understanding a situation. A network insists that such a choice is not risky enough.

One of the more interesting consequences of this shift in our reading practice was the way that the students began to think about how the text, as it progresses, refers or calls upon itself, folding back on itself in a way that undermines the narrative standard of linear development in favor of a nodal economy that's significance resides in its connections to other sites of meaning. We might, for example, think of the fatal rope, whose movement at the end of the novel slips by so quickly that we might not have noticed it had the text not already distracted us with the rope some three hundred pages back. Or have the intervening pages only been a distraction from it? A narrative feint to obscure the connection between the object and the subject it will master? Because there, amid Ishmael's detailed accounts of the minutiae of whaling, he told us the consequences of the line running wrong and now, leading up to the confrontation between the monomaniacal Ahab and his perhaps divine but fully animated foe, the line does indeed run foul. Of the cause of Ahab's death, the text says only that "Ahab stooped to clear it; he did clear it; but the flying turn caught him round the neck, and voicelessly as Turkish mutes bowstring their victim, he was shot out of the boat" (Melville 572). Attending to the rope as *node* not only draws our attention to the narrative potential of non-human actors (the line), but also requires that we consider, at the very end of the tale, the impossible location of what narratology calls the "chronotope" (Bakhtin, 84–85). In studying the novel this way, the space-time of the novel becomes complex, fractured or refracted by the intra-textual network we are describing here. The novel, whose motion has always been chaotic (moving in between the present of the voyage, the past of the individual character, the future-past of the narrator, and the present of narration, to name only a few loci, and not including the ancient history of its allusions as well as other temporalities indicated by the external network), this novel *moves in more than one direction at any given time*, navigating to dispersed points in a sea of information.

Given the argument of the class—that *Moby Dick* was a network—giving students the opportunity to take risks, to trace networks, only made sense. The final projects in the class included a paired term paper and remix, writings that took as their focus a network in the novel (traced through a structure or trope of their own choosing). The goal of this paired assignment was to encourage students to attend not only to the networked structure that they were describing but also the networked structure of their own writing. As with reading, while we tend to look "through" this network in printed writing, the affordances of digital technology can call us to attend to movement and connectivity in new ways, to look *at* this compositional element as participating in instead of separate from sites of meaning. The term paper and its accompanying remix project provided students with an opportunity to see the affordances of each of these types of writing, noticing how they allowed for different engagements with the distractions of the text. One student, Katie McCarty, turned this consideration of the rope into an investigation of narrative structure itself, locating in the twinning of the rope's strands an apt expression of the narrative complexity of *Moby Dick*. Katie's network exposes an argument in the novel *about* narrative complexity. Her remix of her term paper into a presentation allowed her to highlight movement and connectivity, something that was communicated quite differently in the paper itself. While her term paper required her to progress through what seemed like a single argument, her network allowed her to explore the other strands woven into her larger argument but not given the same focus in the printed text. Her attention to the trope of looming, for example, is given new life as she attends to warp and weft as overlapping narrative events. A network is not necessarily an argument (though, it could be). Rather, it is an exposition of relationships, and it opens up a site of knowledge that is not traditionally sanctioned by the university.

DISTRACTION

In *Connected*, Steve Shaviro asks what it means to live in a network society. His answer, as he describes the experience of being online, is that networked life is defined by distraction: "I am continually being distracted. I can no longer concentrate on just one thing at a time. My body is pulled in several directions at once, dancing to many distinct rhythms" (7). For Shaviro, "the networked consumer . . . [is] intensely involved, and maximally distracted, all at once" (26). What we have been suggesting here is that distraction is not necessarily tied to the network society or to digital technologies. *Moby Dick*, as a network, calls for readers to "dance to many distinct rhythms" and to "be pulled in several directions at once." While we might typically associate the reading of novels with Hayles's "deep attention," the practice of slow reading actually demonstrates that the form of the novel carries with it distraction and network connections. As we attend to the networks of the text, we are sent in various directions, and the slow reader learns to follow and trace these paths.

Distraction certainly ramps up in certain digital, networked environments, but it does not originate with the development of digital technology. Rather, these technologies attune us to something that is already present in print texts such as *Moby Dick*, a networked structure of relations that calls for both hyper and deep attention simultaneously. In thinking with the network—that is, attending to networks by tracing and mapping the multiple possibilities that emerge—we can discover how this structure produces meaning in the print text. If we relieve ourselves of the prejudice that networks are emergent with digital technology, then we can, without the threat of anachronism, use networked ways of thinking to find structures or sites of meaning that we might otherwise overlook.

In 1962, Ruben Brower tells parents that the response to the proliferation of information should not be to read *more* but to read *better*, and our response to the challenges of engaging with the network is not far from that. However, we imagine that part of reading better is not disengaging with networks but rather explicitly engaging them *as a way of thinking* and a way to better understand print texts. If the network thrives on distraction, then we are suggesting that the slow reading classroom gives students permission to be distracted, to follow connections, to trace nodes and edges.

Works Cited

Bakhtin, Mikhail. *Dialogic Imagination*. U of Texas P, 1982.

Brower, Reuben. "Reading in Slow Motion." *In Defense of Reading: A Reader's Approach to Literary Criticism*, edited by Reuben A. Brower and Richard Poirier, Dutton, 1962, pp. 3–21.

Carr, Nicholas. "Is Google Making Us Stupid?" *The Atlantic*, Aug. 2008, www.theatlantic.com/magazine/archive/2008/07/is-google-making-us-stupid/306868/. Accessed 13 Aug. 2013.

De Man, Paul. *The Resistance to Theory*. U of Minnesota P, 1986.

Galloway, Alexander R. *Protocol: How Control Exists after Decentralization*. The MIT Press, 2006.

Hayles, N. Katherine. "Hyper and Deep Attention: The Generational Divide in Cognitive Modes." *Profession*, 2007. pp. 187–99.

Latour, Bruno. *Reassembling the Social: An Introduction to Actor-Network-Theory*. Oxford UP, 2007.

McCarty, Katie. "Loose Ends: Weaving the Narrative Network." *Prezi*, 2012, prezi.com. Accessed 13 Aug 2013.

Melville, Herman. *Moby Dick, or The Whale*. Northwestern UP, 2001.

Miller, Richard. "Reading in Slow Motion." *Text2Cloud*. text2cloud.com/wp-content/uploads/2011/01/Reading_in_Slow_Motion_Final-41.pdf.

@Text2cloud. "'Reading in Slow Motion.' Saying good-bye to academic pub-
     lishing." *Twitter*. November 1, 2010, 2:27 PM.
—. "So Much Depends on the Carriage Return: Publishing in the Digital Age."
     Text2Cloud 24 Nov. 2010, text2cloud.com/2010/11/so-much-depends-on-
     the-carriage-return-publishing-in-the-digital-age/. Accessed 13 Aug. 2013.
Sayers, Jentery. Syllabus for HUMA 250, Digital Representation and Creation
     in a Humanities Context: "How to Network a Novel," Spring 2012, http://
     web.uvic.ca/~englblog/huma250s2012.pdf. Accessed 13 Aug. 2013.
Shaviro, Steven. *Connected, or, What It Means to Live in the Network Society*. U
     of Minnesota P, 2003.
Spinuzzi, C. *Network: Theorizing Knowledge Work in Telecommunications*.
     Cambridge UP, 2008.

5 Provocation: Networked History, Networked Humanities

Jim Ridolfo

Summer 1991

For the first time, my father brings his new government-issue laptop home from the office. He has to write a report with a new portable computer and has been dozing off during the day in his mandatory training classes. He takes about an hour to setup the awkwardly large computer on our rickety kitchen table. Moving the computer from the trunk of his brown Malibu into the kitchen was physically challenging for him. For the next two hours he screams at the computer, violently poking at it with his good index finger. The computer physically and mentally exhausts his war-weary body and he goes to sleep.

The next morning the computer is still on the kitchen table. I take the old AT&T rotary phone off the kitchen wall and a few hours later I called into my first bulletin board system. The terminal window was black and white, each line of ASCII text seemed to take an eternity to appear in the command line terminal application.

FALL 2000

I'm in Dr. Galen Johnson's continental philosophy seminar at the University of Rhode Island with illusions that I would continue as a computer science major, but with a dwindling interest in the degree after the dot-com crash just a few months before. Galen is lecturing about place and space, and at some point he tells the class about Samuel Johnson's English definition of a "net work" from 1756:

> Any thing reticulated or decussated, at equal distances, with interstices between the intersections. (18D1r)

I had absolutely no idea what Galen Johnson or this Samuel Johnson character was talking about. If Google Books had existed, I might have found Elbert Hubbard's 1901 book *Samuel Johnson* and his discussion of Johnson's network,

> Quibblers possibly may arise and present Johnson's definition of network — "Anything reticulated or decussated at equal distances with interstices between the intersections," but with the quibbler we have no time to dally. Some people insist on having their literature illustrated, just as others refuse to attend lectures that are not reinforced by a stereoptican. (Hubbarrd, 124–25)

But there was no Google Books, and I didn't connect to Hubbard's entry until 2013 when I searched for commentary on Johnson's definition. However, in the years since 1991, I have made other connections. I've thrown ethernet cable through ceiling ducts, called BBSes all over the world, built local TCP/IP networks, and thought I knew a thing or two about networks. But my philosophy course left me thinking that I had a lot more to learn. I changed my major to philosophy.

WINTER 2013

I'm assistant professor of Writing, Rhetoric, and Digital Studies at the University of Kentucky. My latest book project is on digitizing Samaritan manuscripts. I have boxes full of old hardware and rent colocated servers on two continents. I used to think of every server as an island of unknown potential in the same way some of my colleagues discuss the "deep web" today. When I'm feeling nostalgic, I search YouTube for videos of operating systems booting. Sometime in December, Brian

McNely walked down the hall to my office and asked me to write a few thoughts about a networked humanities. A few hours after saying yes, I opened up Google Drive on my office computer and started to write.

Twenty years ago, I used to know where every file was on every machine. I was concerned about SCSI collisions and the number and type of /dev/tty devices. I'd check blinking hubs daily for packet collision or packet loss through plain old telephone service connections. Today, I think more about knocking on an office door down the hall or how to arrange a flight in such a way that I can make time to see old friends from decades ago. Johnson's definition of a network, as a definition in itself, is no longer interesting to me. What I found interesting about networks before Johnson's definition and after, is not the definition or the digital itself but the surprising potential of professional relationships and friendships: network humanities.

WORKS CITED

Hubbard, Elbert. *Samuel Johnson*. The Roycrofters, 1901.

Johnson, Samuel. *A Dictionary of the English Language., 1756*. 2nd edition, GlasGow University Library Special Collections Dept, Sp Coll Hunterian Dh.1.12–13, Excerpt available: special.lib.gla.ac.uk/exhibns/month/apr2007.html.

6 Networked Asymmetry and Survivability in the Digital Humanities

Nate Kreuter

The paper I presented at #nhuk in February, 2013 was intended as a provocation. And provoke it apparently did, judging from the Twitter backchannel conversations and the discussion period after I spoke, both of which were contentious. After only somewhat seriously titling it "Cosa Nostra: The Digital Humanities as Meta-Cognitive, Navel-Gazing Crime Syndicate," I argued in my presentation that the Digital Humanities (DH) began as a sort of rogue network, much like a criminal syndicate in terms of its organizational structure, and that as it is legitimized within established academic bureaucracies/hierarchies, DH risks some serious growing pains. Institutional affirmation might mean a conservative turn away from DH's original hacker ethos, and from its history of side-stepping the academic norms and bureaucracies that could not, or would not, initially recognize and affirm the methods, work, and publication venues of digital humanists. Unlike the mob going legit though, the Digital Humanities is unusually self-aware (Who are we? What do we do?, it consistently asks, see Kirschenbaum; Fitzpatrick). As both the conversations of the February, 2013 conference and this volume illustrate, self-awareness may mean shaping an emerging discipline in intentional, rather than haphazard, ways, which is an uncommon opportunity if we compare the history of the Digital

Humanities to predecessor disciplines (I don't mean to imply one way or the other whether or not DH is a discipline unto itself—that's another conversation).

As DH—whatever it is—is absorbed by The University, it also turns increasingly to face public audiences as its artifacts are in turn made public, which brings up two more points that are tied in with the process of institutionalization that we see unfolding. In his own blog write-up of #nhuk, Collin Brooke summarized the two additional threads of my presentation this way:

> Our current [publishing] model keeps us silo'ed by default—to my mind, open access isn't just a matter of taking down those walls, but in reimagining the system that defaults to silo in the first place. Nate Kreuter (@lawnsports) talked a little bit about this the following day in terms of considering both material and cognitive accessibility. We can make our work open materially, but without an infrastructure that makes it accessible cognitively, we're not doing as much as we should be.

I would re-state Brooke's summary of my own presentation even more strongly. Cognitive access to DH work and artifacts constitutes a sort of public relations wildcard that, depending upon how it is played, could reinvigorate humanistic inquiry much more broadly, or widen the moat that appears to exist between academe and the public at-large. As the simultaneous processes of institutionalization and going-public occur, issues of open access and cognitive access will be foregrounded. Once scholarship is made public—and current trends suggest that scholarship of all varieties will (and need to) become more publicly accessible over time ("2013 University of California Open Access Policy"; Guess)— some of the audiences accessing the materials of the Digital Humanities will begin to demand cognitive access, will begin to demand understanding of the material that they are accessing, presumably online. Or, even trickier, public audiences demand what they *think* constitutes understanding. These will be politically rocky waters for the digital humanities to navigate, the more so because the DH ship is steered by an anarchic committee, so to speak. As my own home discipline of rhetoric and composition has repeatedly demonstrated, the demand for cognitive access to a text is a political demand, and critiques of difficult-to-access language and styles, like the specialized language of academe, are often political critiques (Barnard; Prendergast; Butler 131–35). Thus, the political/financial pressure currently on the humanities may be increased by the greater visibility of the digital humanities. The era of the so-called Culture Wars does not appear to be over, and with the digital humanities so frequently facing outward, to publics beyond the academy, it is no stretch to imagine that individual projects will come under the scrutiny of special interest groups and individuals who feel they have a stake in scholars' interpretations and arguments. Because DH, by definition, leverages almost entirely new methods of inquiry, these new methods themselves will be subject to outsider scrutiny as well.

All of these simultaneous possibilities and liabilities present themselves at a time when the traditional humanities are under political and fiscal assault, at least within many locations in the United States (Kiley). While some observers debate whether the humanities are indeed on a downswing, defenses of the humanities mount nonetheless (Berube; American Academy of Arts and Sciences). A crisis is perceived by many humanists. Regardless of the numbers, if humanists are to truly justify the work we do, we must face the public and explain in far more concrete terms what it is we do and why it matters. A first step is initiated simply by being public, by publishing our artifacts in open-access forums, rather than esoteric, paywall defended journals. The need to face the broader public, in addition to our peers, already seems to be a common ethos amongst digital humanists, who seem largely supportive of the open-access movement and the notion that public scholarship, often conducted directly or indirectly with public funding, ought to be publicly available and not hidden behind the paywalls of traditional publishers. Having to face and engage with broader publics though will also shift the nature of our own work in unforeseeable ways, making us more accountable to non-experts. As our network expands, it will become more asymmetric. Instead of the peer-to-peer connections that largely characterize the traditional humanities, the digital humanities network will include many expert-to-non-expert connections, where power and access are unequally held. And it might just be the only chance for long-term survival that the humanities has. The digital asymmetry may save the humanities.

While I stand by the theses I offered in February, 2013 (sort of surprisingly to myself, actually), the experience of #nhuk leads me now to see the issues that I originally raised as even higher stakes than I saw them at the time, which brings me to the title of this essay. The terms *asymmetry* and *survivability* are carefully selected. Networks are quite efficient at leveraging unequally distributed resources. Through a variety of types of network connections, a researcher, for example, at a relatively small, cash-strapped university can utilize software or expertise developed at a research university with the resources to develop new tools and methodologies. Similarly, expertise can travel through a network from where it originates to where it is needed. Asymmetric connections within a network, I contend, are more inherently valuable than symmetric connections. Equally weighted nodes, regardless of what quality we're measuring, are less in need of connection than unequally weighted nodes, which stand to benefit more through the sharing of their disparate resources/expertise. Networks don't only transport though. When operating efficiently, they alert those within the network who need the distant solution, and then deliver it. Networks, it almost—but doesn't quite—go without saying, allow information, expertise, and tools to move between the two locations (whether physical or digital or cognitive) where local conditions might be dramatically different. Asymmetric connections in particular help to ensure the long-term survivability of networks, a point that I will return to momentarily.

When I considered the networked nature of the digital humanities for my presentation in February, 2013, three intertwined problems dominated my concerns: (1) how will increasing institutional acceptance within broader university culture affect the somewhat renegade nature of the digital humanities?; (2) how will the open-access movement, whose own values parallel the digital humanities' values so closely, re-arrange the network?; (3) in an era when the humanities more broadly are scrutinized by some policymakers as inefficient, as a luxury, or as actively harmful, how will the digital humanities respond to political demands from non-academic audiences that their artifacts/products be not only materially available, but also cognitively available (and meaningful) to these disparate, non-academic audiences? I doubt that these problems can be "solved" in any discreet sense (I would bet heavily though and give odds that the first and last items on my list will be brutally difficult negotiations).

But before I follow these three threads any further, and hash out the details of the argument I'm already making, let's turn back for a moment to the organizing concept of the February, 2013 conference at the University of Kentucky (and this volume), which I've already referred to more than a little: the network. Networks occur in nature. But they are also man-made, and I've provided an image of basic network structures below. Ever since the first humans or proto-humans became cognitively sutured together through the first gruntings of language, we've been networked.[1] Within the US, the golden age of the man-made network began in the atomic age, as vastly networked interstate highways (for moving troops during invasions) and networked communications systems (which eventually became the internet) were designed to help the country survive nuclear war, by distributing people, resources, and access to both. In the graphic below we quickly grasp that a distributed network is the most survivable form a network can take. None of its nodes relies exclusively for connectivity upon central or hub nodes. Even when one or multiple nodes are sacrificed, the network survives intact, with all remaining nodes still able to reach all other remaining nodes through established, backed-up (although perhaps decreasingly efficient) paths. Questions that we need to consider when we take stock of the networked nature of the digital humanities are "What type of network do we have?" and "What type of network do we want?" While the connections between the nodes of the Digital Humanities might generate organically, in unplanned ways, we do have considerable power to shape the network additionally in conscious, intentional ways, which is an exceptional opportunity.

---

1. Yes, I'm implying that language is the fundamental thread of the network in this case. If I'm correct in that implication, it begins to explain why some disciplines, particularly disciplines explicitly oriented around the study of language, seem disproportionately drawn to the digital humanities. My own discipline of rhetoric and composition has been accused over over-representation within DH conversations. However, if the threads linking nodes within human networks, like the DH networks, are fundamentally threads of language, that linguistic threading might explain why those who study the constitutive power of language have gravitated toward DH conversations and happenings. Such exclusivity, however, ought not to be encouraged, particularly as I argue that asymmetric connections are of higher value than symmetric ones. That is, a connection between a rhetorician and a physicist is more valuable within my argument here than a connection between two rhetoricians.

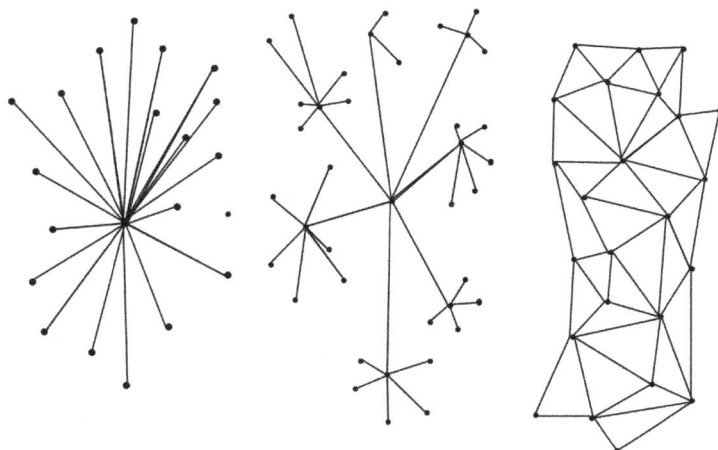

Figure 1. From left to right, centralized, decentralized, and distributed networks. Image adapted from Baran, Paul, "On Distributed Communications Networks." *IEEE Transactions on Communications Systems, 12.*1 (1964): 1–9. Print.

I argue that we need to cultivate a fully distributed network, to ensure the greatest network efficiency for moving around information and ideas and to ensure that the work and ethos of the digital humanities survives as local conditions change unpredictably at individual institutions. We need to shape the DH network such that it takes on a distributed form.

Which brings us to my next point, literally the points, the nodes, of the network. Notice something else in the illustration above. All the nodes in the networks depicted are of equal weight, visually signified by the same size dots. While they are of equal weight, they are not necessarily of equal importance. The central node in the centralized network is key. If it fails or disappears, the entire network fails with it. Similarly, the decentralized network relies upon more hub nodes, and the loss of any one hub significantly reduces the connectivity (and thus the efficiency) of the network (anybody who has experienced a flight delay at Chicago's O'Hare or Atlanta's Hartsfield airports knows the vulnerability of hubs). The only one of these three networks that is truly robust, truly survivable, is the distributed network, wherein all other nodes remain connected even when any single node disappears. Many node failures would be required to bring down or reduce the efficiency of the distributed network. In practical terms though, few networks are really comprised of equally weighted nodes. No matter the distribution pattern, some nodes are likely to be more qualitatively important than others, depending upon which quality we're measuring.[2] It's my contention that a truly healthy network, for our purposes, will be one connecting a wide spectrum of differently weighted nodes.

When we talk about any networked system, we might need to talk about the network as a whole, the nodes within the network, and/or the links between nodes. In reality, we are almost always talking about multiple networks. We could, for example, conceive of the digital humanities as a network of people, as a network of institutional actors, as a network of both, or as multiple networks of people and institutions that interconnect and disconnect. All networks, though, develop preferred paths, preferred ways of connecting nodes. By privileging certain channels and blocking access to others, networks have a predisposition toward creating powerful status-quo scenarios, which computer scientist and Silicon Valley lay-philosopher Jaron Lanier has dubbed "network effects" ("network effects" is sort of a general term, but I'm only really interested in Lanier's definition here). According to Lanier, once the pathways of a dominant network or pathway within a network are established, and once that particular network begins carrying a critical mass of communicative traffic, shifting the network or its traffic onto new paths becomes prohibitively difficult, even when such a shift is widely recognized as desirable.

In Lanier's book *Who Owns the Future?* he uses the example of Facebook to illustrate how a network carrying a "critical mass of conversation" might make it prohibitively difficult to shift or rearrange a network or conversations within a network, or to switch over to using a different network. He answers those who might contend that Facebook does not monopolize conversations, but merely hosts so many because of the popularity of its interface, thus:

> You might further object that it's based on individual choice, and that if Facebook wants to offer us a preferable free service, and the offer is accepted, that's just the market making a decision. That argument ignores network effects. Once a critical mass of conversation is on Facebook, then it's hard to get

2. A particularly accessible explanation of how networks function for humanists is physicist Albert-László Barabási's popular accounting, *Linked: How Everything Is Connected to Everything and What it Means for Business, Science, and Everyday Life.*

> conversation going elsewhere. What might have started out as a choice is no longer a choice after a network effect causes a phase change. After that point we effectively have less choice. It's no longer commerce, but soft blackmail. (207)

Lanier explains how network effects, which are essentially exponentially compounding forces, conspire without a central planner or architect to establish a certain technological status quo that in turn entrenches a cognitive and/or intellectual status quo. Network effects are not inherently positive or negative (though, Lanier treats them as consistently negative), but by entrenching status-quo scenarios, they make it difficult to effect change within a network when such change is desirable or necessary. Soft-blackmail, though, *is* negative, and counter to the ethos of academic inquiry, let alone the open-access ethos that DH allies closely with. Once network effects trigger a phase change (think back to high school chemistry), there is almost no going back, as the network takes on a new form and smaller, less dominant nodes die off. Blackboard, the widespread but often unpopular learning management software, benefits from network effects, as smaller, less established competitors cannot carry enough traffic within their networks (in the sense of garnering enough human participation) to compete. Therein is the danger for the digital humanities. This danger pertains not only to networks of infrastructure (such as digital humanities computing software developed at one institution and shared amongst others) and people (human DH actors), but also applies to a more abstract type of network, a network of cognitive access. Open access advocates, by producing credible alternatives to the traditional publishing model that universities are beginning to buy into, have shown that reversing entrenched network effects within the academy is indeed possible.

Within the digital humanities, the most distributed of our networks are individuals, people who work in the digital humanities who connect via digital technologies, web-based interfaces, and other social interfaces. Then there are institutional networks, by which I mean more formal networks of connection between universities, computing centers, government agencies, independent museums, and the like. These types of networks, or categories of nodes within a network, might be subject to network effects. As Lanier writes of network effects, "In the network age there can be collusion without colluders, conspiracies without conspirators" (72). In some ways, academe is already a conspiracy without conspirators, by which I mean that academic work has historically been cut off from larger publics. Our task here, perhaps, is to conspire, to collude, to shape the network in intentional ways.

What I'm advocating is the humanistic side of the digital humanities. If common calls to defend the humanities are to be credible, then our own organizational structure needs to better reflect the values of open access and democratization that defenders of the humanities claim to value (Franke; Borgman). One of the strengths of networks is their ability to avoid redundancy and thereby promote efficiency. So long as a node is secure and can be readily accessed, information does not need to be duplicated, for the other nodes within the network can always access the original source (of course, nodes sometimes fail, and so backups are a necessity). Such efficiency could be encouraged by cultivating a more asymmetric, fully distributed network, which would be politically, financially, and intellectually savvy. An asymmetric, distributed network—a fully distributed network comprised of nodes and links of different "weights."

Asymmetric relationships will ensure the survivability of the digital humanities, and perhaps even the humanities writ larger. Asymmetry is a good thing. Large universities' partnerships with small universities and institutions create financial efficiency while distributing expertise and artifacts and the opportunities to access both. By making a self-conscious effort to partner with different types of institutions, individual institutions can help to ensure a robust, survivable DH network, a network strong enough to weather local and state threats to humanities funding (whether digital or otherwise), by shifting resources and expertise in response to local events. Moreover, once asymmetric paths are established, such shifts would not need to be consciously planned but would be natural to the traffic patterns and data flows within networks.

If readers are unconvinced that asymmetric questions between institutional DH actors will contribute to the survivability of the humanities, hopefully they will at least agree that such partnerships are good politics. Broadening the cognitive access of DH work will help to reverse the criticisms of many lay-readers that the academy is aloof, impractical, and elitist. Which brings me to the second, most minor, and least controversial of my three theses. Open access will force unforeseeable changes upon the digital humanities. Because they developed in parallel as movements, and are movements often populated by the same actors, the DH and open accesscommunities have much in common in terms of values. Many DH publishing models are simultaneously open access models. So, how will the production of openly available DH artifacts change the DH network? We can't say exactly, but the question springs me forward to my third, final, and more troubling thesis: with material access to DH artifacts, non-expert audiences (that is, people who do not produce DH work professionally) will begin to demand cognitive access to the works they encounter, a demand that will create a set of political pressures much harder to confront or solve than those that the open access movement appears to gradually be overcoming (such as the network effect that, at least within higher education, has privileged antiquated, centralized, expensive, limited-access, traditional publishing models).

Despite aspirations of public access and engagement, which undergird the ethos of the digital humanities, not all DH work is or will be cognitively accessible to all internet-accessing publics. Indeed, digital humanities work could not be all things to all people, just as no utterance of language can. But there will be pressure for exactly that. We need look no further than the debate over "clarity" (cited earlier) within my home discipline of rhetoric and composition to know that similar demands of total cognitive accessibility will be expected of the publicly funded and publicly available work that the digital humanities produces over time. But such complete accessibility is of course a rhetorical and cognitive impossibility, entirely unattainable. As rhetoricians have noted, public arguments over clear or obfuscating writing are not about prose at all, but about political and cognitive capital, and about which audiences should reasonably be able to expect access to particular texts (Kintz, "Clarity"; Kintz, "Finding the Strength"; Crowley 146–7). If my own state of North Carolina is at all representative, politically motivated scrutiny of humanities work will focus the attention of academic outsiders upon our work. As the network of accessibility is expanded to non-academic audiences, as the paywall of traditional journals is breached, we will become responsible to a new set of interlocutors for the implications of our work. I want to suggest that this new, outsider scrutiny is neither good nor bad, but loaded with both liabilities and opportunities for the humanities.

One infamous case is illustrative of the tensions presented by our (I believe) healthy trends toward both open and cognitive access. In 2000, Michael Bellesiles, then an Emory University professor of history, published *Arming America: The Origins of a National Gun Culture*. *Arming America* was published by Knopf, a popular press with a reputation for publishing well-researched academic works with the potential to appeal to broader audiences beyond academe. There was a reasonable expectation by Knopf that the book would interest many more Americans than just those working in the field of history, given that it explored a subject that many Americans feel strongly about—guns and gun control. Bellesiles's project was not a digital humanities project, neither in the methods the scholarship deployed, nor in the mode of its publication. It was, in fact, a very traditional monograph. Shortly after its publication though, the book became embroiled in a controversy that unfolded primarily within digital venues. The controversy, and how that controversy played out within the digital environment, is instructive in terms of how it indicates some of the types of conflicts likely to occur over scholarly artifacts when those artifacts are made public, and particularly when the artifacts are connected to volatile political or social issues. The Bellesiles case illustrates what happens when public audiences demand cognitive access to a scholarly artifact and apply their own, outsider critiques to the artifact.

Upon its publication, *Arming America* garnered widespread attention, far more than is probably typical of a history monograph. Part of *Arming America*'s appeal was that it overturned much of the conventional wisdom about the history of guns in America. Bellesiles argued that the advent of a "gun culture" in the United States was a relatively recent development that was not, as many believe, rooted in America's Colonial past. Instead, Bellesiles wrote, America's gun culture is the legacy of a federal government campaign to arm citizens that began just prior to the Civil War (5). Bellesiles went on to argue that guns in Colonial America were rare, expensive, unreliable and their ownership often regulated by the state, both before and after the Revolutionary War. If Bellesiles's revision of the historical record had held up to scrutiny, even a foundationalist reading of the Constitution would have had to concede that the Second Amendment had not been intended by the Framers of the Constitution to allow individual private citizens to arm themselves, but provided the right to bear arms only to state militias. Such a sweeping reevaluation of the context of the Second Amendment could have had a tremendous effect on contemporary gun control debates, a point that was not lost on Bellesiles (5).

There were two almost immediate reactions to *Arming America* when the book was published. Initially, reviews in scholarly and popular forums written by academics praised the work. Perhaps not coincidentally, these reviews were published within "old media" venues, pay-accessed print publications and traditional academic journals. Celebratory reviews of *Arming America* written by three exceptionally prominent historians appeared in *The New York Times Book Review*, the *New York Review of Books*, and *The Los Angeles Times*, not to mention a slew of praise from academics whose prepublication compliments appeared on the first edition's dust jacket (Anderson; Morgan; Wills). Additional praiseful, but more measured, reviews appeared exclusively in scholarly publications, among them the *Journal of American History* (Lane). Bellesiles's book was also awarded the prestigious Bancroft Prize for History by Columbia University in 2001. Published as a traditional codex text, the so-called "establishment" reviews of the text appeared within similarly traditional venues, paper-and-ink publications with editorial teams and formal vetting processes. Nothing about the book, or its professionally conducted reviews, was recognizably open access or linked to the just-nascent digital humanities movement that was concurrent with the book's publication in 2000.

The online, digitally hosted reaction to Bellesiles's work, however, was quite different. While academics (all of them humanists) were publicly celebrating the book within traditional publishing venues, a vocal contingent of amateur historians and partisan pro-gun organizations, including the National Rifle Association, began to call into question the legitimacy of Bellesiles's research. The contingent's attacks ran the gamut, from accusations of having fabricated historical evidence to *ad hominem* attacks. While the personal attacks were quickly discredited or appropriately ignored, some very serious objections to Bellesiles's research and data analysis lingered. The fallout is thoroughly documented in historian Peter Charles Hoffer's book *Past Imperfect: Facts, Fiction, Fraud—American History from Bancroft and Parkman to Ambrose, Bellesiles, Ellis and Goodwin*. Hoffer documents how fellow professional historians eventually determined that Bellesiles had outright fabricated or misrepresented key evidence, including his analysis of Colonial probate records, upon which his thesis that guns were rare in Colonial America largely rested (147–51). However, such scrutiny from disciplinary peers might never have occurred if not for a series of discussions and allegations that arose in online forums such as H-Net (more on which in just a moment). *Arming America* was eventually thoroughly discredited: Bellesiles lost his post at Emory after an internal investigation, the Bancroft Prize was revoked, Knopf dropped the book, and the discipline of history suffered a tremendous credibility loss in the eyes of those publics that paid attention. The incident was high-profile enough to elicit widespread news coverage in mainstream media (Worth).

Importantly for our consideration of the digital humanities here, the initial insights into the fraud were the result of amateur scrutiny of Bellesiles's book that took place primarily on H-Net, and on the History News Network, both prototypical digital humanities enterprises that originated before *DH* was such a bandied term, where professional historians and the interested lay-publics regularly interacted online, primarily through message boards. While perhaps not initially created to fulfill a "digital humanities" role, the function of these message boards in the Bellesiles case indicates some of the tensions that seem likely to crop up as digital humanistic work expands within the public realm and increasingly faces public, rather than exclusively academic, audiences. Quite significantly, the realization that there were serious inconsistencies in Bellesiles's references occurred to partisans outside of academia before it occurred to the trained professional historians who reviewed *Arming America* for a variety of publications. Only later did professional historians confirm what the amateurs had initiated through the asymmetric connections between amateur and professional historians enabled by the distributed network that H-Net, in particular, created. Perhaps it was their partisanship, their irreverence toward a text with all the hallmarks of serious, stuffy research, but the uncredentialled amateurs caught problems in the Bellesiles text that had evaded reviewers and professional academic reviewers. Networked expertise is greater than the discreet expertise of individuals, and can be applied to discredit work, as in the Bellesiles case, or to build work up further.

As the digital humanities matures, broadens, and produces more artifacts for various publics to encounter, more episodes like the Bellesiles case will occur. Not because humanists are crooked or because there is any reason to believe that such academic fraud is on the uptick, but because more encounters with more publics will mean more encounters with skeptics, and more opportunities for cases of fraud or, more likely, sloppy scholarship to be revealed. It will become part of the cost of doing business, and of doing business publicly in digital environments where virtually everybody has physical access, even if not necessarily cognitive access, to the artifacts that digital humanists produce. And even when publicly available scholarship is airtight, in terms of the validity of its data and methodologies, some scholarship will come under fire as never before because of publics and lay readers that take issue with its conclusions or implications. Equally significant, methodologically bullet-proof scholarship (pardon the pun) will also come under scrutiny and, in all likelihood, politically motivated attack.

With open access though, public audiences are likely to demand cognitive access. Put more simply, public audiences will demand understanding of what we publish. The disciplines of English and history already understand this pressure—public critiques of both disciplines often contend that if one knows English or a bit of history, one ought to be able to read the literature of either discipline and understand it, an expectation that is not often placed, for example, upon physicists. Humanists who publish in open forums will have to walk a careful line between disciplinary rigor and public accessibility, for if our work is not also cognitively accessible to interested publics, we further marginalize the humanities in the eyes of critics. The achievement of open access will only succeed if we (digital) humanists can simultaneously make our ideas accessible, and not only physically available, to the publics we frequently claim to serve. What's most important in the Bellesiles example, at least for the purposes of understanding the implications of the digital humanities' networked structure, is how the fraud was discovered, pursued, and unfolded within an environment that only could have existed because of digital interconnection and information sharing.

On the one hand, it is easy to see the Bellesiles case as a failure of the humanities. A humanist scholar of (then) high reputation published a monograph with all the hallmarks of serious scholarship with a popular publishing house in order to reach a broader audience. Even though it was published as traditional text, *Arming America* at the time of its publication contended to be a serious piece of historical scholarship published by popular press, cultivating an ethos of accessibility and public availability that many of today's digital humanists would both recognize and sympathize with.

On the other hand, we might view the Bellesiles case as an early but fraught win for the digital humanities and a testament to the potential of a networked digital humanities to benefit from its connections to interested communities of non-experts. Notice, again, that the connections between amateurs and professionals within H-Net were asymmetric, and it might have been the amateurs' amateur status that allowed them to cry foul where professionals had not. The attacks on and original inquiries into the research of *Arming America* were initially highly partisan and ideologically motivated. Amateur historians and gun enthusiasts who saw the colonial re-interpretation as a threat to contemporary interpretations of the Second Amendment set out to dismantle the research. But, when you're right, you're right. Despite the ideological motivations, the fabricated research *had been fabricated*, and the amateurs found it, and quite reasonably discredited the work. Without that intervention, which was enabled only by the discussions and information sharing that took place on the digital forums of H-Net, *Arming America* would likely have entered the scholarly canon, surrounded by its praise from within the academy, and would have influenced subsequent scholarship and historical interpretations while its problematic foundation went unnoticed, perpetuating indefinitely a piece of fraudulent scholarship. The public, despite its lack of formal training, got it right. This is the great promise of a truly networked humanities, that disciplinary outsiders,' and academic outsiders,' critiques and readings might be incorporated into our own, might even over time shift the very nature of the work we do and the forms that our work takes.

But the untrained horde's discovery of what professional historians had failed to notice—for whatever reasons—threatened the credibility of the discipline of history. Such incidents, while hopefully never common, will be inevitable. And the more publicly available a work is, the more likely problems are to be rooted out. So, is the solution for digital humanities projects to be even more carefully vetted than traditional projects, or is the solution to allow the collective network to sort things out, to separate the good from the bad and the outright rotten after the fact? It's a tall order to ask scholars to achieve a higher level of academic rigor, while simultaneously making their work cognitively accessible to non-expert publics. Instead, we may perhaps have to engage in more dialogue with interlocutors from outside the academy, updating and curating pieces of scholarship after the event of publication, rather than trying to anticipate all possible critiques and abandoning the piece to the public upon publication. The demands of new audiences will shift the DH network in even more dramatic ways than DH has already shifted the traditional humanities model. And this asymmetrically induced shifting might need to be welcomed.

The Bellesiles case demonstrates to those who might fear a lowering of academic standards with open access publishing that the contrary is true: openly available works will be more rigorously scrutinized, both in terms of the quality of research itself, and in the expectation that the research be presented in such a way that intelligent lay-readers can access it. But the form of scrutiny will be very different from the insular scrutiny of traditional peer review. Whereas in traditional academic publishing models review occurs largely prior to publication, in the form of double-blind peer review, within the new model the essential reviewing might occur after publication, when a work comes into contact with publics outside of academe, who will undoubtedly scrutinize it in entirely different ways than disciplinary peers might. Such new scrutiny, hardly a threat to competent work, may lead to a strengthening of both of our research methods and our ability to communicate our research and its significance to new and broader publics of interested non-experts.

Networks are inherently and ultimately about survival and survivability, whether they're ecological networks or communications networks conscientiously designed to survive nuclear attacks. Given the current economic climate, within which the Great Recession has served as a cover for cutting the funding of the humanities in general, and the political climate within which culturally conservative forces have dubbed the humanities impractical or unnecessary, we should expect to see some nodes disappearing from the networks of the humanities (which is something even larger than the digital humanities). The Digital Humanities will be further legitimized, both within the institution of the modern university, and with the broader public,

Being networked means being connected to non-professionals, to the general public and lay readers, and to all of the various degrees of expertise and interest and interpretive skill that such readers may bring with them when they encounter a product of the digital humanities within, presumably, a digital environment. These encounters will inevitably trigger new connections, as an astute reader with their own specialized knowledge makes a contribution to a digital humanities project, or simply re-circulates a piece, as networks so efficiently do, to a new audience. But there will also be tension. How will the networked digital humanities cope with the interventions and critiques of outsiders, and non-professionals, some of whom will be cranks with little credibility and some sort of ideological axe to grind, and others of whom will possess self-cultivated expertise that rivals professionally accredited expertise? I hope that we will "cope" by welcoming the intersection, by welcoming the asymmetry. I suspect that the collective response to that question will determine whether or not the (digital) humanities survives, and in what form.

WORKS CITED

"2013 University of California Open Access Policy." Office of Scholarly Communication, U of California, http://osc.universityofcalifornia.edu/open-access-policy/. osc. Accessed 21 Aug. 2013.

American Academy of Arts and Sciences. *The Heart of the Matter: The Humanities and Social Sciences for a Vibrant, Competitive, and Secure Nation.* American Academy of Arts & Sciences, 2013.

Anderson, Fred. "Guns, Rights and People." Review of *Arming America: The Origins of a National Gun Culture*, by Michael Bellesiles. *Los Angeles Times*, 17 Sept. 2000, articles.latimes.com/2000/sep/17/books/bk-22272/3. Accessed 21 Aug. 2013.

Barabási, Albert-Lászlo. *LInked: How Everything Is Connected to Everything Else and What It Means for Business, Science, and Everyday Life.* Plume, 2002.

Barnard, Ian. "The Ruse of Clarity." *College Composition and* Communication, vol. 61, no. 3, 2010, pp. 434–51.

Bellesiles, Michael A. *Arming America: The Origin of a National Gun Culture.* Knopf, 2000.

Berube, Michael. "The Humanities, Declining? Not According to the Numbers." *The Chronicle of Higher Education.* Chronicle of Higher Education, 1 July 2013, chronicle.com/article/The-Humanities-Declining-Not/140093/. Accessed 21 Aug. 2013.

Borgman, Christine L. "The Digital Future Is Now: A Call to Action for the Humanities." *Digital Humanities* Quartlery, vol. 3, no. 4, 2009, www.digitalhumanities.org/dhq/vol/3/4/000077/000077.html. Accessed 21 Aug. 2013.

Brooke, Collin Gifford. "Networked Humanities @ UKentucky (#nhuk), Spring 2013." *Collin Gifford Brooke*, Version 2.0, Collin Gifford Brooke, 25 Feb. 2013, www.cgbrooke.net/2013/02/25/networked-humanities-ukentucky-nhuk-spring-2013/. Accessed 21 Aug. 2013.

Butler, Paul. *Out of Style: Reanimating Stylistic Study in Composition and Rhetoric.* Utah State UP, 2008.

Crowley, Sharon. *Toward a Civil Discourse: Rhetoric and Fundamentalism.* U Pittsburgh P, 2006.

Fitzpatrick, Kathleen. "The Humanities, Done Digitally." *Debates in the Digital Humanities*, edited by Matthew K. Gold, U of Minnesota P, 2012, pp. 12–15.

Franke, Richard J. *Democratic Vistas for the Humanities.* Issue brief no. 1. Imagining America, n.d.

Guess, Andy. "Harvard Opts in to 'Opt Out' Plan." *Inside Higher Ed*, 13 Feb. 2008, www.insidehighered.com/news/2008/02/13/openaccess. Accessed 21 Aug. 2013.

Hoffer, Peter Charles. *Past Imperfect: American History from Bancroft to Parkman to Ambrose, Bellesiles, Ellis and Goodwin.* PublicAffairs, 2007.

Kiley, Kevin. "Another Liberal Arts Critic." *Inside Higher Ed*, 30 Jan. 2013, www.insidehighered.com/news/2013/01/30/north-carolina-governor-joins-chorus-republicans-critical-liberal-arts. Accessed 21 Aug. 2013.

Kintz, Linda. "Clarity, Mothers, and the Mass-Mediated National Soul: A Defense of Ambiguity." *Media, Culture, and the Religious Right*, edited by Linda Kintz and Julia Lesage, U of Minnesota P, 1998, pp. 115–39.

—. "Finding the Strength to Surrender: Marriage, Market Theocracy and the Spirit of America." *Theory, Culture & Society*, vol. 24, no. 4, 2007, pp. 111–30.

Kirshenbaum, Matthew. "What Is Digital Humanities and What's It Doing in English Departments?" *Debates in the Digital Humanities*, edited by Matthew K. Gold, U of Minnesota P, 2012, pp. 3–11.

Lane, Roger. Review of *Arming American: The Origins of a National Gun Culture. Journal of American*, by Michael Bellesiles. History, vol. 88, no. 2, 2001, pp. 614–15.

Lanier, Jaron. *Who Owns the Future?* Simon, 2013.

Moore, Shawn W. "#nhuk—Twitter Archive & Visualization." *Shawn W. Moore*, Shawn W. Moore, 20 Feb. 2013. www.smoores.org/nhuk_archive/. Accessed 21 Aug. 2013.

Morgan, Edmund. Review of *Arming America: The Origins of a National Gun Culture*, by Michael Bellesiles. *New York Review of* Books, vol. 47, no. 16, 2002, pp. 30–32.

"Partnerships." *Maryland Institute for Technology in the Humanities*, n.d., mith.umd.edu/community/partnership/. Accessed 21 Aug. 2013

Prendergast, Catherine. "Fighting Style: Reading the Unabomber's Strunk and White." *College* English, vol. 72, no. 1, 2009, pp. 10–28.

Spiro, Lisa. "Getting Started in Digital Humanities." *Journal of Digital* Humanities, vol. 1, no. 1, 2011. journalofdigitalhumanities.org/1-1/getting-started-in-digital-humanities-by-lisa-spiro/. Accessed 21 Aug. 2013. Spiro, Lisa. XXX

Wills, Garry. "Spiking the Gun Myth." Review of *Arming America: The Origins of a National Gun Culture*, by Michael Bellesiles. *New York Times*, 10 Sept. 2001, late ed., sec. 7: 5.

Worth, Robert F. "Historian's Prizewinning Book on Guns Is Embroiled in a Scandal." *New York* Times, 8 Dec. 2001, Books: n. pag.

7 Provocation: Networked Humanities, Past and Present

Devoney Looser

Like many literary historians, I have a knee-jerk response to being asked to define something. I turn to the *Oxford English Dictionary* *(OED)*. The *OED* illuminates both *network* and *humanities*, past and present, although separately, without considering what they might mean in tandem.

Network seems the more interesting of the two words. It enters the English language in the sixteenth century as a textile-based term, describing interlaced threads in fabric or, literally, the interlaced parts of a net. In the middle of the seventeenth century, network starts to refer to living things: the laced structure in animal or plant tissue. At a very early point in its history, "net-work" also took on negative connotations. A great obsolete meaning from 1675 indicates that network meant complicated or involved. The *OED*'s example is from theologian Richard Baxter, who satirically opines, "You will have more solid truth than such Writers do teach you in their learned Net-work treatises."

The definition most of us imagine today—"A chain or system of interconnected immaterial things"—dates back to 1817, with an example from Samuel Taylor Coleridge's *"Blessed Are Ye that Sow Beside All Waters!": A Lay Sermon Addressed to the Higher and Middle Classes, on the Existing Distresses and Discontents.* By the 1880s, network had come to describe interconnected groups of people, as well as things that were electrically connected. The first use of network to mean electrically connected communications systems dates to 1914. "A system of interconnected computers" dates to 1962. To engage in "networking" socially or professionally goes back to the 1980s. So does the meaning of networking involving linking computers together "to allow the sharing of data, interactive operation, and efficient utilization of resources; to incorporate into a computer network." Networked as an adjective dates only to the 1960s.

Humanities has a much shorter, perhaps less complicated, and much better- known history. In the plural, usually coupled with "the," it means "the branch of learning concerned with human culture; the academic subjects collectively comprising this branch of learning, as history, literature, ancient and modern languages, law, philosophy, art, and music." The humanities "are typically distinguished from the social sciences in having a significant historical element, in the use of interpretation of texts and artefacts rather than experimental and quantitative methods," says the *OED*. Such meanings date from the mid-nineteenth century. They certainly persist, although reasonable people may disagree about the extent to which humanists remain committed to making the "historical element" "significant" in our field.

As a scholar of the eighteenth and nineteenth centuries, I already knew that this period saw the rise of the modern postal service, of intricate systems of roads, and of what we now think of as tourism, so it seemed unsurprising to me to learn that this was the period that fostered modern meanings of networks. The networks we look at most often in literary studies prior to the mid-nineteenth century involve readers, books, letters, and letter writers. We study the networks of collectors and antiquarians, often drawing on the expertise of today's collectors, cataloguers, and archivists to do so. We examine the rise of the circulating library. We look at how information traveled by the voice (in conversation or lecture), the page, the pen, the horse, and the sea.

How do we learn about these networks of the past? To do so, we must create a network *to the past*. We use networks that were built at every moment in between. This usually involves seeking out information and materials that are housed in today's libraries and archives or, more rarely, in a private family's papers. Some of these materials have now come to be "housed" digitally, whether available only to that institution's community or available to all. Google Books, and, more recently, the National Digital Public Library of America, have held out the hope of universal access to universal information. Indeed, some of our students (and even the occasional colleagues) seem to believe that all of the important stuff has already been digitized.

But much of the information that historically invested scholars require is not (yet?) digitally available. A 2011 survey of special collections and archives in the United Kingdom found that sixteen percent of books and a whopping thirty-nine percent of manuscripts had no online catalog records. (http://www.slideshare.net/oclcr/special-collections-and-archives-in-the-uk-ireland). This is a worse condition than being undigitized. These materials had no online *record*, no digital footprint. Lest we think that this is a problem reserved for scholars who study pre-1900 materials, it is important to recognize that the percentages reported were even worse for audiovisual, cartographic, and born-digital items, which were the least likely to have an online catalog record. Nearly half of the surveyed special collections units reported that they had some full-scale digitization projects completed, but almost forty percent reported that they hoped to conduct them in the future, and nearly fifteen percent had no plans to do so or weren't sure. As one librarian put it, "Special collections are in danger of being left behind with . . . increasing *expectation* that *everything* will be available *online*."

What does this mean for the networked humanities? One project in which I was involved at my former employer, the University of Missouri, sought to bring together scholars, librarians, and students to make more archival materials available digitally and to make them more findable and visible. We were attempting to link up people on campus who shared interests, problems, and concerns to also share equipment, data, and expertise—to form teams of teams, as well as to save data or create new data out of old data. We convened at a conference on "The Future of Archives in a Digital Age" in February 2011 to compare perspectives, insights, and achievements (http://www.muconf.missouri.edu/futureofarchives/index.html).

By the fall of 2013, my involvement in the project ended, as I had joined a new network, having taken a position at Arizona State University. In my first weeks on the job, I had an experience that, to me, exemplifies both the beauty and difficulty of what "networked humanities" might be. I contacted the head of ASU's Special Collections, Kathy Krzys, to seek materials that could be shown to my eighteenth- and nineteenth-century British literature students. I wanted students to see what the texts they were studying looked like in their first print incarnations, to consider what might be gained by studying the history of the book.

I wanted to show the students period letters, too, to demonstrate that there remains much information in manuscript form that is untapped and to introduce them to postmarks, watermarks, and paleography.

I told Kathy that I'd located an online library record that said that a letter from novelist and critic Margaret Oliphant (1828–97) was tipped in to a book held in ASU's Special Collections. The electronic record for Oliphant's *Literary History of England in the End of the Eighteenth and Beginning of the Nineteenth Century* (1882) indicated, "Holograph letter pasted on t.p. of vol. 1." I asked Kathy if we might inspect the book. I thought I might show students that you could be reading any book and discover that an original, unpublished letter was hidden inside of it. Kathy retrieved it, but much to our chagrin, there was no Oliphant letter in the book. Both of us were horrified, adducing that it must have been stolen and lamenting that such a book would once have been shelved in the circulating stacks.

As we worked to collect materials, Kathy had another idea. She retrieved a big stack of printed cards from the former card catalog. She explained that she was among those who'd argued to keep the printed card catalog, even after the digital records had been created. She often found the cards useful, she said, when looking things up in particular ways. She brought me the cards that had "Eighteenth Century" as a subject heading. Naturally, I found many things in them that a digital search had not turned up. As most librarians (but perhaps not many scholars) know, when digital records were created for materials at libraries, they were often purchased in generic form from a vendor, not transcribed from the printed card catalog. Much unique information about the holdings at libraries was lost in this transition. The digital subject headings were not as detailed; information about unique features of books was not necessarily retained.

Glancing though the cards, I came upon the one for the book we had been so horrified to inspect, Oliphant's *Literary History of England in the End of the Eighteenth and Beginning of the Nineteenth Century* (1882). There, on the printed card, below the note that the book contained an added manuscript letter, I noticed a further handwritten note. It was written in pencil, perhaps added by a past librarian. The note said that the Oliphant letter had been removed to the MS file. I called Kathy over to look at the card, and we both got excited. She sought out where she thought something called the manuscript file could be. As it turned out, the manuscript file was actually several file drawers, containing not just one but dozens and dozens of letters, many of which had been removed en masse at some point from ASU-owned books. We found unpublished letters not just from Oliphant but from William Wordsworth, Leigh Hunt, and Lady Byron. These letters had never been catalogued. They had been removed from the printed books and had been carefully filed, but were, eventually, entirely forgotten.

It was the combination, then, of a miscellaneous note on a digital catalog record (one of the few among dozens and dozens of notes like this that made it from the print to the digital record); the expertise of a backward- and forward-thinking librarian; and the pencil markings on a printed card catalog card that brought these materials back to light. This story, for me, has almost become a parable—a perfect example of what a "networked humanities" means now. No matter how much digitizing libraries and institutions do, scholars and students will never have access to "everything online." My experience convinces me how important it is to humanities scholarship that we emphasize the need for understanding networks to the past. We do so by training ourselves how to seek, use, and preserve information from the many networks that have come into being since before the word was first coined.

NETWORKED MATERIALISMS

8 New Materialisms, Networks, and Humanities Research

Laurie Gries, Jenny Bay, Derek Mueller, and Nathaniel Rivers

As an interdisciplinary theory being taken up across multiple fields such as political science, women's studies, social science, history, and, as of late, rhetorical studies, new materialism is pushing humanities research in exciting directions. In a general sense, new materialists challenge the modernist paradigm—heavily influenced by Descartes and Kant—that perpetuates dualist kinds of thinking. As Bruno Latour explains in *We Have Never Been Modern*, modernity tries to divide the world into separate, opposing spheres with humans/subject/culture on one side and things/object/nature on the other. New materialists reject such dualism, as it fails to acknowledge the ontological hybridity that constitutes reality. In order to make sense of the complex material realities we face in the twenty-first century, new materialists focus on what Donna Haraway calls "naturecultures," or what Latour calls collectives, to acknowledge the complexity of materialist factors that shape society and constrain human experiences.

New materialism is motivated to a great extent by an emergence of complex phenomena such as climate change, genetically modified foods, and e-waste, all of which are constituted by a complex, dynamic assemblage of discursive, material, natural, social, and political actants and activities—an entanglement that Andrew Pickering might call a mangle. But new materialists recognize that mangles are not specific to such recent phenomena of pressing concern. As Susan Hekman notes so succinctly, "Mangles are everywhere. They construct the world we inhabit in all of its complexity" (*Material* 126). Such complexity cannot be investigated solely through social constructivist methodologies, which tend to give too much weight to language's ability to account for reality, agency, and ontology. Nor can such mangles be "understood in the modern metaphysics that distributes Nature and Society into pure ontological zones . . . and allows us to disavow our responsibility for the consequences of our sociotechnical activity" (Herndl). For new materialists, then, new kinds of empirical investigations that foreground complex relations and attend to nonlinear processes of materialization are needed to make sense of our contemporary existence.

Networked relations are foundational to new materialism in that new materialists are committed to models and methods that privilege immanent and emergent relationality (Tianen and Purikka). Rather than reduce the world to symbolic, signifying structures or representations, reality is studied as a dynamic and open network of concrete, material, physical, digital, and physiological apparatuses that work alongside signifying discourses as well as other things with ontological import to create change (Tianen and Purikka). From a new materialist perspective, networks take on significance, then, for a couple of important reasons. In one sense, networks become the "object" of study. Whether new materialists are speaking of collectives, assemblages, aggregates, or meshworks, scholars investigate how networks of heterogenous actants, each with their own distinct and vital constitution, emerge and interact to materialize change. Such focus helps to not only give material things their due but also identify the complex, unfolding, distributed material practices that contribute to any given natural cultural phenomenon of humanist concern.

In a second sense, network becomes a new mode of inquiry, a way of constructing knowledge. This network sense (Mueller) emerges, in part, because new materialists embrace what Timothy Morton calls the ecological thought—"the thinking of interconnectedness" (7). As Morton contends, "The ecological thought doesn't just occur 'in the mind.' It's a practice and a process of becoming fully aware of how human beings are connected with other beings . . ."(7). New materialists also recognize distributed causality and embrace what Levi Bryant refers to as parity reasoning—a form of reasoning that refuses to grant one sort of agency control of development (*Democracy* 201). In conjunction with one another, as we have gestured here, ecological thinking and parity reasoning force scholars to acknowledge that a network of interlocking factors and an ecology of interacting entities contribute to the existence and outcome of any given phenomenon. For new materialists, then, networks are also important in that they influence how research is conducted and knowledge is produced.

In this chapter, we shed light on how new materialism can push humanities research in productive directions and where the humanities might push back (or at least bring to bear on new materialism projects such as feminism). As new materialist rhetoricians, we are particularly committed to exploring how the propensities, affordances, and affectivities of nonhuman entities co-constitute and help (re)assemble collective life. We are also committed to experimenting with new research methods that can reinvigorate the humanities in this unique historical moment. As a collaborative endeavor, we offer four vignettes that explore how we might employ new materialisms in and across a variety of disciplinary contexts.

SYMMETRICAL HUMANITIES

[H]e therefore vigorously strode to the apt door, turned the knob and pulled on the release bolt.

The door refused to open. It said, "Five cents, please."

He searched his pockets. No more coins; nothing. "I'll pay you tomorrow," he told the door. Again he tried the knob. Again it remained locked tight.

[. . .]

From the drawer beside the sink Joe Chip got a stainless steel knife; with it he began systematically to unscrew the bolt assembly of his apt's money-gulping door.

"I'll sue you," the door said as the first screw fell out.

Joe Chip said, "I've never been sued by a door. But I guess I can live through it."

—Phillip K. Dick, *Ubik*

> On a freezing day in February, posted on the door of the So-
> ciology Department at Walla Walla University, Washington,
> could be seen a small hand-written notice: "The door-clos-
> er [a mechanical device] is on strike, for God's sake, keep the
> door closed."
>
> —Jim Johnson (Bruno Latour), "Mixing Humans and
> Nonhumans Together: The Sociology of a Door-Closer"

These two abridged scenes, which taken together blend science fiction
with sociology, speak to what new materialism might bring to the digital
humanities. In each instance, we see a certain sort of negotiation taking place: a negotiation that spans the human and nonhuman, treating
each symmetrically. The methodology of symmetry (taken from Bruno
Latour's actor-network-theory [ANT]) requires that humans and nonhuman actors be treated alike when tracing a network of relations. The
door and Joe Chip are accounted for in similar ways. Sonorous with
Joe, a door can speak, enter into contracts, and then litigate or go on
strike when that contract is violated. Both scenes dramatize the need for
humans and nonhumans to negotiate, to get along. In this section, we
touch on the work of Latour and Jane Bennett to argue that the digital
humanities needs to treat nonhumans (e.g., digital technologies) as equal
partners capable of doing unexpected things. DH projects must account
not only for the human but the nonhuman as well, and, just as importantly, must count them in symmetrical ways. The digital technologies
humanities scholars enroll are not mere putty in their hands; they are
what Bennett calls vibrant matter.

Before moving on, however, it is important that we return to the
two scenes above: they also reveal how symmetrical accounts are shot
through with competing and mixed motives, different capacities, and
unexpected twist and turns. Although no one in rhetoric perhaps needs
to be told this, compromise is always hard won if and when it is ever
reached. This difficulty, this litigation and labor dispute, is, in fact, how
both Latour and Bennett generally introduce the vibrancy of things. "To
put it crudely," Latour writes, "human and nonhuman actors appear first
of all as troublemakers" (*Politics* 81). Just as importantly, we see in these
scenes that the very shape and tenor of symmetry itself is always already
bound-up in the number and kind of parties involved.

Teasing out this notion of the troublemaker in terms of symmetry,
Bennett writes, "Latour's later work continues to call for people to imag-

ine other roles for things besides that of carriers of necessity, or 'plastic' vehicles for 'human ingenuity,' or 'a simple white screen to support the differentiation of society'" (*Vibrant* 30–31). In the case of DH, such work would entail describing projects as more than the application of digital technologies. This approach ignores the troublemaking capacities of such technologies and their abilities to do unexpected things. "For instance," Latour writes, "fisherman, oceanographers, satellites, and the scallops might have some relations with one another, relations of such a sort that they make others do unexpected things" (*Reassembling* 106). By virtue of Latour's symmetrical tracing, objections like "'things don't talk,' 'fish nets have no passion,' and 'only humans have intentions'" are unproductive (*Reassembling* 107). "There might exist many metaphysical shades between full causality and sheer existence," Latour writes. "In addition to 'determining' and serving as a 'backdrop for human action,' things might authorize, allow, afford, encourage, permit, suggest, influence, block, render possible, forbid, and so on" (*Reassembling* 72). Efficacy needn't be asymmetrically confined to the particular abilities of humans.

Bennett's own political ecology of things moves in the same directions, and she offers a compelling example of how asymmetrical accounts of action remain incomplete. Bennett argues that our political and philosophical work needs to attend to the agency—the vibrancy—of objects, which she describes as their thing-power. Bennett explores the force of things such as minerals, fatty acids, and electricity. For instance, a response to the 2005 North American blackout cannot only apportion responsibility to human actors or motivations (e.g., the incompetence or greed of electric companies), but to "the cascade of effects" that includes humans and nonhumans: "electricity too contributed swerves and quirks" ("Agency" 451). A focus on human actors and human motives leaves unexplored and underdeveloped the contributions of nonhumans such as electricity. Asymmetrical accounts may generate satisfying attributions of praise or blame, but they limit our ability to imagine other ways of responding. Bennett prods us to ask, "What difference would it make to the course of energy policy were electricity to be figured not simply as a resource, commodity, or instrumentality but also and more radically as an 'actant'?" (*Vibrant* viii). DH needs to be asking the same questions.

When we embark on a digital humanities project, then, we must not lose track of the nonhuman, their quirks and contributions. The digital humanities is not simply the humanities plugged in, but the humanities seeking out a kind of seduction: to be drawn into new relations that will invariably produce unexpected outcomes. DH is not doing the same work differently; *it is different work done differently and with new partners.* Work like Latour's and Bennett's attends explicitly to these sorts of reciprocal relations, attuning us to how we are not simply using or applying digital technologies but continually enrolling them as we negotiate together what the humanities will be. We'd wager that such an attunement ratchets up the inventional potential of the digital humanities.

Respons-Able Humanities

As we embark on adventures of invention in the digital humanities, it is especially important to keep in mind just how integral the digital technologies we work with matter to our research findings and the ongoing configuration of collective life. As evident in the digital humanities barn raising event called One Week/One Tool that took place in July of 2010 at George Mason University, in conjunction with the Roy Rosenzweig Center for History and New Media (CHNM), digital humanists love to build digital tools. Digital-tool building, in fact, according to some digital humanists, is what differentiates digital humanists from other kinds of humanist scholars. At the very least, it is believed that "computational tools have the potential to transform the content, scope, methodologies, and audience of humanistic inquiry" (Burdick et. al. 123). As such, digital-tool building has become a big business in the digital humanities. From Lev Manovich's and the Software Studies Initiative's work with ImagePlot to CHNM's work with Zotero and Omeka, new technologies are popping up to help humanities scholars do their work differently.

In light of such rampant tool building, new materialism encourages scholars to interrogate the very concept of *tools*, as tools are generally thought of as being inert, passive things that scholars with full-blown agency use to produce knowledge. From a new materialist perspective, the computational things with which we enter into negotiation are important actants that co-constitute any phenomenon under study. They, alongside us, in other words, are not exterior to any phenomenon under investigation; they both help co-produce our very object of study and co-determine our research findings. Karen Barad's work with agential realism perhaps does the best job in making this point clear.[1] Influenced by Neils Bohr's work with quantum physics, agential realism attempts to reconfigure our relations with our "objects of study" by pointing out that *we are a part of that nature that we seek to understand* (Barad 27). In one sense, the physical boundaries that we like to imagine existing between us and any singular thing do not ontologically or even visually exist (Barad 156). In a second sense, the research methods we deploy, the digital technologies we build to collect, analyze, and visualize data, the political discourses that are already mapped onto "our" object of study, the theoretical perspectives from which we choose to think about it—all these factors and entities (as well as unmentioned others) influence what it is that we think we are studying.

As an example, Barad discusses the role of the sonogram in disclosing the reality of a fetus, which is never simply a reality produced by the biological process inside a mother's womb but rather is the culmination of biological, scientific, technological, political, and cultural forces. Such a networked perspective and agential realist understanding of epistemological and ontological matters is especially crucial for humanities research because the things we study are not determinate things that embody specific, fixed characteristics and properties, which we can investigate without influencing. Rather such things are phenomena,[2] constituted by an ongoing historicity and caught up in a process of becoming, that we and other entities in our research process intra-act with. In these intra-actions,[3] our "objects of study" *only* become temporarily determinate when we make an "agential cut," marking off our objects of study from us (subjects) as well as the digital things and other entities involved in the phenomenon under study. In actuality, the things we intra-act with are both phenomena in their ongoing materialization and part of an ongoing reconfiguring of the world that our research can never fully capture and in which our research is always embroiled. We need to be conscious, then, of how the digital things we build play a vital role in our research process by disclosing, or bringing to light, a specific reality that itself takes on material consequences as it both pushes back on our research objects and findings and generates new matters of concern (Hekman 92).

The challenge, then, for the digital humanities is to be acutely conscious of our entanglements with the digital things we build. Ethics, as Levinas teaches us, is always about relationality and responsibility. How then, we might ask, do the things we build construct certain ways of seeing and knowing? How do they influence what is believed to be real? How do they afford some potentials and preclude others? How also do they impact the world beyond our present use? From a new materialist perspective, the digital things we build are not innocent bystanders. In any given enactment, they are vital actors that, alongside us, are responsible for shaping not just the humanities but the ongoing mattering of the world. In this sense, they are response-able—capable of being influenced and influencing. From an ethical standpoint, we owe it to the digital thing we build and to ourselves to acknowledge and confront this immense and complex response-ability.

EMBODIED HUMANITIES

While new materialism in general pushes us to think more seriously about research actants, feminist new materialism forces us to attend to the specificities of embodiment. The following scenes engage key questions about how the networked humanities must also be an embodied humanities.

Scene 1: "The Strike"

In this well-known *Seinfeld* episode—most often referred to as the Festivus episode—Jerry dubs his new girlfriend, Gwen, "two-faced." Two-face literally has two faces; sometimes Gwen shows up and is model-gorgeous, very feminine, and attractive. At other times, she looks hideous, haggard, dark and sallow-skinned—almost masculine. The difference, of course, is the lighting. The lighting not only makes her look different; she becomes a different person, to Kramer and to others. Gwen has no clue of the effects of the lighting on how she looks, nor does she have any conscious control over the situation.

This example shows us in a basic way some of the precepts we have been discussing: how the lighting technology and the material environment in which the lighting functions constructs Gwen's gender and race. Feminist theory has shown us that gender is mutable, undulating, shifting according to the collection of materialities present; it is not predetermined. But moreover, it also demonstrates that the lighting environment works outside of what we might see as subjective agency; it has its own important part in the construction of bodies and rhetorical environments. As we emphasized earlier and as Karen Barad more eloquently states in *Meeting the Universe Halfway*, "Individuals do not preexist their interactions; rather individuals emerge through and as part of their entangled intra-relating" (ix). In simpler terms, as Jerry says, he never knows which Gwen is going to show up.

Calling attention to the co-constitutive role that technological objects play in forming our worldly entanglements is essential to new materialism, but less attention has been paid to the way such objects are key co-actants in the construction of the gendered assemblages we call bodies. One of the claims of feminist new materialism is that gender and race are material constructs; neither completely discursive nor linguistic, they are formed through a nexus of bodies, objects, cultures, and technologies. In short, gender is a materialized and constantly materializing process. In our attempts to involve non-human elements in the thinking and doing of humanities work, we sometimes eclipse the intra-active becomings of bodies, especially their historical and biological specificities. So, we need a different kind of attention to bodies, to the ways in which material objects allow and constrain the possibilities for creating inhabitable worlds—and what that might mean for imagining a digital or networked humanities.

Scene 2: "This is my weapon and this is my gun; one is for fighting and one is for fun"

One of the most often cited examples of human-nonhuman entanglements today is Bruno Latour's citizen-gun, as illustrated in *Pandora's Hope*. Latour sets up his discussion of human and non-human collectives by invoking the ontological underpinnings of the arguments made for and against the gun lobby. In one argument, the agency lies in the human being holding the gun; in the other, the gun transforms the citizen carrying the gun. In Latour's translation model, though, the responsibility for action is shared; thus, as he explains, the actant becomes the gun-citizen or the citizen-gun: "You are different with a gun in your hand; the gun is different with you holding it" (179), he claims.

But there is more at stake in Latour's example than the collective agency among humans and objects, especially in today's transnational contexts. Latour switches back and forth between gender-specific pronouns, which makes it seem as if it doesn't matter whether the citizen is male or female. But in the US context, Latour's citizen is most likely a man. In our country today, statistics show that only twenty-three percent of women own a firearm (Saad). Gun violence is mostly male; thus, Latour's gun-citizen is implicitly male (and also white). But how did this assemblage become male?

Barad explains that *"matter is substance in its intra-active becoming—not a thing, but a doing, a congealing of agency. Matter is a stabilizing and destabilizing process of iterative intra-activity.* Phenomena come to matter through this process of ongoing iterative intra-activity" (210). In this sense, the object is a process in relation to the human and to other objects. As such, the intra-action between object, human, environment, and culture works to create what we understand to be the material. Feminist new materialism, then, tells us that biological specificities will affect the intra-action between these elements. In short, the body holding the gun *matters.*

So, what happens when the human being interacting with the gun is a woman? Or what happens when the human is a young black male on the south side of Chicago? The gun object in this instance changes just as much as the human in possession of the gun. In the first instance, the collective possibilities afforded to the woman are different. A woman is less likely to become a mass murderer-gun; in all likelihood, the gun in her hand will show up as self-defense, or unfortunately, she most likely would be on the other side of the weapon. In the second instance, the black male holding the gun can easily become the gun-criminal or the criminal-gun. The brown body holding the gun easily becomes the gun-terrorist, and of course the larger material environment will further constitute this becoming. Some differently-abled bodies may not even be able to hold a gun. Bodily specificities matter, and incorporating this difference makes the apparatus rhetorically rich. That richness becomes inseparable from circulating cultural norms and biases, contributing to them and perpetuating them.

Barad argues that our methods allow us to see or not see matter's agentiality. She calls us to interrogate the methods by which these materialities come into being. That is, the method by which we examine and understand the emergence of gendered or biological forms will let some things show up and others not; of course, this is also Haraway's argument in "Situated Knowledges." As we consider new approaches to the digital humanities, how do we account for bodies in the rhetorical assemblages we analyze? In short, what will be the process of *mattering* in the digital humanities?

Scene 3: Technology Matters

Here's a common everyday scene from any university today. A young woman in the library takes a break from studying to pull out her smart phone, turn on the reverse camera function, and look at herself on the screen. She turns her head from side to side to get a complete view of what she looks like. One could argue that Kim Kardashian serves as the spokesperson for this method of what could be termed *becoming female.*

The cellphone as compact mirror serves as an apparatus of bodily production and lets us witness the mattering of gender. Bodies and technologies co-constitute one another: the camera constructs the female body on the screen, but the body's use of the camera genders the technology. Thus, the body becomes the digital image, and the smartphone in the woman's hand becomes a compact mirror. The boundaries between the two are unclear.

But the key here cannot be an objective discussion of how human and non-humans interact; it must attend to gender as a process brought into being by the interaction of the human and non-human. Race even comes into the equation since most digital cameras do not process dark skin tones in the same ways that white skin tones are processed. Donna Haraway tells us, "What constitutes an apparatus of bodily production cannot be known in advance of engaging in the always messy projects of description, narration intervention, inhabiting, conversing, exchanging, and building. The point is to get at how worlds are made and unmade, in order to participate in the process, in order to foster some forms of life and not others" ("A Game of Cat's Cradle" 62).

As we consider how the digital humanities leverage new technologies and new affordances such as big data, ANT, object-oriented ontologies, et cetera, what forms of life are fostered and what forms are not? In other words, what worlds do our approaches and methods allow to come into being and what are foreclosed?

Scene 4: Display Out of Order

Chocked full of displays of bizarre and long-forgotten technologies, The Museum of Jurassic Technology in Los Angeles asks visitors to question both the concept of the museum and also our trust in technology's potential for innovation. One of the first exhibits one encounters is a microscope, in which the objective piece has been pushed down on the stage clip so far that it has crushed the specimen and the glass holding it. The label on this exhibit declares "Display out of order!"

Part of considering what forms of life the digital humanities fosters lies in our methodological approaches to the phenomena under consideration. As iterated above, what we understand to be phenomena must include the measuring technology; it must include the apparatus. We cannot just look at the microscope as an objective technology of measurement, nor can we look at the data it produces as independently meaningful. Rather, the entire apparatus and the human being looking through or at it constitute meaning together. And in many ways, as this exhibit shows, the technological apparatus does not necessarily constitute positive relationships among bodies and objects; instead it can literally be crushing—or out of order.

Barad writes, "Apparatuses are not merely about us. And they are not merely assemblages that include nonhumans as well as humans. Rather, apparatuses are specific material reconfigurations of the world that do not merely emerge in time but iteratively reconfigure spacetimematter as part of the ongoing dynamism of becoming" (142). As we consider applying new materialist methods to the digital humanities, what will be our technological apparatuses for understanding gender and sex? How will we account for gender as iteratively reconfigured and becoming? And what worlds will the resulting phenomena foster?

Crowned Humanities

As we have established, new materialism offers a theory and method for apprehending things unto themselves and things as entangled in networks. These networks are suspended among and teeming across conglomerations of actors, human and non-human alike. Oriented in terms of discipliniography—or the systematic inquiry into disciplinary formation, maturation, and persistence including the ways such formations are inscribed and historicized—new materialism may productively estrange us from established, conventional approaches that tend to elevate humans and, consequently, eclipse nonhumans. This estrangement is valuable because it unsettles disciplinary orthodoxies and invites reconsideration of the variety of networks that constitute disciplinarity. New materialism, with its radically simplistic concern for things, is particularly well suited to helping us conceptualize and enact an alien discipliniography.

Sitting with Things, Disciplinarily

Alien discipliniography draws its primary influence from Ian Bogost's *Alien Phenomenology*, a primer on object-oriented ontology and its emerging philosophical premises, which has much in common with new materialism. By focusing on phenomenological wonder, Bogost's account seeks perspective on what it is like to be a thing (this is the monograph's subtitle). At this point it is pertinent to recall that "theory" comes from a family of Greek words connoting perspective and looking. As Sharon Crowley and Debra Hawhee remind us, theory comes from *theorein*, "which literally means 'to sit in the highest row of bleachers'" (53). With this literal definition in play, Bogost's theorizing of alien phenomenology is akin to sitting in the highest row of bleachers, but in a strange, out-of-this-correlationist-world, *things-only* section of the stadium.

Alien *discipliniography* seeks perspective on disciplinary formation, maturation, and persistence from a seat in this same, oddly populated row. That is, new materialism ushers us—theoretically—to this *things-only* section from which we can inquire anew into what a field, such as rhetoric and composition, looks like from here and how agencies cascade across this alien section. Understood in this way, alien discipliniography specifies an opportunity for speculating differently—and more strangely—than we have before into a disciplinary arena. It does not, however, require us to reduce humans to irrelevance or to run ramshackle over the more conspicuously human-focused approaches widely valued in rhetoric and composition. We do not need to call StubHub for a refund; *these* seats need not be life-long season tickets to be useful. That is, being disciplinarily curious *from this networked, thing-ed mezzanine* can help us grasp the field as a complex ecology with divergent, materially complex actors.

Crowned Ontologies

Few field narratives to date have operated with new materialism as theory and method. Those that have come closest have gravitated to theoretical perspectives that foreground human actors—or, in keeping with the stadium seating metaphor, that too briefly invite objects to pass through the Anthropocene Suite. Consider as a recent example an article published in *College English* in 2012, "Evocative Objects: Reflections on Teaching, Learning, and Living in Between." Three prominent scholars in rhetoric and composition—Doug Hesse, Nancy Sommers, and Kathleen Blake Yancey—took turns "choosing objects unconstrained by academic purpose," to consider each object's "gravitational force" on "shared professional identity" (326). Hesse meditated on a pipe cleaner and crayon project his son made in 1990, Sommers considered a series of family photographs, and Yancey reflected on an illustration of tectonic plates. Initially, this has the appearance of seeking perspective from the position set up earlier—the position identified with alien discipliniography. Yet, after the objects have spoken, they exit, return quietly to their hiatus, probably in the *things-only* section.

While Hesse, Sommers, and Yancey's collaboration takes an interest in objects, their effort embarks only part-way down the speculative aisle new materialism opens up for us—the "gravitational force" of their chosen objects reads as passing and impactful foremost on their human subjectivity. For Bogost, alien phenomenology assumes a perfectly flat ontology, or an undifferentiated existence-scape, and alien discipliniography should aspire to the same. But "Evocative Objects," drawing its influence from Sherry Turkle's work by the same title, and similar accounts operate more like *crowned ontologies* than flat ontologies. Crowning names the slight curvature of a field of play. A crowned ontology, in this sense, is flat-seeming even as it bears out a nearly imperceptible curve. The anthropocentrism that new materialism disavows resurfaces in the end. As such, there are other gestures toward ecological understandings of the field, but even though ecological gestures have become increasingly influential, there remains a nascent disciplinary opportunity born of new materialism to depict "the nonhumanity that flows around and through humans," as Jane Bennett puts it ("Force" 349).

Ontographs

In "Ontography," Bogost introduces five concrete examples of ontography—a practice of writing and illustration emphasizing the existential aspects of things. Although the chapter does not directly consider methods, it does lay out in sections five examples of ontography: 1) Tobias Kuhn's graphical notation system, which is called Ontography, 2) Latour Litanies, which are short lists of objects named in succession as if at random, 3) visual ontographs, or image registries, 4) exploded views, like the sort of thing you might find when you are putting together cheap furniture, and 5) what Bogost calls ontographic machines, puzzle toys and games whose operations "map abstract gestures to concrete meanings" (52).

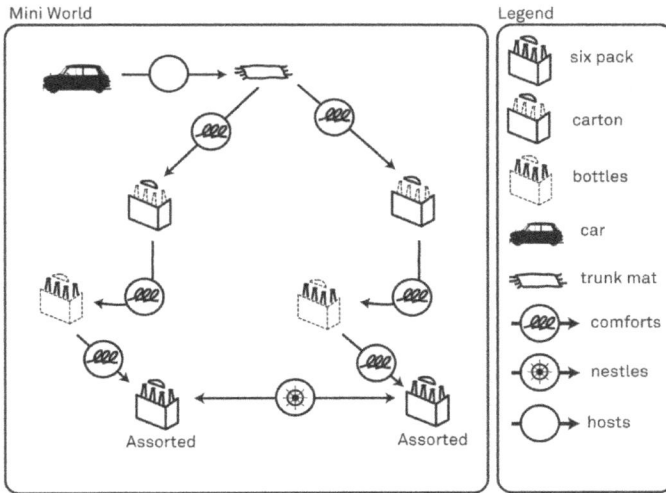

Figure 1. An experimental ontograph, or simple visual model, wherein isolated object-interactions schematizes everyday disciplinary activities. Figure by author (Mueller).

To illustrate the application of ontography for alien discipliniography, consider this adaptation of Kuhn's graphical notation system, ontography, to a mundane disciplinary encounter—a beer swap at an academic conference (Figure 1). Kuhn's system features a materially-intensive network-like depiction of mini-worlds, which are designed to be simple, formal, and highly specific, although they assume a parallel syntax in language that emphasizes subjects and verbs, or, if you are familiar with Joseph Williams' work, characters and actions. Ontographs operate with the bold assumption—requiring a suspension of disbelief—that there is nothing outside the mini-world, and no possibility for negating the operations depicted therein. An ontograph like this is a provisional attempt at connecting new materialism's concerns to a practice of alien discipliniography, a connection made stronger by the insistence upon featuring nonhuman actors in the mini-world. Though the mini-worlds are bounded, we can imagine scenarios comparable to the one shown here that would reveal "the rich variety of [disciplinary] being," to redraw Bogost's chapter's subtitle.

For digital humanities scholars attending to questions of disciplinary formation, maturation, and persistence, new materialism offers a theory and method for teasing out commonplaces about the presumed-to-be-natural actors and the networks they constitute in a given disciplinary domain. This is but one application of new materialism that has the potential to recast histories and field narratives in a new, alien light. Such deliberate ecological gestures prompt new perspectives on disciplinary formation and persistence—perspectives especially useful for casting ordinary networks in sharp relief against a surfeit of subject-focused disciplinary accounts.

CONCLUSION

The impetus behind this chapter and its arrayed vignettes is to demonstrate the remarkable methodological variety available through new materialisms. The humanities is at a tipping point, it seems, and everywhere our value is under re-evaluation. How might the humanities continue to make a place for itself in the world, which is work it has always and ever done? In a recent and widely circulating defense of the humanities, *New Republic* literary editor Leon Wieseltier, at the May 19 commencement ceremony at Brandeis University, asked, "Has there ever been a moment in American life when the humanities were cherished less, and has there ever been a moment in American life when the humanities were needed more?" After a litany of challenges facing the humanities (namely the encroachment of capital and technology), Wieseltier concludes, "Use the new technologies for the old purposes." While there might be much to admire in his defense of the humanities, this final note remains inadequate. This line of argument presumes that the humanities and the question of the human have been settled and so the work of the humanities remains to defend them—to circle the wagons. We would argue (and have here argued) that the humanities need new approaches that do not merely honor "the quest for the true and the good and the beautiful" (Wieseltier), but which seek ways to ever re-compose the good, the true, and the beautiful. Focus less on what the humanities have been: work to define what they will be. Our wager is that the humanities will become increasingly mangled as humans are called upon to deal with ever more complex, hybrid phenomena such as climate change, which involve potent combinations of science, law, politics, engineering, and religion. In response, as we have gestured here, we'll need to embrace networks in theory and practice to develop new approaches for addressing such complexities.

NOTES

1. Agential realism is an epistemological-ontological-ethical framework developed by Barad that helps deepen understandings of the role that human and nonhuman, material and discursive, and natural and cultural factors play in scientific and other social-material practices. See page 26 in *Meeting the Universe Halfway.*

2. In light of such claims, Barad suggests we think of things as "things-in-phenomena." See page 140 in *Meeting the Universe Halfway.*

3. Barad argues that a crucial perceptual shift occurs when we think in terms of intra-action versus interaction. Interaction "presumes the prior existence of independent entities" (Barad 815). Intra-action, on the other hand, recognizes that the boundaries and properties of the "components" or relata become determinate with time and space and within phenomena. Such relata, in other words, do not preexist relations; they do not lead an independent, self-contained existence. Rather individuals emerge through and as part of specific phenomena in which they are intra-acting with an entanglement of other entities. See pages 139–40 in *Meeting the Universe Halfway.*

WORKS CITED

Barad, Karen. *Meeting the Universe Halfway: Quantum Physics and the Entanglement of Meaning and Matter.* Duke UP, 2007.

Bennett, Jane. "The Force of Things: Steps toward an Ecology of Matter." *Political Theory*, vol. 32, no. 3, 2004, pp. 347–72.

—. *Vibrant Matter: A Political Ecology of Things.* Duke UP, 2010.

Bogost, Ian. *Alien Phenomenology, or What It's Like to Be a Thing.* U of Minnesota P, 2012.

Crowley, Sharon, and Debra Hawhee. *Ancient Rhetorics and Contemporary Students.* 2nd Ed., Allyn & Bacon, 1998.

Dick, Philip K. *Ubik.* Random House Digital, 2004. EPUB.

Burdick, Anne, Johanna Drucker, Peter Lunefeld, Todd Presner, and Jeffrey Schnapp. *Digital_Humanities.* MIT Press, 2012.

Haraway, Donna. "A Game of Cat's Cradle: Science Studies, Feminist Theory, Cultural Studies." *Configurations*, vol. 2, no. 1, 1994, pp. 59–71.

Hekman, Susan. *The Material of Knowledge: Feminist Disclosures.* Indiana UP, 2010.

Hesse, Doug, Nancy Sommers, and Kathleen Blake Yancey. "Evocative Objects: Reflections on Teaching, Learning, and Living in Between." *College English*, vol. 74, no. 4, 2012, pp. 325–50.

Herndl, Carl. "Rhetoric and the New Materialism." 2012 Rhetoric Society of America Conference. Philadelphia, PA. 26 May 2012. Conference Presentation.

Johnson, Jim (Bruno Latour), "Mixing Humans and Nonhumans Together: The Sociology of a Door-Closer." *Social Problems*, vol. 35, no. 3, 1988, pp. 298–310.

Kuhn, Tobias. "How to Evaluate Controlled Natural Languages." *Controlled Natural Languages 2009*, edited by Norbert Fuchs, Springer-Verlag Berlin Heidelberg, 2010, pdfs.semanticscholar.org/df4a/f470698a4462387a7ba4d-b588d1d48b4ee58.pdf.

Latour, Bruno. *Pandora's Hope. Essays on the Reality of Science Studies*. Harvard UP, 1999.

—. Politics of Nature: How to Bring the Sciences into Democracy. Harvard UP, 2004.

—. *Reassembling the Social: An Introduction to Actor-Network-Theory*. Oxford UP, 2005.

Morton, Timothy. *The Ecological Thought*. Harvard UP, 2010.

Mueller, Derek. "Views from a Distance: A Nephological Model of the CCCC Chairs' Addresses, 1977–2011." *Kairos*, vol. 16, no. 2, Jan. 2012. kairos. technorhetoric.net/16.2/topoi/mueller/

Saad, Lydia. "Self-Reported Gun Ownership in U. S. Is Highest Since 1993." *Gallup.com*, 26 Oct. 2011, news.gallup.com/poll/150353/self-reported-gun-ownership-highest-1993.aspx. Accessed 14 Aug. 2013.

Turkle, Sherry. *Evocative Objects: Things We Think With*. MIT, 2007.

Wieseltier, Leon. "Perhaps Culture is Now the Counterculture." *New Republic*. 28 May 2013, newrepublic.com/article/113299/leon-wieseltier-commencement-speech-brandeis-university-2013. Accessed 1 Aug. 2013.

9 Provocation: Teaching Networked Humanities through Interdisciplinary Projects

Paul Gestwicki

The humanities have always recognized that their impact is not limited to the classroom, but that the impact of a humanities-rich, liberal education should resonate through a lifetime. Conventional university education divides coursework around academic distinctions between disciplines: a history department offers a course on medieval Spain, a philosophy department offers a course on the ethics of war, and so on. These tidy distinctions are artifacts of academic epistemology and university structure. They tend to vanish outside of academia, where problems exist in messy, interdisciplinary problem spaces. Networked humanities recognizes that that these spaces present opportunities to deploy humanistic discourse in practical contexts.

For the past several years, I have had the privilege of mentoring student teams in the development of educational, humanities-oriented video games. Designing and developing educational games is an interdisciplinary problem space in which the humanities naturally fit. Jesse Schell, for example, includes anthropology, history, and creative writing in his litany of skills required for game designers, and in their widely-adopted textbook on games, Salen and Zimmerman devote a chapter to discussing games as cultural artifacts. My teams are multidiscplinary and composed primarily of undergraduates, and our studio environment provides the crucible in which their humanistic values are tested. Studying how these teams collaborate and coordinate activity provides us with an authentic assessment (Wiggins) of their humanities education.

Consider the case of the lone humanities major—a history major—on the team who developed *Museum Assistant*. This game was designed to teach children about exhibit design and the inner workings of museums (Gestwicki and McNely). The history major had no prior experience with museum studies, education, or game design, yet the work she did reflects her disciplinary training. She gathered information from a variety of resources and synthesized this information into reports, presentations, and game design recommendations. The team recognized and valued these contributions as highly as any art, music, or programming assets, and they serve as undeniable evidence she was able to apply humanistic methods outside of traditional humanities coursework.

Students from non-humanities disciplines sometimes struggle to recognize their engagement in humanist endeavors. The team that developed *Morgan's Raid*—a game about Indiana's Civil War history—consisted of art and computer science majors, and two historians served as design consultants (Gestwicki and Morris). Although the entire project constituted legitimate historical interpretation, from game design to art direction, there is little evidence that the team recognized this or reflected on it. Tasks that appeared to be "history work," such as locating period maps and census records, were delegated to the history consultants while the computer scientists focused on the programming. These students did not engage in any meaningful humanistic inquiry or reflect critically on their role as interpreters of history; though the project was successful in meeting its stated goals, there is little evidence from it that the students recognized the opportunity to apply the methods of the humanities. This stands in stark contrast to the team who developed *Children of the Sun*, a game about Middle Mississippian culture. This team also contained no humanities majors and had access to consultants; however, when faced with uncertainty regarding the Middle Mississippians, this team went to the university library to read archaeological reports and field studies. What they learned from these readings manifested in significant and intellectually vigorous debate regarding the game design and learning objectives. These team members explicitly reflected on their role as interpreters of the past, and their actions demonstrate lived humanist values.

It should come as no surprise that some student teams successfully deploy humanistic methods while others do not; clearly, not everyone with a university education lives by the values of humanist discourse. This is partially a matter of transfer—applying what one has learned in one context to another. Although these educational game development experiences were designed to mimic industrial practices, they were still grounded in an explicitly educational, credit-bearing, university-situated experience. If a student cannot transfer an understanding of the humanities here, then they are unlikely to do so outside the university environment. The ecological approach to perceptual learning (Gibson) provides a useful insight to addressing transfer, that in order for a person to meaningfully act, the person must first perceive the affordance for action. Teaching students to recognize the opportunities for humanistic inquiry, then, must be a primary educational objective of networked humanities.

Teaching networked humanities is therefore not merely a matter of guiding students through challenging disciplinary content: it must explicitly educate students to recognize the affordances, in different contexts, where the intellectual tools of the humanities can be applied. This requires designing deliberately scaffolded learning experiences that incorporate interdisciplinary problems. By doing this, we prepare students to be continuously-learning reflective practitioners (Schon) and to recognize the value of the humanities to their own networks.

Works Cited

Gestwicki, Paul, and Brian McNely. "A Case Study of a Five-Step Design Thinking Process in Educational Museum Game Design." *Meaningful Play 2012 Conference Proceedings*, Michigan State University, 2012, meaningfulplay.msu.edu/proceedings2012.

Gestwicki, Paul, and Ronald Morris. "Social Studies Education Game Development as an Undergraduate Immersive Learning Experience." *Handbook of Research on Serious Games as Educational, Business, and Research Tools: Development and Design*, edited by M. M. Cruz-Cunha, IGI Global, 2012, pp. 838–58.

Gibson, James J. *The Ecological Approach to Visual Perception*. Houghton Mifflin Harcourt, 1979.

Salen, Katie, and Eric Zimmerman. *Rules of Play: Game Design Fundamentals*. MIT Press, 2004.

Schell, Jesse. *The Art of Game Design: A Book of Lenses*. CRC Press, 2008.

Schon, Donald A. *The Reflective Practitioner: How Professionals Think in Action*. Basic Books, 1983.

Wiggins, Grant. "Teaching to the (Authentic) Test." *Educational Leadership*, vol. 46, no. 7, 1989, pp. 41–47.

10 Ripple Effects: Toward a *Topos* of Deployment for Feminist Historiography in Rhetoric and Composition

Tarez Samra Graban

THE "PROBLEM" OF DIGITAL RECOVERY IN FEMINIST HISTORIOGRAPHY

I n *Theorizing Histories of Rhetoric* (2013), fifteen scholars of rhetoric and composition argued for re-examining the historian's role in writing history, each describing an approach that ranged from textual, to ambient, to trans-historical, to cross-cultural.[1] This volume followed on the heels of *Feminist Practices: New Horizons for Rhetoric, Composition, and Literacy Studies* (2012), in which Jacqueline Jones Royster and Gesa Kirsch called for more critical imagination in feminist historiographic work. Buoyed by decades of experience, Royster and Kirsch argued that today's historical methodologies must reflect "tectonic shifts" in the field, enabling historians to construct new topographies that reflect their beliefs about what counts as knowledge, how knowledge is made, and how it is transferred. Both books reflect a methodological moment in which rhetorical historians are encouraged to (1) become more conscious of how they interact with their histories and subjects, and (2) ensure that these interactions do not merely perform the same dialectical recovery in new ways. The trajectory outlined by both books creates a legitimate dilemma: How can historians operate on a different temporality than dialectical recovery, without working *ahistorically*?

As research in the humanities turns simultaneously dialectical and digital, raising historians' consciousness of their own involvements in reconstructing disciplinary histories through digital means (Cohen, *et al*), the dilemma becomes enhanced for feminist historiography. On the one hand, digital recovery serves an important function in feminist historiography. Owing in part to the emergence of accessible digital tools that enable historians to *build exhibits and displays*, and to *observe* the evolution of rhetorical treatises in primary and edited forms through the Internet Archive (https://archive.org/), scholars of rhetoric and composition do have some creative and critical control over women's rhetorical histories, fulfilling an important feminist historiographic imperative to achieve recovery in many forms, including offering a more complex representation of under-served figures. On the other hand, while such tropes as *building, exhibiting*, and *observing* can lead to mobile and effective projects, feminist historiographies that merely digitize analogue desires can remain stuck in a notion of recovery that privileges cumulative advantage, whereby one narrative is replaced by a more complex (or reverse-privileged) corrective that brings forgotten figures back into the dominant conversation.

We already know that the mere digitization of archives does not overcome the principles of cumulative advantage that reinforce historical neglect in our field. We also know that feminist subjects frequently reside in the digital "dark spaces" of institutions, their collections, and their published histories (Earhardt; Golbeck; Queen; Theimer; and Yakel, to name only a few). Yet our attempts to reveal them principally through the ideology of exhibited representation may subdue them further by unwittingly stabilizing figures and texts in linear time, space, or geography resonant with historiographers' desires to capture and preserve a more "'complete' historical picture" (Skinnell 113), overlooking the constraints on what has, historically "count[ed] as legitimate geographical knowledge" and knowledge production (Rose 2). Ekaterina Haskins, in reflecting on the construction of crowd-sourced archives, has predicted that the "preservation of large quantities of digitized materials does not [automatically] translate into a usable past" (419), given that even the most extensive data gathering project is at best a fettered historical process (Earhart 310). And Jessica Enoch and Jean Bessette have more recently observed that the availability of digital tools does not automatically lead to more meaningful engagements for feminist historians unless they are willing to rehearse new practices (such as "non-reading"), that will better attend to the social circulation of figures and their texts and develop their critical imagination about how historical influence can even circulate at all (646). It follows, then, that a more ontologically demanding task for the networked humanities is to contend with recovery *pan-historically* (Hawhee and Olson), by revisioning, reinvesting, and destabilizing the timing of our iconoclastic tendencies (Skinnell 119).

In response, this chapter considers archival metadata as a destabilizing influence, by merging historians' coordinates with those of their subjects through the *topos* of deployment (Barad, *Meeting*; Graban and Sullivan; Rose). Specifically, this chapter outlines two arguments. First, because of their performative nature, visualizations of archival metadata have the potential to place rhetorical historians and their subjects in the same critical space without presuming only a (temporal) dialectical approach to recovery. Second, the critical problem of *what* and *how* to visualize reveals that there is a rhetoricity to historical data work that is unique to our field, and especially evident as we grapple at the convergence of space, digitality, and critical consumption.

DEPLOYMENT AS A *TOPOS* FOR THE NETWORKED HUMANITIES

A conception of recovery that is grounded in *deployment* may offer one step towards developing a feminist historiography for the networked humanities that does not become objectified or fixed. Unique to rhetoric and composition, "deployment" privileges a production-oriented stance towards history-writing, describing research methodologies that stem from our interests in disciplinary ecologies (Blythe; Edbauer); in the circulation of rhetorical performances (Ridolfo, "Rhetorical"); in the postcritical tensions between theoretical and empirical approaches to knowledge building (Sullivan and Porter); in an understanding of "text" as im/material imaginaries (constructed through the circulation and reception of cultures, ideologies, and beliefs) (Miller; Ong; Taylor); and in our understanding that historical events often occur as outcomes of our archival interventions in them.[2]

As a *topos*, deployment is similar, in kind, to Jim Ridolfo's "textual diaspora" for its emphasis on situating the "past, present, and future of texts in relationship to the changing rhetorical goals ... of cultural stake-holders" ("Delivering," 137), though not intended to be text- or artifact-driven. It is evident in Patricia Sullivan's thought experiment when she conducted digital-only recovery of a rhetoric instructor by the name of Frances Perry, where the question of what it means to *do history digitally* burgeoned into something like an epistemology for tracing digital records in ways that challenged bibliographic sovereignty (Sullivan and Graban 4). It enables us to theorize historical and technological interactions for the sake of expanding the texts, themes, and groups normally studied in relation to communication and writing (Sullivan and Porter). And it reflects the bold, almost anti-territorial claims of Jay David Bolter ("Remediation"; *Remediation*), Richard Grusin ("Radical"), and Collin Brooke ("Discipline") in the ways that these scholars encourage an understanding of media studies to be set apart from static, print-book-driven economies that solidify the very networks they encourage us to relinquish.

Yet axiomatically, a *topos* of deployment differs from what motivates digital history writ-large. For, it is also evident in Lynée Lewis Gaillet's survey of ten years' worth of scholarship produced within rhetoric and composition that claims disciplinary agency in archival work, not only by re/defining what it means to do archival work but also by complicating the traditionally distinctive roles of archivist and researcher ("(Per)Forming"). It is evident in a 2012 special issue of *Advances in the History of Rhetoric* focusing on the "Doing of History and the Making of Historians in Rhetoric," which included Janine Solberg's Google-enabled investigation of Frances Maule as a case study for shifting conditions of findability and a rethinking of historical *proximity* (53), as well as Roxanne Mountford's ("Mentoring," 101) and Debra Hawhee's ("Hackers," 119) recommendations for teaching, training, and mentoring rhetorical historians according to practices more in line with hacking than with handing over stable traditions or beliefs. And it is evident more recently in Michelle Baliff's renewing of rhetoric's imperative to take up (and re-write) histories that help us metatheorize ("Introduction," 1), as well as in Hawhee's and Christa Olson's work putting histories, artifacts, and whole archives in motion to result in historical *topoi* that are not limited to a single temporal scope ("Pan-Historiography," 90) or geographic space (92). It is the principle that allows us to view archives as critically networked, self-reflexive, prototypical, democratic, and animated: as entities that simultaneously are constructed and deconstruct. In sum, *deployment* describes a special interest not in finding new ways to historicize others' performances, but in *finding new ways to perform others' histories.*

THE METADATA MAPPING PROJECT AS A PROTOTYPE FOR DEPLOYMENT

In her prologue to *Graphesis* (2014), Johanna Drucker differentiates between a diagrammatic image that *"produces the knowledge it draws"* and a digitally rendered image of Web traffic that *"only displays information,"* potentially "conceal[ing] the decisions and processes on which it was based" (1, italics original). For Drucker, our images—like our networks and queries—are situated: those that aim to *construct* information require strategies for reading and understanding their situatedness. Rhetorical historiography has much to contribute to this distinction, given that its data needs are pan-historiographic in their tendency to meta-theorize, not merely to re-present. Our data needs simultaneously find disciplinary agency in historical work and complicate the distinctive roles of historical agents.

An interest in this kind of networked data performance now seems plausible for rhetorical historical work, and I argue for its untapped potential in tracing the im/material circulations of feminist subjects. While the impetus for interpreting large amounts of data in rhetoric and writing studies is often to find answers to questions of student performance, programmatic growth, and assessment, the impetus or need for interpreting smaller sets of data in historical studies of women pedagogues is (in my mind) to complicate or destabilize data categories, demonstrating the fragility and mutability of data patterns. This fragility is best seen in Haskins' argument that, without exercising appropriate discernment, our historiographic traditions are, like any others, at risk of hyper-digital representation (418). If they are not guided by an ethic of reflexivity, our digital networked projects can easily result in what Daniel J. Cohen might call "losing the historical present" ("Interchange") and what Andreas Huyssen might call the "disappearance of historical consciousness" (*Twilight Memories* 253, qtd. in Haskins 406).

As such, I argue for using metadata to understand the intellectual migrations of women's work in more rhizomatic ways.[3] In *Mechanisms,*

Matthew Kirschenbaum asks theorists to understand digital objects (archival and otherwise) as instances of propagation and belief (23) that have the capacity to point to their own processes of inscription and fabrication (2). By the same token, *networked historical subjects* have the capacity to store and retrieve understandings of the present in views of the past.[4] The *metadata network* especially supports the idea of feminist archives as immaterial cultural forms inasmuch as it mediates between readers, writers, texts, ideas, and the principles underlying their circulation (Johnson 105-6; Lang and Baehr 174; Graban 186). For feminist historiographic work in rhetoric and composition, metadata networks can describe information sets that are *implicit*, enabling what Derek Mueller calls an "inventorying or re-inventorying" of the loci through which disciplinary knowledge circulates, gains, attention, and gains or loses status (196). In spite of the necessity for archival metadata to document or substantiate the physical existence of text-objects (OCLC 4), most metadata networks are simultaneously denotative and ontological in that they reveal how categories or terms are at best manifestations of (often complex) ideologies. Their power lies in providing organizational and kairotic snapshots of activity, rather than in serving as stable or sovereign tools with which to name items and establish relationships beyond evolution or doubt.

In a deployment paradigm, these snapshots of activity become mobile performances that carry evidence about their diffusion—how archivists' habits of storage and retrieval reveal relationships between historical fact and fiction (Theimer; Cohen, *et al.*), and how users' behaviors reveal relationships between actors and their disciplines (Bollen, *et al.*). I learned this performativity first-hand while developing a prototype called the MetaData Mapping Project (MDMP, pronounced "MID-map"), a crowd-sourced tool with dual functions.[5] Primarily, MDMP was intended to help trace the nuanced contributions of women pedagogues to rhetorical education in the nineteenth and twentieth centuries, when they are defined by transient careers or when their activities have historically been blunted by bibliometric thinking (Urban, *et al.*; Roemer and Borchardt). Secondarily, it was intended to help its users observe their own and others' historiographic assumptions by enabling the construction of taxonomies and the visualization of small data sets reflecting how disciplinary foci have changed (or not changed) over time ("Ecologies and Ontologies"). As a mechanism for noticing archival uptake and accretion, then, MDMP was intended to represent *intellectual influence* as a highly mobile commodity, best sought out in the gaps caused by publishing trends, by existing archival or institutional legacies, by the temporal nature of women's positions in the university, or by lingering assumptions about the class and rank of certain pedagogues over others.

For example, three iterations of an unpublished curriculum might migrate to three different schools in three different states, but the migration is only traceable in an administrative memo or a vita line stored in another institution's archive. By capturing and visualizing provenance information on obscure primary source materials such as textbooks, primers, unpublished curriculum, annual faculty reports, administrative papers, and other unprocessed references to their work, MDMP sought to reveal those performances that we might know only by inference—by their mentions, citations, or even acknowledgments in other out of print works—and that remain masked by how we do history, how we determine rank and class, how we measure bibliographic circulation, and how we trust archives to reveal or conceal our disciplinary interests. Thus, MDMP was envisioned as a tool that could help its users to recognize the migration of feminist work through the various evidences they might gather or collect in less traditional venues than the scholarly monograph, the permanent faculty file, or even the Modern Language Association or NCTE member lists.

The greatest challenge in constructing this project came in trying to model a gestalt that was based in the performance and circulation of research practices, rather than in the stasis of geography. From January 2013 to June 2014, I collaborated with an independent data designer, Alli Crandell, on the construction of MDMP's interface. Motivated by a shared interest in deployment, we investigated how to represent metadata relationships that did not rely only on standard bibliographical and geographical descriptors, and much of this investigation centered on building a flexible ontology that showed the periodic redistribution and hierarchical reordering of key concepts and terms. Ideally, the ontology would illustrate potential relationships between a document's historical ecology and the disciplinary assumptions underlying it. If a user came to MDMP to browse, for example, s/he might search terms or topics on any level (e.g., "Current-Traditionalism," "grammar instruction," "letter writing," "foreign English," "folkloric writing," "creative writing," "administration," "NCTE," etc.), resulting in a list of relationships between data fields contributed by other users. As each data set was opened or explored, a corresponding set of data fields would become visible for browsing. This correspondence, in turn, would enable another user to witness how ontologies can be formed or reformed based on trending or fluctuating queries, as the ontological relationships would change with each new query, or each batch of contributed records. Appendix A shows the ontology lists derived from MDMP's data sets while it was still an active prototype. The hierarchical ordering of topics reflected in its stored data showed a different ordering of fields and subfields from the Library of Congress subject headings—awarding a different status to rhetoric, composition, and communication studies in relation to other humanities disciplines—and making frequent re/orderings necessary because MDMP functioned as a performative historical tool.[6]

Crandell and I also considered how to visualize intellectual provenance and migration as feminist archival reconstructions based on a series of relationships between bibliographic references and users' activities. We considered heat maps to imply pan-historical concentrations of activity and topic models to imply the weightedness or influence of specific curricula.[7] In practice, MDMP's interface would have to offer researchers a way to contribute metadata about particular texts or figures or archival locations while also offering their own "affiliations and motives"—their own coordinates, so to speak—as part of the metadata record informing a document's or pedagogue's history, and thus as traceable information within the archive ("Ecologies and Ontologies"). To visualize that history, a user might set one or more search parameters, resulting in dynamic illustrations such as the one shown in Figure 1, where various icons depict various aspects of a document's historical coordinates or various evidences of its circulation.

In MDMP's lexicon, these visualizations were known as "ecologies" rather than "maps" or "landscapes," representing pedagogical histories as assemblages that relied on ecological thinking to show movement between the temporal and the spatial, and the individual and the collective. This lexical disruption seemed necessary because mapping remains a pervasive and uncomplicated epistemological tool in many digital projects. While the recurrence of the "landscape" metaphor in feminist historiographic work has demonstrated its significant potential for disruption (Glenn; Glenn and Enoch; Gold; L'Eplattenier and Mastrangelo; Royster), when applied to metadata work it implies the preservation of stable relationships between persons, places, and things. As we gathered and tested sample data sets for MDMP, we realized the need to construct a different set of icons for privileging motive, purpose, and use—for depicting digital locatability as *a disruption* of iconic relationships, rather than *an intimacy* among them.

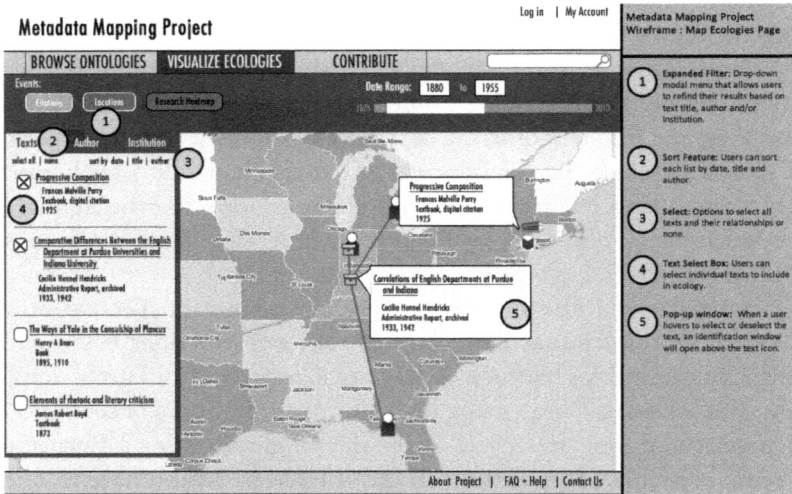

Figure 1: Prototype Visualization of MDMP's functions, by Alli Crandell, 2013.

The resulting ecologies favored terms that could account for documents' or pedagogues' actual and perceived circulation, as well as their *residual value*. Rather than showing a series of object relationships (i.e., *How did Text A get to Location B?*), the ecologies reflected how specific activities have moved through historians' disciplinary and critical consciousness (i.e., *How do Texts/Locations A and B reflected in this metadata record lead us to discover Topic C?*). They demonstrated a layering of relationships having to do with the emergence of a curriculum and its retroactive study; thus, they were less a geographical construct than a historiographic performance, an attempt to "notic[e] how the changing locations of our disciplinary queries might influence or be influenced by the topics we regularly research and teach" ("Ecologies and Ontologies"). Beyond the storage, retrieval, and visualization of user-contributed metadata, what gets democratized through this performance is not only the archive or artifacts being traced, but also their associations and reconstructions (Kirschenbaum, ".txtual").

Disrupting Idioms of Participation and Use: The Spatial, The Digital, and Critical Consumption

When I first envisioned MDMP as a prototype, I did not envision a *built thing*, i.e., an exhibit, repository, or collection, but a tool for composing, realizing, and disrupting idioms of participation and use, and I had hoped it would harness the energy of the vernacular Web in doing so. Such realignment and refocusing of visualized metadata is not only timely for promoting the kinds of archival recovery efforts that are already underway in feminist rhetorical studies, it is also necessary for representing the textured, layered, and unstable subject positions of locatable agents, past and present. I also did not assume that MDMP's visualizations would merely reinforce the humanities' "spatial turn" (Bodenhamer, "Space")[8] or enable speculative arguments about who had access to whose texts and who was interested in what figure, although I find no fault in these kinds of archival imaginings in light of recent calls on feminist scholarship. True to data-mining goals, MDMP invited its users to contribute and note patterns of activity (Juby). But true to feminist rhetorical epistemologies, MDMP sought to rearticulate historical involvement from multiple standpoints (including but not limited to the user's) and to reveal *archival interspaces*—the differends between what motivates certain trends in our historicizing, and how those trends get circulated or constrained. Institutions, citation patterns, location(s), and metadata factors become the new genres of information around which we should build our historical models and tools. Nathan Johnson calls these rhetorical "factors of influence" that require a reorientation to infrastructure and data collection (Johnson 97); we can now find them in our own disciplinary narratives (Geisler; Kennedy; Lang and Baehr).

The resulting metadata network may help historians realize their own spatial engagements and digital constraints, troubling how historiographers take up digital/spatial metaphors such as *distance, zoom*, and *scale*. Without discounting the importance of the digital for this work, I offer that a deployment-driven methodology transcends the digital for the networked by blurring methodological distinctions between "organizing, analyzing, and using historical information" (Graban, *et al* 239). Rhetoric and composition's own "digital archival turn"—assuming we agree there is one—may have begun to disrupt these idioms by shifting emphasis from accessing and witnessing archival information to participating in the formation of digital archives, and I advocate for an additional shift, from constructing digital archival exhibits to developing tools that aid their critical consumption.

I borrow Cathy Davidson's notion of "critical consumption" from a discussion she posted to the HASTAC Consortium several years ago, in which she outlined a definition of 21st-century literacies that would require new metrics for evaluating educational benchmarks. Davidson's writing may have been an extension of the mood developed in her 2008 discussion in *PMLA* about differentiating between "Humanities 1.0" and "Humanities 2.0"—based on the simultaneous usability and malleability of "unfinished" scholarship (713). The post itself was likely a precursor to her 2011 monograph *Now You See It*, in which she would eventually depart from Howard Rheingold's "digital literacies" to suggest a set of core competencies for information literacy among millennials. Whatever Davidson's motivations, she succeeded in building a vocabulary for what constitutes "doing" digital humanities, and she identified a set of ten competencies, among them "network awareness" and "critical consumption" (how to take information in and assess it credibly without gatekeepers). The usefulness of this vocabulary extends beyond the digital humanities, towards more networked projects. While it may seem altruistic or naïve to assume that "network awareness" and "critical consumption" could operate together without systematic gatekeeping, these competencies have significant implications for feminist historiography. They begin to move information literacies toward outcomes that are achieved *in collaborations*, through *itinerant technologies*, and via *crowdsourced labor*.

As a case in point, when I first described MDMP to a colleague in the Information School, Richard Urban, he quickly drew a domain model that reflected information standards emerging from traditional bibliographic-archival relationships. According to these standards, documents' histories could be witnessed and measured in terms of intellectual migration, where intellectual capital was based in the circulation of document-like objects (see Figure 2). After several discussions on the project and for the sake of comparison, Urban sketched a more detailed model that emerged partly from a cultural-heritage orientation toward data and partly from a rhetorical orientation toward the archives, where he identified intellectual migration as occurring through a series of fluctuating (non-static) relationships between physical agents and conceptual activities, all operating within the same domain (Crofts, *et al.*) (see Figure 3). In the process, Urban demonstrated that projects like MDMP might help trouble particular terms and agents, even in data paradigms that acknowledge the complex lives often lived by material cultural objects, inspiring more rhetorical approaches to platform architecture.

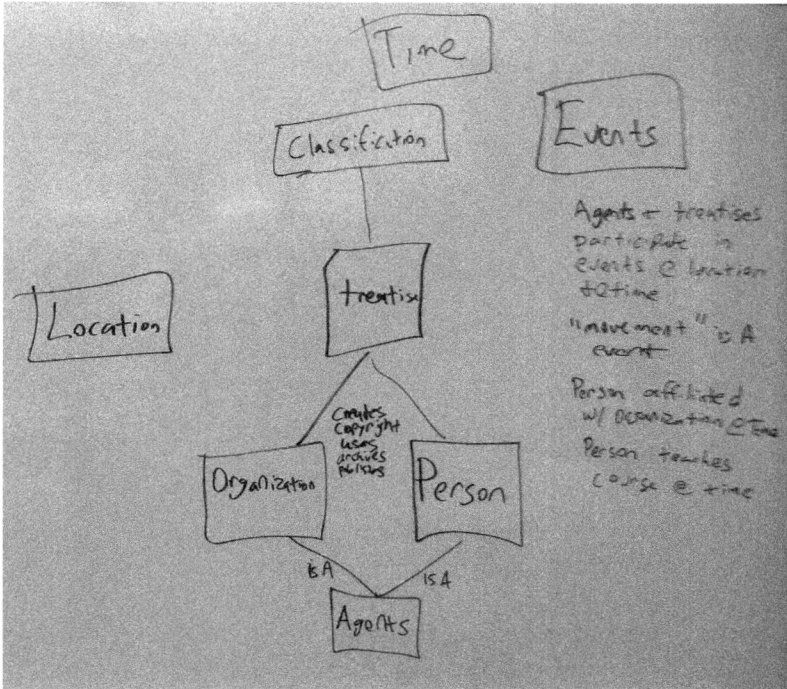

Figure 2: Richard Urban's initial sketch of an object- (treatise-)based Domain Model for MDMP.

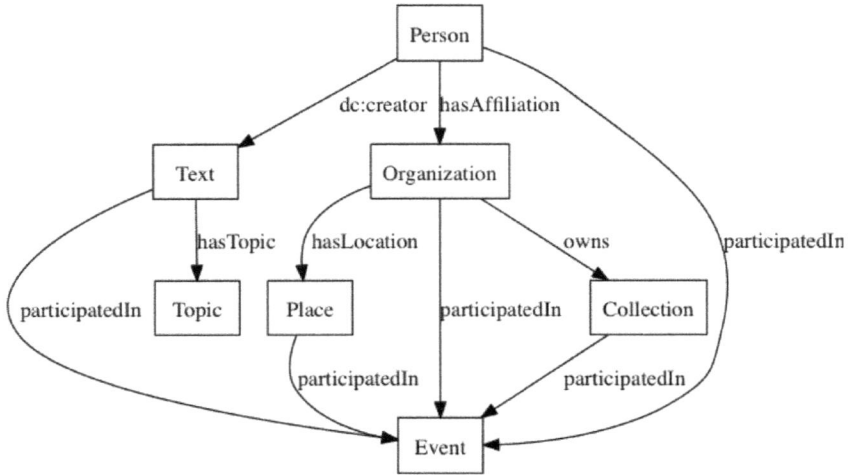

Figure 3: Richard Urban's comparative sketch of an activity-based Domain Model using MDMP's actual experimental data sets

A side-by-side comparison of both models demonstrates how complex the act of recovery can be when it is approached as a kind of *critical consumption of interrelationships*, where all records are given the status of events. For example, in an event describing curricular influences that can be traced back to a female pedagogue's brief tenure as writing program administrator while completing her doctorate, who makes up the "person entity" and how would they differ from "organizations" if the only information MDMP collects is an agent's institutional affiliations? In an event describing archived references to the recirculation of a Midwestern pedagogue's professional writing primer by a now-defunct publishing company in the East, what distinguishes "collections" from "text" entities if our definition of text remains open? In an event that cites a newspaper clipping about a pedagogue's post-retirement projects and travels, what distinguishes "topics" from "terms," and how can we distinguish *places* from *events* when the latter may range from a single citation to a series of archival documents to an entire oral history project?

In short, the kind of idiomatic disruptions that reject stable descriptors for discussion of "events" are what make this a uniquely rhetorical project. The feminist historiographic potential of deployment shows up on this second model in Figure 3—and through Urban's questions—as an *interstitial* layer: a dual perspective, putting close and distant views in the same interpretive network of expectations about what should appear in relation to what else. It points to a perception of historical tools that reflects what Kirsch and Royster call "strategic contemplation," by allowing the researcher to "engag[e] in inquiries that permit [her] to gain perspective from both close and distant views of a particular rhetorical situation or event" ("Feminist" 659). Kirsch and Royster describe this as a back-and-forth movement between varying points of interrogation, analytical and embodied, dialogical and dialectical: "in this case between critical analyses of a rhetorical performance and the recognition of the passionate attachments and ethical commitments that [those who are analyzing the performance] claim and hold" (659). It was our efforts to articulate this duality that inspired the further development of MDMP's prototype into the "Linked Women Pedagogues" (LWP) project, investigating relationships among researchers' motives and various mindsets about how metadata function for historiography, no matter the platform.

CELEBRATING DIFFRACTION OVER FACT: OFFERING *DEPLOYMENT* AS A FEMINIST ETHIC FOR KNOWLEDGE MODELING

My ultimate objective with a prototype like MDMP was to promote more feminist metadata standards that enabled circulatory looking, where *feminist* means *un-engendered by traditional data modeling mindsets* (Bath 1). Traditional mindsets typically encourage the construction of distinct containers, linear pathways among them, and stability—rather than disruption—of those pathways. In contrast, a feminist metadata standard reflects an historical paradigm that operates on extraction rather than containment, and this is the principal reason why I argue for metadata visualization as research in its own right. As a form of deployment, metadata provide us a method for recovery by disrupting several assumptions: that historical relationships are drawn according to traditional taxonomies of storage, ordering, and use; that an amassing and representation of data will make our histories more accurate or complete; and that disciplinary impact and historical agency are measured through the visible circulation of published scholarship, or through moving electronic data in the same ways it moves through print.

As Derrida reminds us in *Archive Fever*, "archivization produces as much as it records the event" (17). It exists in the future perfect, always prompting the question: "What will it have meant?", or—for Jennifer

S. Milligan—reminding us that "'archive' stands as a metaphor for all things historical ... [I]t is above all an institution with a history of in-stitutionalization" (160). The dual archive—*ideas and spaces together*—is open, incomplete, and in constant flux. Such incompleteness and fluc-tuation underlie what Corinna Bath has recently proposed as a feminist ethic of knowledge modeling for scholars in library sciences and infor-mation technology. If scholars want to achieve something close to a fu-ture web, or Web 3.0, Bath argues, they need to envision a web that does more than invoke the image of an intelligent social machine (1). Her resulting *feminist web ethic* operates according to physicist Karen Barad's "agential realism" (Barad, "Getting" 89; Bath 5), through which phenomena get realized and become possible through *intra-acting* as opposed to *intentional* agencies. Whereas Web 2.0 might describe an increase of social software applications to be used by historians, Web 3.0 might suggest a framework that operates on fluctuating linked open data, where historians do not necessarily begin with a dominant or static originary inquiry. For Bath, network and web users are not just observ-ers or non-observers according to the choices they make when operating digital tools; rather, they are co-creators of new information that changes how the tools work.

However, Bath is not convinced that a feminist web ethic can be achieved on the basis of information technology principles alone, ar-guing that information technology devalues diffraction as a historical paradigm. To illustrate, she makes the analogy of throwing stones into a pond. Depending on our disciplinary paradigm, we will either see the expected (i.e., the stones breaking water) or see the unexpected (i.e., the interference that occurs in forms of ripples or waves), but not both at once. The question of metadata ownership for information scientists, she argues, is more tied to their belief that metadata are *facts*—thing-objects, like the stones that break the water and hence have certain preservation properties and mobile characteristics—rather than *relationships*—the re-fractions rippling on the water's surface that point to potential spaces where other objects reside.

Bath's "ripple effect" challenges normalized activity and reveals gaps in users' activities, rather than only trusting in object-oriented histories (Crofts, *et al.*). It describes what happens when users of a particular tool reinscribe certain historical values as they make navigational decisions. I argue that it is a uniquely rhetorical concept because it operates on principles of critical consumption. Whether rooted in the digital or in the networked, feminist historiographic recovery is a celebration of *diffraction*, not of fact, relying more on the prevalence of humanistic ideals than on the success of computational relationships. It occurs through fluctuating relationships between material agents and immaterial activities, that do not exist only in bibliographic form. Thus, what could be seen as competing or dissonant desires in our work—dilemmas between dialectic and atemporal, spatial and interstitial, digital and physical, stable and unstable—more likely points to an ethic of deployment and a compulsion for feminist scholars to use metadata when performing their historiographic ideals.

NOTES

1. This chapter would not be possible without the significant contributions—both intellectual and technical—of Alli Crandell and Richard Urban to the Metadata Mapping Project. From 2013-2014, Crandell was a full collaborator on the development of MDMP's visualization and ontologies into a basic prototype, and Urban was a valuable and frequent advisor on MDMP's methodological dis/similarities with metadata and information studies.

2. Sullivan and Porter have already established the need for a simultaneously critical and reflective research methodology in composition research– a "postcritical" attitude towards research that exposes the disciplinary, environmental, methodological, and relational tensions undergirding the rhetorical situation of writing studies research (164). Here, I extend that attitude towards historical queries and rhetorical environments.

3. According to the Online Computer Library Center and the National Information Standards Organization, "metadata" refer to "structured information that describes, explains, locates, or otherwise makes it easier to retrieve, use or manage an information resource" (NISO 1), and this typically includes the fifteen terms defined by the international Dublin Core. These metadata terms, all dedicated to describing the thing or the object (the text or the artifact), primarily report preservation characteristics. However, metadata can also be used more flexibly to describe relationships beyond thing-objects and, as evidenced in the metadata-inspired recovery projects already named above, they can be more user-driven and relational (Smith-Yoshimura and Shein 10-11), structured so as to support an analysis of the information networks in which various texts or artifacts reside.

4. To wit, digital interfaces such as the ArchiveGrid (https://beta.worldcat.org/archivegrid/), the IMLS Digital Content Collections Project (http://dpla.grainger.illinois.edu/), the University of Oxford's "Relational Museums" Project (http://history.prm.ox.ac.uk/), the U.S. National Archives' "Citizen Archivist" Project (http://www.archives.gov/citizen-archivist/), Alex Gil's

"Around DH in 80 Days" (http://www.globaloutlookdh.org/around-dh-in-80-days/), and Colin Wilder's international "Republic of Literature" offer more than digitized collections and museums. They offer discovery systems and network analysis tools, reflecting the belief that *digital histories*, and more specifically *the work of digital historicizing*, is a simultaneously informed and imagined articulation of possible relationships among texts, their users, and the ideologies that help them circulate.

5. MDMP's prototype has since evolved into a larger project called "Linked Women Pedagogues" (LWP), which is currently described at http://lwpproject.org/wp. LWP includes a more extensive investigation of researcher behaviors and metadata mindsets. The old MDMP prototype is viewable at its archived URL http://tsgfolio.com/mdmp/.

6. There is an element of ethnographic observation to the prototype's functioning, yet I maintain that MDMP's interest in drawing digital locatability differs from ethno-historiography, strictly speaking.

7. One visualization, for example, might offer a shaded map showing variable concentrations, by state, of post-secondary institutions with rhetoric instruction—in writing, English, or speech. Another visualization might depict, by region, variable concentrations of rhetoric and writing programs established in a given window of time, or alongside the number of research queries stemming from or made about those regions.

8. Informatics historian David Bodenhamer has argued for a spatial turn that occurred in the 1990s, as humanities disciplines such as archaeology, cultural studies, and archival studies began to privilege space, over time, as a critical lens, and as they became interested in finding ways to integrate or merge non-standardized data ("Potential," 18). I would not narrate the development of humanistic scholarship in such a fashion that bifurcates space and time; I might even argue that historiography in these disciplines had already moved towards spatial literacies and epistemologies in advance of Bodenhamer's claim, and thus were already focused there before the so-called postmodern data deluge of the 1970s. However, the MDMP prototype embraced Bodenhamer's notion that the historical junctures out of which the spatial humanities emerged were characterized by a continuous re-orientation of scholarly practices towards using and circulating data. These scholarly practices—for example, GIS mapping, data visualization, and topic modeling—were meant to encourage historians to realize "regions" of data as multilayered and collaborative "contact zones," in turn drawing attention to what occurs between the regions of metadata ("Potential," 21).

WORKS CITED

Ballif, Michelle, ed. *Theorizing Histories of Rhetoric.* Carbondale: Southern Illinois UP, 2013.

Ballif, Michelle. "Introduction." In Balliff, ed. 1–7.

Barad, Karen. "Getting Real: Technoscientific Practices and the Materialization of Reality." *Differences* 10.2 (1998): 87-128.

Barad, Karen. *Meeting the Universe Halfway: Quantum Physics and the Entanglement of Matter and Meaning.* Durham, NC: Duke UP.

Bath, Corinna. "Towards a Feminist Ethics of Knowledge Modeling for the Future Web 3.0." Unpublished paper, Institute for Advanced Studies on Science, Technology and Society. 20 June 2011. Accessed 15 June 2013. http://www.ifz.tugraz.at/ias/content/download/5300/47331

Blythe, Stuart. "Agencies, Ecologies, and the Mundane Artifacts in Our Midst." *Labor, Writing Technologies, and the Shaping of Composition in the Academy,* eds. Pamela Takayoshi and Patricia Sullivan. Cresskill, NJ: Hampton P, 2007. 167-86.

Bodenhamer, David J. "The Potential of Spatial Humanities." In *The Spatial Humanities: GIS and the Future of Humanities Scholarship,* eds. David J. Bodenamer, John Corrigan, and Trevor M. Harris. Bloomington: Indiana UP, 2010. 14-30.

Bodenhamer, David. "Space, Time, and Place: The Emergence of the Spatial Humanities." Institute for Digital Arts and Humanities. Wells Library, Bloomington, IN. Web. 18 February 2010. Brownbag lecture. http://breeze.iu.edup95926181/

Bollen, Johan, Herbert Van de Sompel, and Marko A. Rodriguez. "Towards Usage-based Impact Metrics: First Results from the MESUR Project." *JCDL* (June 2008): 231-240. Web.

Bolter, Jay David, and Richard Grusin. "Remediation." *Configurations* 3 (1996): 311-58.

Bolter, Jay David, and Richard Grusin. *Remediation: Understanding New Media.* Cambridge, MA: MIT, 1999.

Brooke, Collin G. "Discipline and Publish: Reading and Writing the Scholarly Network." *Ecology, Writing Theory, and New Media,* ed. Sid I. Dobrin. New York: Routledge, 2012. 92-105.

Cohen, Daniel J., Michael Frisch, Patrick Gallagher, Steven Mintz, Kirsten Sword, Amy Murrell Taylor, William G. Thomas III, and William J. Turkel. "Interchange: The Promise of Digital History." *Journal of American History* 95.2 (2008): 452-491.

Crofts, Nick, Martin Doerr, and Tony Gill. "The CIDOC Conceptual Reference Model: A Standard for Communicating Cultural Contents." *Cultivate Interactive* 9 (2003). Web. Accessed 15 January 2014. *Comité International pour la Documentation.* http://www.cidoc-crm.org/docs/martin_a_2003_comm_cul_cont.htm

Davidson, Cathy N. "Humanities 2.0: Promise, Perils, Predictions." *PMLA* 123.3 (2008): 707-717.

Davidson, Cathy N. "Twenty-First Century Literacies." *Cathy Davidson's Blog.* HASTAC. Web. 12 February 2010. http://www.hastac.org/blogs/cathy-davidson

Derrida, Jacques. *Archive Fever: A Freudian Impression.* Transl. Eric Prenowitz. Chicago, IL: U Chicago P, 1996.

Drucker, Johanna. *Graphesis: Visual Forms of Knowledge Production.* Cambridge, MA: Harvard UP, 2014.

Earheart, Amy E. "Can Information Be Unfettered? Race and the New Digital Humanities Canon." *Debates in the Digital Humanities,* ed. Matthew K. Gold. Minneapolis: U of Minnesota P, 2012. 309-318.

"Ecologies and Ontologies." *MetaData Mapping Project,* 1 September 2014, http://tsgfolio.com/mdmp/ecologies-and-ontologies/

Edbauer, Jenny. "Unframing Models of Public Distribution: From Rhetorical Situation to Rhetorical Ecologies." *Rhetoric Society Quarterly* 35.4 (2005): 5-24.

Enoch, Jessica, and Jean Bessette. "Meaningful Engagements: Feminist Historiography and the Digital Humanities." *College Composition and Communication* 64.4 (Jun. 2013): 634-60.

Gaillet, Lynée Lewis. "(Per)Forming Archival Research Methodologies." *CCC* 64.1 (September 2012): 35-58.

Geisler, Cheryl. *Analyzing Streams of Language: Twelve Steps to the Systematic Coding of Text, Talk, and Other Verbal Data.* New York: Longman, 2003.

Glenn, Cheryl, and Jessica Enoch. "Invigorating Historiographic Practices in Rhetoric and Composition Studies." In Ramsey, *et al,* 11-27.

Glenn, Cheryl. "Mapping the Silences, or Remapping Rhetorical Territory." In *Rhetoric Retold: Regendering the Tradition from Antiquity Through the Renaissance.* Carbondale: Southern Illinois UP, 1997.

Golbeck, Jennifer. "Analyzing Networks." In *Introduction to Social Media Investigation: A Hands-on Approach.* Walton, MA: Syngress, 2015. 221-36.

Gold, David. "Remapping Revisionist Historiography." *College Composition and Communication* 64 (2012): 15-34.

Graban and Sullivan. "Deploying the Digital Humanities," English Department Digital Humanities Lecture Series, Indiana University, February 24, 2010.

Graban, Tarez Samra, Alexis Ramsey-Tobienne, and Whitney Myers. "In, Through, and About the Archive: What Digitization (Dis)Allows." In Ridolfo and Hart-Davidson, eds., 233-44.

Graban, Tarez Samra. "From Location(s) to Locatability," *College English* 76.2 (Nov. 2013): 171-193

Grusin, Richard A. "Radical Mediation." *Critical Inquiry* 42.1 (2015): 124-48.

Haskins, Ekaterina. "Between Archive and Participation: Public Memory in a Digital Age." *Rhetoric Society Quarterly* 37.4 (2007): 401-422.

Hawhee, Debra, and Christa J. Olson. "Pan-Historiography: The Challenges of Writing History Across Time and Space." In Ballif, ed., 90-105.

Hawhee, Debra. "The New Hackers: Historiography Through Disconnection." *Advances in the History of Rhetoric* 15.1 (2012): 119-25. Web.

Hayles, N. Katherine. *How We Think: Digital Media and Contemporary Technogenesis.* Chicago, IL: U Chicago P, 2012.

Johnson, Nathan. "Modeling Rhetorical Disciplinarity: Mapping the Digital Network." In Ridolfo and Hart-Davidson, eds., 96-107.

Juby, Dianne L. "Memory, Arts, Electronic Topoi, and Dynamic Databases." *Making and Unmaking Prospects for Rhetoric: Selected Papers from the 1996 RSA Conference.* Eds. Theresa Enos and Richard McNabb. Mahwah, NJ: Lawrence Erlbaum, 1997. 186-96.

Kennedy, Krista. "Textual Machinery: Authorial Agency and Bot-Written Texts in Wikipedia." *The Responsibilities of Rhetoric: Proceedings of the 2008 Rhetoric Society of America Conference,* eds. Michelle Smith and Barbara Warnick. Waveland P, 2009. Retrieved from SURFACE: Writing Program Series at http://surface.syr.edu/wp/1/

Kirsch, Gesa E., and Jacqueline J. Royster. "Feminist Rhetorical Practices: In Search of Excellence." *College Composition and Communication.* 61.4 (2010): 640-72.

Kirschenbaum, Matthew G. *Mechanisms: New Media and the Forensic Imagination.* Cambridge, MA: MIT P, 2008.

Kirschenbaum, Matthew. "The .txtual Condition: Digital Humanities, Born-Digital Archives, and the Future Literary." *DHQ* 7.1 (July 2013). Web. http://www.digitalhumanities.org/dhq/vol/7/1/000151.html

L'Eplattenier, Barbara, and Lisa Mastrangelo, eds. *Historical Studies of Writing Program Administration: Individuals, Communities, and the Formation of a Discipline.* West Lafayette, IN: Parlor P, 2004.

Lang, Susan, and Craig Baehr. "Data Mining: A Hybrid Methodology for Complex and Dynamic Research." *CCC* 64.1 (Sep. 2012): 172-94.

Miller, Susan. *Trust in Texts: A Different History of Rhetoric.* Carbondale: Southern Illinois UP, 2008.

Milligan, Jennifer S. "'What Is an Archive?' In the History of Modern France." *Archive Stories: Facts, Fictions, and the Writing of History,* ed. Antoinette Burton. Durham, NC: Duke UP, 2005. 159-83.

Mountford, Roxanne. "Mentoring Rhetoric's Historians." *Advances in the History of Rhetoric* 15.1 (2012): 101-108. Web.

Mueller, Derek. "Grasping Rhetoric and Composition by Its Long Tail: What Graphs Can Tell Us about the Field's Changing Shape." *CCC* 64.1 (Sep. 2012): 195-223.

National Information Standards Organization. "Understanding Metadata." Bethesda, MD: NISO, 2004. Accessed 1 January 2013. http://www.niso.org/publications/press/UnderstandingMetadata.pdf

OCLC/RLG Working Group on Preservation Metadata. "Preservation Metadata for Digital Objects: A Review of the State of the Art." Unpublished white paper, 31 January 2001. Accessed 1 January 2013. http://www.oclc. org/content/dam/research/activities/pmwg/presmeta_wp.pdf

Ong, Walter. *Rhetoric, Romance, and Technology: Studies in the Interaction of Expression and Culture.* Ithaca, NY: Cornell, 1971.

Queen, Mary. 2008. "Transnational Feminist Rhetorics in a Digital World." *College English* 70.5: 471-89.

Ramsey, Alexis E., Wendy B. Sharer, Barbara L'Eplattenier, and Lisa Mastrangelo, eds. *Working in the Archives: Practical Research Methods for Rhetoric and Composition.* Carbondale: Southern Illinois UP, 2010.

Ridolfo, Jim, and William Hart-Davison, eds. *Rhetoric and the Digital Humanities.* Chicago: U of Chicago P, 2015.

Ridolfo, Jim. "Delivering the Textual Diaspora: Building Digital Cultural Repositories as Rhetoric Research." *College English* 76.2 (Nov. 2013): 136-151.

Ridolfo, Jim. "Rhetorical Delivery as Strategy: Rebuilding the Fifth Canon from Practitioner Stories." *Rhetoric Review* 31.2 (2012): 117-29.

Roemer, Robin Chin, and Rachel Borchardt. "From Bibliometrics to Altmetrics: A Changing Scholarly Landscape." *College & Research Libraries News* 73.10 (November 2012): 596-600. Accessed 10 April 2013. http://crln.acrl. org/content/73/10/596.full

Rose, Gillian. *Feminism and Geography: The Limits of Geographical Knowledge.* Cambridge, UK: Polity, 1993.

Royster, Jacqueline Jones, and Gesa E. Kirsch. *Feminist Practices: New Horizons for Rhetoric, Composition, and Literacy Studies.* Carbondale: Southern Illinois UP, 2012.

Royster, Jacqueline Jones. "Disciplinary Landscaping, or Contemporary Challenges in the History of Rhetoric." *Philosophy and Rhetoric* 36.2 (2003): 148-67.

Smith-Yoshimura, Karen and Cyndi Shein. "Social Metadata for Libraries, Archives and Museums Part 1: Site Reviews." Dublin, Ohio: OCLC Research, 2011. Accessed 23 January 2012. http://www.oclc.org/research/publications/library/2011/2011-02.pdf

Solberg, Janine. "Googling the Archive: Digital Tools and the Practice of History." *Advances in the History of Rhetoric* 15 (2012): 53-76. Web.

Sullivan, Patricia, and James E. Porter. *Opening Spaces: Writing Technologies and Critical Research Practices.* Westport, CT: Ablex, 1997.

Sullivan, Patricia, and Tarez Samra Graban. "Digital and Dustfree: A Conversation on the Possibilities of Digital-Only Searching for Third-Wave Historical Recovery." *Peitho* 13.2 (Dec 2011): 2-11.

Taylor, Charles. *Modern Social Imaginaries.* Durham, NC: Duke UP, 2004.

Theimer, Kate. "Two meanings of 'archival silences' and their implications." *Archivesnext.com*, March 27, 2010. Accessed 13 January 2012 http://www.archivesnext.com/?p=2653

Urban, R. J., Piotr Adamczyk, and Michael B. Twidale. "Designing and Developing a Collections Dashboard." *Museums and the Web 2010: Proceedings*, ed. Jennifer Trant and David Bearman. Denver, CO: Archives & Museum Informatics, 2010. http://archimuse.com/mw2010/papers/urban/urban.html

Yakel, Elizabeth. 2010. "Searching and Seeking the Deep Web: Primary Sources on the Internet." In Ramsey, *et al*, 102-118.

Appendix A: MDMP's Experimental Ontology Lists

Composition, Rhetoric, and Literature
- English Literature
- Pedagogy
  - Grammar
  - Letter Writing
  - Punctuation
  - Rhetorical Models

English Composition
- History and Theory
- Pedagogy
  - Advanced composition
  - Army and Navy English
    - English 61
    - English 62
  - Basic Writing
    - English 1
    - English 2
    - English 101
    - English 102
  - Essay writing
    - Handbooks
    - Modes of Exposition
      - Short and Long Exposition
    - Paragraphing
  - First-year composition
- Teacher Preparation

Folklore and Ethnography
- Cultural Research
- Family Development
- Island Development
  - Palau Islands

Institutional Research
- Continuing Education
- G.I. Bill
- Higher Education
  - Enrollment Patterns
  - Entrance Requirements

- o   Recent Trends
- o   Junior Curriculum
- Humanities Revival
- Institutional History
- Public School Administration
- Secondary Education
    - o   Recent Trends
- Women's Education
- Writing Program Administration
    - o   Placement
    - o   Assessment

Language
- History and Theory
- Pedagogy
    - o   English as a Second Language
    - o   Linguistics
    - o   Writing for Foreign Students
- Philology
    - o   Dictionary Editing
    - o   Translingualism
- Teacher Preparation

Philanthropy

Politics

Professional Writing
- Business Writing
- Creative Writing
    - o   Nature Writing
    - o   Writers' Conference
    - o   Writing Editorials
- Journalism
- Technical Writing
    - o   Scientific Essay Writing
- Writing for the Professions
- Writing for Women

Rhetoric
- Argument

- Criticism
- History and Theory
  - o Memory
- Pedagogy
  - o Belletrism
  - o Critical Writing
    - ▪ Forms of Discourse
    - ▪ Modes of Exposition
  - o Logic
  - o Prose Composition
    - ▪ Handbooks
  - o Style

11 Provocation: "We have mult[i] ple nets to fit into": Understanding Networked Claims

Clay Spinuzzi

In *Networked: The New Social Operating System*, Lee Rainie and Barry Wellman argue that networks among people have transformed how we connect with each other, both personally and electronically. People, they argue, "have become increasingly networked as individuals, rather than being embedded in groups. In the world of networked individuals, it is the person who is the focus: not the family, not the work unit, not the neighborhood, and not the social group" (Rainie and Wellman 6). Networked individualism requires new strategies and skills for solving problems (Rainie and Wellman 9). And it involves a "triple revolution": We can reach beyond tight groups; We have new communication power and information-gathering capabilities; and information and communication technologies (ICTs) are a "bodily appendage," always accessible (Rainie and Wellman 11–12). Like Castells, Deleuze, and other commentators, Rainie and Wellman argue that this emergent networked individualism shifts us away from central authorities and toward more multidimensional loci of trust and authority.

This erosion of central authority has a number of ramifications, but one is briefly explored in this December 2013 Twitter exchange between Wellman and his interlocutor, Philip Mai:

Barry Wellman @barrywellman · 7 Dec 2013   ⌄
Reading about Milgram started me thinking of problem of authority in a
networked, non-hierarchical world

   ♡ 1   ↻   ♡ 1

Philip Mai @PhMai · 7 Dec 2013   ⌄
@barrywellman Milgram's world was more top down. Since Enlightenment that
world has been waning, replaced now by "networked individualism"

   ♡ 1   ↻ 1   ♡ 1

Barry Wellman   (Follow)   ⌄
@barrywellman

Replying to @PhMai

.@PhMai Milgram explicitly responding to issues of conformity & the Holocaust. With net individualism, we have multple nets to fit into.

9:14 AM - 7 Dec 2013

2 Likes

♡   ↻   ♡ 2

Figure 1. Twitter exchange between Barry Wellman and Philip Mai, December, 2013.

The Milgram experiments examined how far people would follow the commands of an authority figure when the commands violated their own consciences. But Wellman asks: how authoritative are these authorities? The tweet echoes what Rainie and Wellman argue in their book: "In the less hierarchical and less bounded networked environment—where expertise is more in dispute than in the past and where relationships are more tenuous—there is more uncertainty about whom and what information sources to trust" (18). Rather than a single authoritative hierarchy, "we have mult[i]ple nets to fit into."

That's not to say that the Milgram experiments would necessarily fail today. The appeal to authority is weaker, but it is not dead. Yet, networked individualism means that *different networks of authority overlap*: we occupy different networks simultaneously, networks with different frames, assumptions, and logics. And in these overlapping networks, the claims that circulate most in a networked age are often the ones that gain strength through resonance across these networks, supported by reasons that are often incompatible or incoherent because they draw on the different frames of the different, overlapping networks.

One example is supplied by David Ronfeldt and his colleagues at RAND in their analysis of the Zapatista netwar (Ronfeldt et al. 1999). The Zapatistas (EZLN) began as a traditional Marxist insurgency, arranged along Maoist lines in which guerillas would build up forces and eventually form regiments and divisions to confront the enemy. Unfortunately for the EZLN, this strategy was not working. But the EZLN found that it gained traction among nongovernmental organizations (NGOs) interested in various issues, such as indigenous rights, human rights, and anti-NAFTA sentiment. These NGOs did not necessarily agree with each other about many things, but they did detect a shared set of propositions—which the EZLN quickly clarified as its own, shifting its objective from revolution to reform, jettisoning much of the Marxist language and demands along the way. As Ronfeldt et al. put it in the Zapatista study, "NGO coalitions arose that were characterized by 'flexible, conjunctural [coyuntural], and horizontal relations' held together by shared goals and demands" And, "To some extent, this was a compromise agenda" (Ronfeldt et al. 51).

Let's think about this, tentatively, in rhetorical terms. Under classical (and arguably institutional) rhetoric, arguments are expected to be internally coherent. We can use Stephen Toulmin's structure as an example: A well-formed argument has a claim supported by data. Connecting the claim to the data is a warrant, an assumption shared by both the speaker and the listener. The more data supporting the claim, the better. In a well-formed argument, none of these bits of data contradict each other.

But in the Zapatista example, we see something rather different. True to network principles, different actors cross boundaries to collaborate on a single set of shared goals and demands. Let's call this set of goals and demands the claim. The NGOs are largely single-issue: indigenous rights, human rights, anti-NAFTA, etc. They come from different regions, are based in different countries, and reflect different ideologies. But they are all *interested* (to use actor-network theory's terminology) in the same problem or proposition or claim; they all define it and are in turn defined by it. So, in Toulmin terms, each contributes warrants and data. But *these components do not have to be coherent* with the components of the other NGOs. NGOs A, B, and C may have completely different logics, ideologies, warrants, evidence, etc. But they swarm the claim and lend their support to it.

Since this networked argument is not coherent, it provides a much more difficult target. It may not even appear rational to an institutional actor, and in fact it's probably a poor argument by institutional (classic rhetorical) standards. To use terms that I introduced in my 2008 book: institutions expect a *woven* argument; networks deliver *spliced* arguments.

Castells similarly examines another case of netwar, the World Trade Organization protests in Seattle. This case was characterized by

> a vast coalition of *extremely different, and even contradictory, interests and values*, from the battalions of the American labor movement to the swarms of eco-pacifists, environmentalists, women's groups, and a myriad of alternative groups, including the pagan community" (Castells 141; emphasis added; cf. Castells' examination of other networked groups in Castells, "The Power").

Other examples of such spliced arguments include "open source warfare" (Robb), Occupy Wall Street, and the Tea Party. At present, such movements tend to be united in tactical opposition rather than strategic objectives. In these movements, individuals come into contact and network with those who have similar tactical goals through information technologies that also help them to rapidly coordinate.

Such networked arguments, I believe, will become more common in the future, as networked individuals overlay more and more of their networks, more and more of their authoritative loci, and produce claims that splice together these different networks, the different "mult[i]ple nets" into which the interlocutors fit. As the cases above suggest, networked arguments have thus far tended to be disruptive, reactive, and tactical, and I don't see hope for more ideologically coherent or lasting movements based on them. Since it's easier to protest what is than to build what isn't, in the short term these protests are more likely to encourage gridlock and inaction than they are to move us toward productive development. That is, networked claims are easier to pull together, but harder to build on.

What is the role of the networked humanities here? I propose that one role is to map out the fundamentals of networked claims—their characteristics and structures, their tactics, their deployment—and to explore ways to make them more productive. A good first step is Jones' (2013) exploration of the tactic of "switching" in Twitter arguments, but more work needs to be done if we are to understand and improve argumentation among networked individuals.

Works Cited

Castells, Manuel. *The Power of Identity*. Blackwell, 1997.

— . *The Internet Galaxy: Reflections on the Internet, Business, and Society*. Oxford UP, 2003.

Deleuze, Gilles. *Negotiations, 1972–1990*. Columbia UP, 1995.

Jones, John. "Switching in Twitter's Hashtagged Exchanges." *Journal of Business and Technical Communication*, vol. 28, no. 1, 30 Aug. 2014, pp. 83–108. doi:10.1177/1050651913502358.

Rainie, Lee, and Barry Wellman *Networked: The New Social Operating System*. MIT Press, 2012.

Robb, John. *Brave New War: The Next Stage of Terrorism and the End of Globalization*. Wiley, 2008.

Ronfeldt, David, John Arquilla, Graham E. Fuller, and Melissa Fuller. *The Zapatista Social Netwar in Mexico*. Rand Co., 1999.

Toulmin, Stephen E. 1969. *The Uses of Argument*. Cambridge UP.

12 Homeless Infrastructure

Casey Boyle

The rapid growth of the South by Southwest (SXSW) technology and music conference has demonstrated itself in recent years by overloaded and slowed wireless network connections for its attendees. For the 2012 SXSW gathering, a marketing firm responded to the network problem by employing a dozen homeless people to serve as wireless hotspots for conference goers. According to the project's organizers, "Homeless Hotspots" was an attempt to modernize and make digital "Street Newspapers," an existing communication practice—homeless persons distributing newspapers written by and about homeless persons—by equipping those same distributors with/as wireless hotspot hubs and clothing them with shirts instructing, in one instance, "I'm Clarence, a 4G hotspot."

It should be no surprise that traditional and social media venues reacted with outrage to Homeless Hotspots. Several commentators criticized the move as exploitative or, at the very least, insensitive to those it had hired. As seen in this representative comment by Erin Kissane, critics took issue with how the project articulated itself (Fig. 1.).

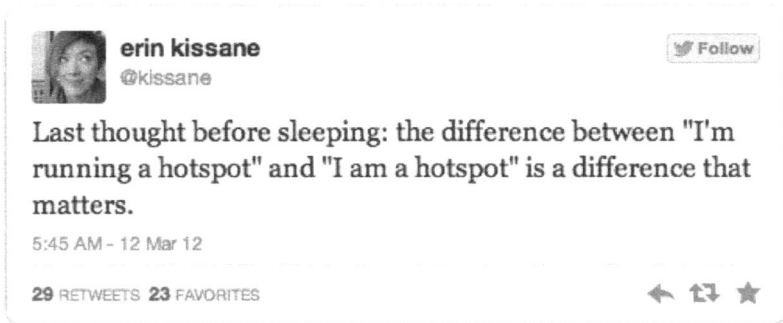

erin kissane
@kissane

Last thought before sleeping: the difference between "I'm running a hotspot" and "I am a hotspot" is a difference that matters.

5:45 AM - 12 Mar 12

29 RETWEETS **23** FAVORITES

Figure 1. Erin Kissane on Homeless Hotspots.

Commenters from Twitter to TechCrunch to Jon Stewart questioned as inhuman/e the notion that an individual human had been reduced to *being* a component in a network infrastructure. Put differently, Homeless Hotspots seemed to jeopardize the very notion of the human by succumbing to an assumed inhuman logic of technological connection. The underlying assumption for this reaction relies on an understanding of the human as a unique actor who is separate from the nonhuman technology with which that actor may or may not *choose* to engage. Maintaining the difference between the two, as Erin Kissane curtly states, *matters*.

Of course, the difference matters, but the difference matters differently than we might first understand. In response to Kissane's representative comment, I submit that the two sentences—I'm running a hotspot & I am a hotspot—are not mutually exclusive. In addition to the common reaction against "I am a hotspot," we find that the human and nonhuman frequently intermingle despite our many attempts to impose and sustain distinct categories. In fact, we could write these sentences any number of additional ways and still find it difficult to compose even one version of the sentence that is not, at least in some sense, *true*. Such an exercise would show that categories between the human and the nonhuman are confused and difficult to keep separate.

Toward examining this confusion, Matthew Wilson, a critical geographer, wonders if Homeless Hotspots is "perhaps illustrative of the peculiar pervasiveness of digital culture, wherein the demands of connectivity necessitate new, innovative infrastructures, and new vehicles to serve the throng of digital technophiles on the move" ("Geospatial technologies" n.p.). Wilson goes on to argue that researchers and GI-Sciences "have a responsibility to interrogate the increasing interplays between socio-technical systems like location-based services (LBS) and everyday life" (n.p.). Thus, Homeless Hotspots is not an event to guard humanity against but perhaps an example of humanity's contemporary networked condition.

We do not have to look far to witness that the rise of mobile devices like phones, tablets, and laptops reorganize infrastructure and alter the character our most entrenched institutions. For instance, several universities have leveraged the rise of mobile technology by eliminating phones in many of its faculty office phone lines (if not the offices themselves) by relying instead on the mobile devices provided to or by that faculty. Nor is it uncommon for universities to no longer provide email to its students or employees since "free" options have become widely accessible. Consistent with this infrastructural creep into our previously separate lives, we find a more expansive homelessness roaming through institutions of higher learning where a mobile army of part-time and partially invested instructors replace previously stabilizing lines of tenure-track faculty. This condition is by no means germane to universities and colleges as we see outside of academia an even greater erosion of full-time employment, pensions, and benefits give way to increased corporation-friendly part-time labor. Homeless Hotspots then might be informative of something other than what we might immediately—even if rightly—critique or dismiss. Just as Wilson finds in Homeless Hotspots a need to develop methodologies to account for the "interplays" between human and non-human actors as a "socio-technical system," so too must the humanities more generally develop pedagogical and ethical responses for those infrastructural interplays exemplified by *homelessness*.

An emerging networked humanities persuades us to not only become aware of technological dynamics, but they also compel us to become attuned to new ways of knowing and generating knowledge in response to what Wilson calls "continuous connectivity" (543). We typically understand the network as the capacity to connect to more things. This appeal to more connection is especially the case in discussions of new media writing. Toward this end, Jeff Rice righty extols the network's ability to serve as our guiding metaphor to refigure writing for contemporary communication practices. In place of *topos* and rigid knowledge categories, Rice argues that new media and English (we might consider English here to be an easy stand-in for any humanities discipline) "should be the study of the mixing and remixing of connections" across a host of different situations, including "popular culture and the university" from "geography to politics" and from "celebrity to noncelebrity," and so on ("Networks and New Media" 132). Rice's call is usually taken up as support for making disparate connections that would then challenge existing structures and *status quos*. However, along with the logic of "mixing and remixing" underlies another version of the network that is less discussed in humanities scholarship. This version Rice later characterizes as being "as much a supporter of as a challenger to contemporary notions of structure" (*Digital Detroit* 31). In addition to networks that seek difference through growth, networks are just as important producing difference to sustain certain kinds of engagement. Peter Galison describes this other capacity for networks by examining how the United States dispersed its infrastructure from urban centers amid fears of nuclear catastrophe, summarizing that "[d]ispersal could aid in reconstruction and also prevention—a stronger nation 'protected in space' (as the phrase went) would deter any attacker" ("War Against the Center" 22). To put it too simply: the network ensured homes by decentering the home. America and other countries prepared for nuclear conflict by becoming homeless.

The remainder of this chapter will attempt to explore what homelessness offers for networked humanities. I will examine and extend this notion of network as itself a humanities practice that relies less on tracing connections in an attempt to categorize and know a network and instead engage in an exercise towards developing a comportment, an attunement to the many connections available as being a chief practice of an emerging networked humanities.

INFRASTRUCTURE AS CRISIS

A conversation has emerged over the last decade concerning institutional dynamics of infrastructure as creating conditions for networked writing. This conversation, while somewhat new to the humanities, is important because as writing studies define writing more broadly, its scholars and teachers need to become more aware of the wider networks. Much of this scholarship offers valuable modes of intervening in institutional practices that open spaces and opportunities for engaging those infrastructural networks in ways that help support a reconfigured humanities agenda. Toward this end, Danielle Nicole DeVoss, Ellen Cushman, and Jeffery T. Grabill use Susan Leigh Star and Karen Ruhleder's understanding of infrastructure—an institution's embedded and transparent systems of technologies, polices, practices, and values—as a spatio-temporal analytic that helps "[make] strange the taken-for-granted, often invisible, institutional structures implicit in the teaching of new-media composing" ("Infrastructure and Composing" 19). DeVoss et al., find infrastructure as the site that conducts, supports and/or obstructs networked writing in the academy. To participate in those dynamics, an infrastructural framework helps expand the scope of writing to intervene in the institutional structures by revealing the dynamics of institutional activity and making visible the limitations or obstructions for teaching new media composing. Their representative example involves how a routine course assignment helped re-negotiate an institution's network infrastructure because that infrastructure's limits become known and negotiated, showing "how composing and compositions change shape within the complex dynamics of network" (37). A catalyst for this kind of intervention surfaces when some tool or process breaks down or becomes suddenly unavailable—be it a hammer, bridge, paperwork protocol, or web server. It is those moments of breakdown, rupture, and loss that allow otherwise ignored infrastructure to be foregrounded and made apparent to our conscious attention. Without the breakdown or rupture that allowed for a network to become visible, participants could not have successfully argued for a change in policies.

The visibility of an infrastructural problem—here, technological policies that resist pedagogical goals—is the chief heuristic for enacting change. Stuart Selber extends these tactics by proposing "postmodern mapping" (visual-spatial maps) as a method for tracing the multiple overlapping and interwoven contexts in which infrastructure unfolds. Mapping allows Selber to visually define the positions and relationships of key components shaping academic computing, components that include both institutional and personal devices. For instance, Selber finds that "something unexpected happened when faculty started to integrate computers into administrative work" because, at times, "documents actually became less public and less accessible, dispersing into personal computers with tendencies toward individuation and customization" (27). The mappings help identify spaces of ambiguity wherein competing infrastructural contexts impede an institution's aims. Defining and interrogating these interwoven contexts proliferating in academic computing (and we can extend to any other contemporary context) offer Selber the sites for the interplay of non-official and official uses of technology to agonistically play out a drama that renegotiates established contexts for achieving administrative or pedagogical goals. *As rupture helps make network infrastructures visible, making infrastructures visible helps show that ruptures help make network infrastructures.*

As read above, it is commonly understood that networks and infrastructure are understood best when breakdown occurs or when that infrastructure is visibly rendered to show ongoing ruptures; however, recent theorists have begun to complicate those notions as it becomes more difficult to step back and separate oneself from those networks, especially when one is afforded instances of disruption. Kacyz Varnelis, an architectural theorist who has written extensively on network culture, characterizes networks and infrastructure as being perhaps always in constant crisis (Fig. 2).

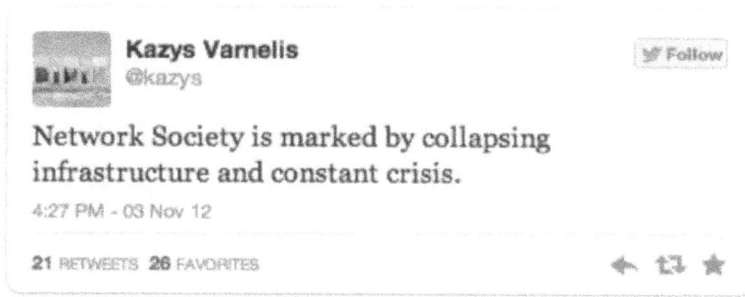

Kazys Varnelis
@kazys

Network Society is marked by collapsing infrastructure and constant crisis.

4:27 PM - 03 Nov 12

21 RETWEETS 26 FAVORITES

Figure 2 - Kazys Varnelis and Network Society.

Varnelis posted this brief statement in the days after Hurricane Sandy had caused wide damages, especially to the region's communication and electrical infrastructure. Previous modes of intervening in infrastructures and networks would privilege this event as offering a space to interrogate previous assumptions and polices now foregrounded through their breakdown. While the storm disrupted communication networks of all kinds—transportation, electrical, data—what became clear was that the region had the capacity to reconfigure itself. In addition to the destruction caused by high winds and flooding, news reports also circulated surprising images of residents swarming spaces of available electric outlets to recharge phones and mobile devices. These events demonstrate another capacity of the network that is not reducible to what one can see or know.

In opposition to a mode of intervention that relies on rupture or lack to make itself visible and known, I propose that these responses to the aftermath of Hurricane Sandy were not made available because of outages or even ruptures—despite taking place during outage and disruption. Instead, what we witnessed in the aftermath are different capacities of the network. That is, in the event of rupture and disruptions, a capacity for homelessness arose that demonstrated homelessness as an ability to reconnect, to remix, and to refigure even in catastrophic conditions, especially in catastrophic conditions. Within a much larger pre-individual fund of human bodies, mobile devices, and spotty connections, another network exercised itself in the aftermath of Hurricane Sandy. Albeit shifty and not optimal, a homeless network emerged that invites us to consider networked humanities as offering modes of inquiry that rely on more than rupture or lack.

TAKING UP HOMELESSNESS

It might seem odd to consider homelessness as a rhetorical strategy since rhetoricians are usually cast in the role to remedy lack and loss. Such an appeal makes no explicit appearance in any contemporary textbook nor any rhetorical handbook from antiquity. This is not to say we lack resources for taking up homelessness. Media theorist Vilem Flusser offers homelessness as an easy way to explain a contemporary condition marked by an increase in mobility. Flusser, a Jewish man born in Prague, raised in German culture, and eventually taking up residence in Brazil, is himself an accumulation of different places and through those many places has a capacity for enacting different modes of being as a result of having been composed through multiple networks. In his short essay "Taking up Residence in Homelessness," Flusser considers his own exiles, migrations, and movements, and proposes that "I am homeless, because there are so many homelands that make their home in me" (*Writings* 91). Flusser's homelessness speaks to a larger condition in which:

> We are all like this, we nomads who have surfaced after having experienced the breakdown of a settled form of existence.
>   Secret threads tie the person with a home to people and the things of home. They reach beyond the consciousness of our adult life into regions that are at once childish, infantile, and perhaps even fetal and transindividual. . . . (93).

These secret threads are multiple and irreducible to one's conscious understanding and stretch far past one's own individual life and experiences. The multiple threads form an infrastructure and offer an understanding of home not as a geographic place but "rather the function of a certain technique" (93). While paying heed to loss as something we do suffer, Flusser goes on to see such suffering as only increasing since "[t]he migrant is a man of a coming future world without homes." As I mentioned above, we need not look too far to see evidence of this kind of homelessness as the pervading condition of contemporary life—one that speaks toward a permanent mobility that we now see in labor issues, technology affordances, national allegiances, and so on.

It would be easy to understand Flusser's homelessness as an appeal to the benefits of multicultural programs and curricula. Such an appeal to the "social" is one that the humanities has included and praised these last couple of decades as a way to expand the notion of the humanist outwards past its traditional outline of the European intellectual. I would not reject that argument, but I do propose something else might also be happening. While Flusser is here talking about culture and geographic ties, the "invisible" and "secret threads" that tie a person to a place, his account is remarkably consistent with notions of our own technological situations, especially those exhibited through my opening example of Homeless Hotspots. Flusser's understanding that "home is a certain function of technique" and is "transindividual" resonates with more recent writers whose own articulations of the transindividual considers technology and technique to be derived from a larger, pre-individual fund as the dynamic infrastructure that mediates devices, processes, and even biological bodies. Adrian Mackenzie claims that "[t]he notion of the transindividual forms a crucial part of an alternative account of psychosocial experience because it links the emergence of collectives to something that is not fully experienced or perceived by individuals" (*Transductions* 117). In later work, Mackenzie concretizes this argument by turning to wireless networks (like those exemplified by Homeless Hotspots) and argues that wirelessness provides "an experience trending toward our entanglement with things, objects, gadgets, infrastructures, and services" that "affects how people arrive, depart, and inhabit places, how they relate to others, and indeed, how they embody change" (*Wirelessness* 5). These entanglements are vital in that they operate and make themselves known as those ongoing microruptures that call on us (our devices, bodies, software) to reconfigure in slight, barely noticeable ways. These reconfigurations are not to be dismissed as they build up capacities for future reconfigurations. Mackenzie goes on to further characterize these reconfigurations by suggesting that the same conditions of loss and lack we often consider to be in urgent need of fixing are actually the underlying conditions of wirelessness:

> Wi-Fi's limitations and surprising potentials highlight wirelessness as a composite experience animated by divergent processes, by relations that generate transitions and create expectations of more change to come. 'More' includes the 'less' of wirelessness: there will be less wires, less obstacles, less difficulty, less weight, and in general much more of less (5).

The transindividual—both in Mackenzie and Flusser's accounts—offers a figure through which to understand networks without concentrating on individual subject positions or resorting to a structural totality of *culture* or *society*. Importantly, this transindividual does not follow the cyborg model we might have understood as underpinning early post-human notions of subjectivity whose fundamental lack is alleviated by something external to itself. Instead, the transindividual marks out bodies as interwoven collectives that arrive at a (meta)stability only as a result of always shifting distributed agency irreducible to human intentions or nonhuman forces. The transindividual, then, is always certain techniques of relationships that are more *and* less than the sum of its available components.

Flusser returns to the transindividual in a related essay wherein he expands the notion of homelessness to encompass our future cities as configured through networks. "In order to conceive of this new city model," Flusser argues "one must surrender the intellectual categories of geography in favor of topology (177). Here, Flusser abstracts himself further from physical geography as our prime organizing principle, by insisting that as "soon as we are able to think topologically—that is, in terms of networked concrete relationships—the city to be designed allows not only localization, but also localization everywhere in the network" (177). He stresses the importance of topological thought for a future society whose networked connections are abundant with media, people, and infrastructure. Topology, here, refers in part to the branch of mathematics whose study of geometric shapes is undertaken by twisting, folding, stretching, and squeezing that shape to determine its limits. Topology, then, seems to be the mode of inquiry that might best allow us to localize or find residence in an ongoing homelessness.

TOWARD A TOPOLOGICAL PEDAGOGY

Marshall McLuhan reminds us that the "content" of any medium "is always another medium" (*Understanding Media* 8). The same can be said for networks more generally since enacting networks requires a topological capacity that requires becoming different to remain the *same*. This proposition demonstrates itself even in this short chapter as Homeless Hotspots contain Street Newspapers; Flusser was Brazilian in as much as he was first German; official institutional technology is inhabited by any number of unofficial, personal devices. As computer scientists often paradoxically claim that a computer is not necessary to do computer science, we can similarly claim that digital media or global infrastructures are not needed to develop topological thinking. McLuhan offers another example in which the network can be performed without digital media by engaging the practice of topological thinking.

In *Counterblast*, McLuhan cites fifteenth-century humanist Desiderous Erasmus as a model for responding to 1960s media practice. McLuhan finds Erasmus to be an exemplar of emerging media because he allowed and encouraged then nonacademic media and writing practices a place in the academic classroom. McLuhan proposes to his contemporaries that "[w]e could do for the classroom what Erasmus did for the classroom of his day. We could make it the matrix of a cultural flowering much greater than that of the Elizabethan Age. For we possess, and to some degree already experience, the facts of media cross-fertilization." (*Counterblast* 122). That is, Erasmus carved out a space within the academia for material that we typically associate as being outside of it by intensifying the opportunity to experience the interwoven media practices of that day. Following McLuhan's lead, we can look again to Erasmus for how we might think topologically.

In addition to encouraging the mixing of multiple genres and media, Erasmus offered another network exercise. Erasmus's writing manual, *De Copia* or *On Abundance*, outlined techniques for varying sentences and generating subject matter by practicing a system of permutation through metaphor, analogy, amplification, and other figures and tropes. The book's most notable example is Erasmus's demonstration of the *copia* technique by varying the sentence: "I received your letter" over 150 times: I rejoiced exceedingly in your letter; Your letter brought me greater joy than I can express; What clover is to bees, what willow boughs are to goats, what honey is to the bear, your letter is to me. I propose that *copia* offers a linguistic analog to the dynamics inherent to network infrastructure. The practices we find in *copia* are consistent with the momentary, reconfiguring, and topological movements we find in networks. It is a practice that includes but exceeds one's conscious, critical awareness by involving a writer in an exercise of attuning to the differential repetition essential for networked connection. *Copia* then is not concerned with adhering to a topos as much as it is with *exercising* a topology.

Alexander Galloway and Eugene Thacker help us consider what topological thinking means for the network by declaring that "[b]y 'thinking topologically,' we mean an approach that compares the abstract spaces of different structural or architectonic systems" (*The Exploit* 13). They further argue that that the importance of networks lies not in any one individual's ability to control what is or is not contained in a network since "networks operate less through the exception of individuals, groups, or institutions and more through the exceptional quality of networks or of their topologies" and what matters "is less the character of the individual nodes than the topological space within which and through which they operate as nodes" (44). As Mackenzie says above, the transindividual is a temporal collection of relationships that span human and nonhuman and we can understand a networked humanities as providing spaces to exercise those collectives topologically.

A networked humanities would seek to exploit, not resolve, how our academic networked infrastructures are becoming homeless through an internal proliferation of official and non-official technologies that range from personal to institutional devices. The academic infrastructure of a university, along with the particular space of a networked classroom, offers ongoing events through which an abundance of actors—teachers, students, electricity, IT, computers, wifi, architecture, moods, et al.— fold together network infrastructures that cohere as a single network while also persisting as multiple. A pedagogy for a networked human-ities would not only include one's conscious and critical awareness to trace out these networks—foundational humanities practices that I am not arguing against—but such a pedagogy would also leverage one's dis-parate embodied connections in a kind of exercise remarkably similar to previous pedagogies.

At the risk of repeating myself, again, our current networked human-ities contain the practices of our earliest rhetoricians. The Greek soph-ists, itinerant teachers and practitioners, were literally homeless as they traveled from across the Greek world, breaking the "secret ties" that con-nected them to their past homelands. In opposition to Plato's academy— a place separated from the bustling urban center of Athens—the sophists offered training that leveraged their experience of homelessness to teach others to cultivate habits of timely response. Debra Hawhee highlights the basis for sophistic training as consisting of rhythm, repetition, and response. To quote Hawhee's take on Isocratean pedagogy, "no system of knowledge can teach kairotic response; rather, such response is culti-vated out of repeated encounters with difference—different opponents in different positions at different times and places" (*Bodily Arts* 148). These different encounters are typically thought to be those agonistic engagements we find in wrestling, debating, and in arguing for trials. While those practices can be seen as subtending forms of engagement that seek to remedy lack, we could also benefit from considering the multiple and varied infrastructures as offering occasions for encountering "difference." These differences need not to be different locations, as we might traditionally understand it, but as the repeated encounters that sustain one location. That is, using a networked classroom as an example, we enact and experience an abundance of networks: internets, intranets, extranets. Students collaborate on a discussion forum, through instant message, by passed notes, in shared drafts in material and digital spaces, and on public and personal devices. Each enactment of the network composes another material articulation of "I received your letter" or "I am a hotspot." In place of having students locate the network as residing in one place (social media, mobile devices, instant message), networked humanities would develop exercises of networks that leverage the different networks available as an exercise in relating to and through those interwoven contexts that compose out networked infrastructure. Performing topologically and not just topically would undermine the traditional notion of the humanist subject as contained agent of rational thought. It would render that subject *homeless*.

Networked humanities would displace a humanities that finds home with only concerning itself with the rational humanist subject. This task is only becoming harder to sustain. Rosi Braidotti remarks that our current "identity crisis of the contemporary Humanities," one not unrelated to the exigence of this collection nor this chapter, "is related to the high levels of technological mediation and the multicultural structure of the globalized world" (The Posthuman 153). Braidotti argues that, in place of a stable and rational humanist subject, "posthuman subjectivity reshapes the identity of humanistic practices, by stressing heteronomy and multi-faceted relationality, instead of autonomy and self-referential disciplinary purity" (145). Braidotti's posthumanites would cultivate a nomadic subject considered to be "a radically immanent intensive body [that] is an assemblage of forces, or flows, intensities and passions that solidify in space, and consolidate in time, within the singular configuration commonly known as an 'individual' self" (201).

The nomadic subject is yet one more renewal of a particular mode of inquiry we have seen throughout this chapter. In connecting the many disparate accounts above, I proposed a pedagogy for a networked humanities. This pedagogy relies on an underlying capacity for enacting a topological thinking as seen in the juxtapositions of homelessness, wirelessness, itinerancy, and nomadism. Such accounts are not only the product of an idea or one's labors to build and enact interoperable systems through portable technologies, but they are also processes that seek to share dispositions, orientations, and attunements. These capacities are inherent to the transindividual whose effectiveness is gained through cultivating a homeless infrastructure that operates as sensitivity to those abundant processes and practices that create, maintain, and transform the relations *between* things. Homelessness, then, includes lack not as a problem to solve but as the exigence for continuing an ongoing practice of sifting, remixing, and versioning an abundance of connections.

Works Cited

Braidotti, Rosi. *The Posthuman.* Polity Press, 2013.

DeVoss, Dànielle Nicole, Ellen Cushman, and Jeffrey T. Grabill. "Infrastructure and composing: The when of new-media writing." *College composition and communication*, 2005, pp. 14–44.

Flusser, Vilém. *Writings.* U of Minnesota Press, 2002.

Kissane, Erin (@kissane). "Last thought before sleeping: the difference between "I'm running a hotspot" and "I AM a hotspot" is a difference that matters." 12 March 2012, 5:45 AM. Tweet.

Galison, Peter. "War against the center." *Grey Room*, vol. 4, 2001, pp. 5–33.

Galloway, Alexander R., and Eugene Thacker. *The Exploit.* U of Minnesota P, 2007.

Hawhee, Debra. *Bodily Arts: Rhetoric and Athletics in Ancient Greece.* U of Texas P, 2004.

Mackenzie, Adrian. *Wirelessness: Radical empiricism in network cultures.* MIT Press, 2010.

—. *Transductions: Bodies and Machines at Speed.* Continuum International Publishing Group, 2002.

Rice, Jeff. *Digital Detroit: Rhetoric and Space in the Age of the Network.* SIU Press, 2012.

—. "Networks and new media." *College English*, vol. 69, no. 2, 2006, pp. 127–33.

Selber, Stuart A. "Institutional dimensions of academic computing." *College Composition and Communication*, 2009, pp. 10–34.

Varnelis, Kazys (@kazys). "Network Society is marked by collapsing infrastructure and constant crisis." 3 Nov. 2012, 4:27 PM. Tweet.

Wilson, Matthew W. "Continuous connectivity, handheld computers, and mobile spatial knowledge." *Environment and Planning D: Society and Space*, vol. 32, 2014, pp. 535-55.

13 Provocation: Minding the Network: An Eco-logic for Networked Humanities

Kristie S. Fleckenstein

Words matter. In 1945, Kenneth Burke pointed this out, contending that we craft vocabularies that "will be faithful *reflections* of reality." In the process, we craft vocabularies that are only "*selections* of reality," a sifting process that simultaneously operates as "a *deflection* of reality" (*Grammar* 59; emphasis original). Two decades later, in "Terministic Screens," Burke repeats this claim almost verbatim, emphasizing that "any nomenclature necessarily directs the attention into some channels rather than other" (45). In this brief provocation, I take Burke at his word and ask what insights we glean if we Mind the network, if we use the eco-logical vocabulary of anthropologist Gregory Bateson as a terministic screen for networked humanities.

Bateson's eco-logic, or his central premise that we can keep track of the ongoing development of an individual species only by considering it within the context of the ecosystem as a whole, forms the basis of Mind, and Mind offers an intriguing perspective—or vocabulary—from which to reflect, select, and deflect an identity for networked humanities. Informed by his training in the natural sciences and anthropology as well as his participation in the post-World War II Macy Conferences, Bateson took nascent systems theory and reshaped it to conceptualize living biological-cultural networks as gestalts—as Minds—that function through the self-regulating flow of information. In brief, *Mind* is Bateson's term for the pattern formed when an "aggregate of interacting parts" connect into a whole (*Mind* 92). A new way of thinking in terms of contexts— "pattern[s] through time" (14)—rather than discrete units, Mind exists on multiple transacting levels, from the collocation of cells comprising the human body to the daunting complexity of entire ecosystems. In contradistinction to a Darwinian emphasis on the individual species as the site of evolution (or learning), Mind as dynamic pattern under- scores that the context, not the discrete organism, survives, evolves, or devolves (*Steps* 155). Furthermore, the pattern constituting Mind shapes itself from the communication of information, or what Bateson famous- ly called "differences that make a difference" (*Mind* 105). Via a com- plicated circular causal dynamic, the pattern comprising Mind exists as a result of and only as long as difference circulates. While necessarily reductive, this quick summation of Mind points to the importance of pattern and difference, each of which reflects, selects, and deflects the realities of networked humanities, offering invitations for exploration.

What is the pattern that connects networked humanities? Displac- ing what Bateson called the "obsolete epistemology" that dualistically separated mind and nature, Mind as nomenclature directs attention to the pattern that connects, or "the dance of interacting parts" (*Mind* 14) in networked humanities. As commonly conceptualized, the fledging field currently emphasizes projects and/or the array of digital technolo- gies necessary to bring projects to fruition. Lisa Spiro implies as much in 2011 when she defines the central conundrum of digital humanities as a question of how: how does one create a digital humanities proj- ect? More recently Jessica Enoch and David Gold underscore the use of technology "to develop digital tools and platforms" (106) to build "projects themselves" (108). By this assessment, attention is placed on what Bateson calls quantities, or auditing discrete things that can be counted: strategies, tools, projects, research questions, goals. However, pattern, as he points out, is not about quantity; it is about form. Most of us, he mourns, "have lost that sense of unity of biosphere and human- ity" (17), an aesthetic loss that "was, quite simply, an epistemological mistake" (18). What needs to be investigated and described, he argues, is not quantity, but the "vast network or matrix of interlocking message material" (20).

The pattern that connects summons us to consider networked hu- manities as recursive causal systems, or as relationships among things acting in ways that reflect both backward on and forward to their joint organization. The salient features, then, include more than building a digital interactive site, more than a consideration of technologies, codes, and nodes. The salient features include as well, if not foremost, the ways in which pathways constitute a self-regulating system. The vocabulary of Mind draws us to consider the economics—digital, interpretive, or material—by which pattern forms and reforms. It summons us to inquire into the limitations on its emergence and its stability across time. At the same time, Mind points to the importance of the rain of the random—external and internal—that, for good or ill, threatens the dynamic constituting pattern. Such a vocabulary construes networked humanities not as quantity but as a pattern connecting, and the glue by which the pattern coheres is difference.

What are the differences that make a difference in networked humanities? If pattern constitutes Mind, then pattern, in turn, is constituted by the circulation of information, which Bateson defines as "difference . . . making a difference" (*Mind* 72). This nomenclature holds important implications for networked humanities as a whole, but especially for our understanding of interactivity. As Susan Schreibman, Ray Siemens, and John Unsworth note, the digital media integral to networked humanities foster interactivity because "every point of consumption can also be a point of production." Difference illuminates this interactivity by privileging information not as content or substance but as response.

Difference, Bateson explains, and thus information, lurks within the gaps between. In the world of Mind, for information to exist a relationship must form between two entities or between "a part at time 1 and the same part at time 2" (*Mind* 102). The double description afforded by the relationship between two parts brings into being a third component, which Bateson calls a receiver, such as a sensory end organ. Relationships and receiver are thus co-constituent, "made 'real' by their internal relations and by their behavior in relationship with other things" (64). The receiver comes into existence through its perception of and response to a significant difference between two entities or between one entity at two different times. Furthermore, in a complex play of circularity, difference comes into being only when it is significant to the receiver. To illustrate, the common reed frog exists as female only as long as information within its particular information economy confirms that identity. When that economy changes over time, more specifically when the population of male reed frogs decreases, the female will respond to these differences that make a difference by chemically dissolving her female genitalia and remerging as male. Receiver (reed frog) and difference (population change) exist in complex circular flow of information.

The vocabulary of difference illuminates our understanding of inter-activity within networked humanities. It directs our attention not to the source or presumed content of the disclosed digital message (or project), but to the flow of information. It confirms the importance of asking of any digital project what significant differences evolve, which ones survive, and which degrade. It demands that we consider what double description the user perceives difference through, calling us to explore how that perception in turn shapes the user. In sum, it bids us to address how user and project become "real" together.

Words matter. As we move forward with networked humanities, Burke invites us to reconsider our vocabulary. He invites us to ask whether a "given terminology, or calculus, is suited to the subject matter it was designed to calculate" (*Grammar* 59) and to revise it if, in fact, we miscalculate. Minding networked humanities provides one option for pursuing that terminological assessment. The eco-logic of Mind, Bateson contends, constitutes a new thinking—a new vocabulary—essential for human and ecological survival. Perhaps that eco-logic might help us reflect, select, and deflect the kind of networked humanities we want to survive and flourish.

WORKS CITED

Bateson, Gregory. *Mind and Nature: A Necessary Unity*. E. P. Dutton, 1979.

—. *Steps to an Ecology of Mind. Collected Essays in Anthropology, Psychiatry, Evolution, and Epistemology*. Jason Aronson, 1987.

Burke, Kenneth. *A Grammar of Motives*. U of California P, 1945.

—. "Terministic Screens." *Language as Symbolic Action: Essays on Life, Literature, and Method*. U of California P, 1966, pp. 44–62.

Enoch, Jessica, and David Gold. "Introduction: Seizing the Methodological Moment: The Digital Humanities and Historiography in Rhetoric and Composition." *College English*, vol. 76, no. 2, 2013, pp. 105–14.

Schreibman, Susan, Ray Siemens, John Unsworth, editors. *A Companion to Digital Humanities*. Blackwell, 2004. www.digitalhumanities.org/companion/. Accessed 17 Feb. 2014.

Spiro, Lisa. "Getting Started in Digital Humanities." *Journal of Digital Humanities*, vol. 1, no. 1, 2011. journalofdigitalhumanities.org/1-1/getting-started-in-digital-humanities-by-lisa-spiro/. Accessed 12 Feb. 2014.

14 Provocation: We Are the Network: Creating Gravity in the Digital Humanities

Liza Potts

For the digital humanities to flourish, then we must see ourselves as a network: an organic, cooperative ecosystem of makers, thinkers, and doers. To do so, we must create gravity around our activities, interests, labs, and ideas. In creating gravity, I mean we must focus on collaboration, innovation, and creativity in ways in which we build each other's ideas and refocus our own. In answering Kathleen Fitzpatrick's question of "What Are the Digital Humanities?" (2011) I aim to answer it by simply stating "We Are the Network."

We are still amid the boom period for the digital humanities. I spent the late 1990s/early 2000s working at start-ups during industry's dotcom boom. That experience taught me how brief a boom can last and how critical it is that we focus on seizing this moment to build our networks and be mindful of our investments in time, energy, and yes, money. We have both in different measures, across our labs, our departments, our colleges, and our centers. If the Digital Humanities is in fact a "tactical term" as Kirschenbaum (2012/2013) would have us believe (and I want to believe), then how must we take action in this moment?

My perspective as both an academic and practitioner has taught me that I cannot build alone, I cannot think alone, and I cannot solve problems alone. There is great strength in how we assemble ourselves, our technologies, and our organizations to collaborate on productive, enriching projects. Projects that can bridge these spaces and lead us to new discoveries, new technologies, and new public policy. As Johnson-Eilola and Selber point out, it is through these kinds of experiences that we can "gain the ability not merely to *do* things but to *think about* how you are doing things" (5).

While many of us are already doing this work, many more of us are scraping by, trying to build our ideas with little to no funding and little to no support. We must open our labs, projects, and resources if we are to create this kind of networked cooperation. We must re-examine how we reward this kind of work if we are to encourage participation. Consider the following ideas as a way of thinking about our work as part of this network, creating gravity through these tactics and strategies and building an ecosystem of activity. In doing so, I want to enact the suggestion made by McNely and Teston (2014) that "tactics should be meaningfully and reflexively configured to broader *strategies* of research" (emphasis original).

VALUE EACH OTHER'S WORK

We must value our diversity of thought and production as relevant, pertinent, and critical to the work of the university and the world. To do so, we will need to move beyond the silos of our departments, colleges, and even universities. When we constantly squabble about what "counts" as the humanities, we are only fracturing ourselves. When we debate "hack" vs. "yack" (Cecire 2011), we undermine our ability to do both and create a false binary that serves to divide us. We need both. We often are both. When I conduct a heuristic evaluation of a website, am I not being critical? And when I suggest alternate designs, am I not being a maker? Of course. It takes a team to do the kind of thinking and making that can enrich our work. When we value each other's strengths, we can be open to increasing our shared areas of influence and expertise, rather than cutting out our more innovative scholars out there on the boundaries.

PARTNER WITH EACH OTHER

Rather than establishing new labs, consider partnering with an existing lab. When we compete for resources, we lose time and energy that we could be using to build, analyze, and create. By partnering, we can also tap experts who have been there, done that with regards to project management, assessment, archiving, funding, etc. We are our best resource. Rather than focusing on whether your role is that of a "maker" or a "critic," become a contributor. That contribution might be pointing out better ways to create products, to implement curriculum, or to rethink policies. What matters is that we are partnering and focused on being productive in ways that can lead to positive outcomes.

REWARD COLLABORATIVE WORK

We need to make our collaborative work "count" for merit, tenure, and promotion. The truth is, it is far more difficult to collaborate than it is to work alone on publications. However, it is in that collaborative work that we can come to much richer conclusions, take on larger projects, and broaden our solutions because of these added thinks and makers. We cannot be digital humanists if we do not collaborate; we must align our department by-laws, our college requirements, and our university's policies to reflect our belief in the value of collaboration. We may not even need our university's consideration, since collaboration is already a mainstay in other colleges for good reason.

FOCUS ON HUMAN EXPERIENCES

Our strength in the digital humanities is that we should be focused first and foremost on the human experience. We are humanists, after all. We can build from human-centered experiences, creating better policies and technologies that can address the context in which our participants want to engage with our work (Spinuzzi 2013). And we are storytellers—our ability to build narratives around experiences, research, data, and products is one of our greatest strengths. Let us build websites sharing our research not just with those inside the academy, but also with the general public, the K-12 community, and others who will benefit from it. The better we can become at telling the story of our research with others, the more we can share the value of our work. As humanists and communicators, we need to be these agents of change (Potts 2014).

In building a new undergraduate degree program centered around a concept called *experience architecture*, I wanted us to consider the difference we could make as Humanists within the practice of building new technologies. Partnering across the university with colleagues in computer science, art and design, and philosophy, our goal was to create a program that would ask "what if the humanists were the architects of experience?" I am very much committed to humanists at the center of these conversations, and if we could refocus our efforts in these directions rather than arguing about who is a humanist and what counts as the digital humanities, we will exceed our potential for positive impact in the university and the world.

In closing, I encourage you to reach out across the disciplines for collaborators and co-conspirators who want to make this kind of positive impact. I am not being naïve when I tell you the ideas put forth in this vignette are complicated; I fully realize the challenge ahead. But if the digital humanities boom and bust, we have only ourselves to blame. Let us be better students of history, and focus our efforts on becoming better analysts, makers, and doers. The more we can be our own network, across disciplines and across spaces, the more gravity we can create around our ideas and innovations.

WORKS CITED

Cecire, Natalia. "When Digital Humanities was in Vogue." *Journal of Digital Humanities*, vol. 1, no. 1, 2011, journalofdigitalhumanities.org/1-1/.

Fitzpatrick, Kathleen. (2011). "The Humanities, Done Digitally." *The Chronicle of Higher Education*, chronicle.com/article/The-Humanities-Done-Digitally/127382/. Accessed 8 Jun. 2016.

Johnson-Eilola, Johndan, and Stuart A. Selber. (2013). "Introduction." *Solving Problems in Technical Communication*, edited by Johndan Johnson-Eilola and Stuart A. Selber, The U of Chicago P, 2013, pp. 1–14.

Kirschenbaum, Matthew. (2012). "Digital Humanities As/Is a Tactical Term." *Debates in the Digital Humanities*, edited by Matthew K. Gold, U of Minnesota P, 2012, dhdebates.gc.cuny.edu/debates.

McNely, Brian and Christa Teston. "Tactical and Strategic: Qualitative Approaches to the Digital Humanities." *Rhetoric and the Digital Humanities*, edited by Jim Ridolfo and Bill Hart-Davidson, U of Chicago P, 2014, pp.111–26.

Potts, Liza. "Archive Experiences: A Vision for User-Centered Design in the Digital Humanities." *Rhetoric and the Digital Humanities*, edited by Jim Ridolfo and Bill Hart-Davidson, U of Chicago P, 2014, pp. 255–63.

Potts, Liza. *Social Media in Disaster Response: How Experience Architects Can Build for Participation*. Routledge, 2014.

Spinuzzi, Clay. "How Can Technical Communicators Study Work Contexts?" *Solving Problems in Technical Communication*, edited by Johndan Johnson-Eilola and Stuart A. Selber. U of Chicago P, 2013, pp. 262–84.

15 The Limitations of Choice: Toward A New Materialist Reading of "Mommy War" Rhetorics

Naomi Clark

I t is well established in the humanities and social sciences that language accumulates meaning as it circulates in the material world that is simultaneously shaped by language. Yet, as rhetorician Laurie Gries asks, "[W]hat if we take meaning consequentialism seriously?" (334). That is to say, what kind of methods might we use to study the consequentiality of circulating arguments as they emerge in time and space? Inspired by Gries' question and methodology as presented in her writing and in her presentation at the University of Kentucky's 2013 Networked Humanities Conference (Rivers, Bay, Mueller, and Gries), this essay demonstrates how analysis of circulating political rhetoric in the context of global capitalism is incomplete without including an account of the relevant material, nonhuman forces at work. This accounting can be provided by new materialism, a set of analytical approaches that places a renewed emphasis on physical matter and natural forces that share agency with human actors. What distinguishes this renewed emphasis on materiality from materialist philosophies of the nineteenth century is the way it takes into account new developments in the natural sciences (Coole and Frost). While materialists such as Marx drew on a Newtonian conception of materiality as inert matter, twentieth-century discoveries as well as theoretical physics now see in that matter vibrancy, energy, and movement. Thus, new materialism incorporates these updated understandings of physical matter into theories of social relations as well.

Drawing in part on Bruno Latour's actor network theory, the theories and methodologies of new materialism offer new analytical tools for humanities scholarship to advance beyond post-structuralism's near exclusive focus on the discursive. That is, new materialist approaches theorize the relations between materiality and discourse and the consequentiality that arises from these relations. Furthermore, theorists such as Karen Barad emphasize the already existing entanglements between other dualities as well (i.e., between culture and nature or between the humanities and sciences). Rather than trying to create synthesis between seemingly distinct entities, Barad urges the exploration of how they are already entwined and co-created ("New Materialism: Interviews & Cartographies"). Thus, these approaches not only support the development of interdisciplinary relationships, building more effective bridges within and beyond the academy, but also the explication of relations that are already present but often overlooked. With a new materialist approach, then, the analytical process becomes less about making connections between the humanities within and without the university, and more about tracing relationships between fields, approaches, methodologies, and objects of study that are often studied in virtual isolation from each other.

Diana Coole and Samantha Frost identify within new materialist approaches a vein of critical analysis that is "practical, politically engaged social theory, devoted to the critical analysis of actual conditions of existence and their inherent inequality" (25). The inclusion of critical analysis with a new materialist lens refers in part to theorizing the complex processes of global capitalism, broadly conceived, and the uneven effects of these processes on a local, everyday level. I extend this definition to also include the analysis of language that shapes and is shaped by these unequal conditions. As theory that "insist[s] on the generativity and resilience of the material forms with which social actors interact, forms which circumscribe, encourage, and test their discourses," it is a timely lens for the humanities in an era of globalization with its forces that are irreducible to distinctly discursive, economic, political, or cultural effects (Coole and Frost 26). Crucially, critical new materialism incorporates post-structural critiques in its renewed emphasis on materiality, or, in the words of Julie Torrant, it is a "rethinking of the rethinking" that is sensitive to the particular times and places bodies inhabit (xiv). In other words, critical new materialism turns new materialism's focus on the "entanglement of matter and meaning" to the everyday workings of power. Unlike the style of critique that focuses primarily on exposing the weaknesses of its object of analysis, a critical new materialist approach is more interested in understanding how these networked relations in everyday life came to be, how they function, and what they generate in terms of real life consequences. To demonstrate, in this essay I trace circulating rhetorics about family generally and the so-called "mommy wars" specifically to better understand their role in cultivating a political environment in which United States citizens have difficulty imagining new social policies that might begin to alleviate often unacknowledged economic pressures of global capitalism on US citizens.

NEW MATERIALIST READINGS OF DISCOURSE

One example of a real world situation that merits interdisciplinary analysis is the United States' failure to join other industrialized/post-industrialized nations in establishing the kind of social supports (e.g., paid maternity/paternity leave for new parents; quality, affordable childcare; adequate housing; single-payer health care) that mitigate the pressures of global capitalism on families and individuals. Humanities scholars in cultural, feminist, or transnational studies—not to mention those in my home field of rhetoric and composition—who analyze social policy issues tend to emphasize how language shapes policy. However, a new critical materialist lens expands the scope of analysis to include the material forms in which that language arises and circulates, requiring interdisciplinary inquiry. Calls from university administrators for interdisciplinary scholarship—such as those related to the digital humanities—often risk invoking superficial engagement and/or the privileging of one field over another, thus falling short of the full potential of interdisciplinary partnerships (Grimm). For such scholarship to be genuinely collaborative, researchers must not just appreciate other disciplinary methods, but also adopt elements appropriate to their own research; in other words, interdisciplinary researchers' aims should ideally accommodate other approaches rather than compromise them (Miller et al., 46, Frost and Jean 140, Borrego and Newswander 132). To that end, critical new materialism's embrace of multiple forms of evidence, methodologies, and approaches offers a more level playing field where productive cooperation can take place. In the paragraphs that follow, I demonstrate how a critical new materialist approach can expand the work of rhetorical analysis by drawing more explicitly on related material, economic, and political elements to offer a richer account of the relationship between text and context particularly as it relates to social policy in global capitalism.

In any rhetorical analysis of arguments about social policy, the contributing forces are difficult if not impossible to pinpoint because at once these policies (or lack thereof) can be read in cultural, political, economic, and technological terms just to name a few of the possibilities. Thus, a critical new materialist lens that "track[s] the complex circuits at work whereby discursive and material forms are inextricable yet irreducible, and material structures are simultaneously over- and underdetermined" can expand rhetorical analysis to include the nonhuman forces such as digital and print technologies involved in the distribution, circulation, and adaptation of social policy rhetoric (Coole and Frost 27). However, for a critical new materialist approach, "material" not only refers to the concrete objects we can see and touch, but also to cultural and economic resources and how they are distributed. Thus, conducting rhetorical analysis with a critical new materialist lens involves not only acknowledging materiality in terms of things we can see and touch, but also accounting for how economic systems and social class distinctions that animate the circulation of rhetorics within a given political field influence the framing of social issues in public discourse.

These expressions of material forces figure prominently in Julie Torrant's analysis of discourses associated with the formation of the post-nuclear family. Although Torrant does not claim a new critical materialist approach, her work as a cultural materialist closely mirrors Coole and Frost's definition in the way Torrant incorporates materiality into a post-structuralist reading of discourse about family. She critiques the widely held belief among scholars that families in the late twentieth and early twenty-first centuries are no longer structured around economic need as they had been for millennia. While Torrant celebrates the broadening of the definition of family to include those based on mutual affective attachment and individual choice, she points out that families today are no less constrained by the economic realities of a globalized economy, job shortages, expensive or unaffordable health care, and stagnated wages. Yet, according to Torrant, the rhetorical effect of the "new" family as it is generally represented, "is also an ideological construct that deflects attention away from the deteriorating conditions for working and living in global capitalism and blocks investigation into the cause of these material conditions" (xv). That is to say, when rhetoric about the post-nuclear family is limited to the language of affect or desire to describe its formation and function, it prevents substantive discussion of the constraints global capitalism places on families as well as preventing how we might imagine better public policies to address those constraints.

According to Elizabeth Grosz's new materialist re-imagining of the conventional American conception of freedom, the "new" family that Torrant critiques suffers from an impoverished definition of freedom, the absence of restraint. That is to say, the cultural freedom to expand the definition of family beyond that of a heterosexual two-parent household does not guarantee that this "new" family of the twenty-first century has cast off all its material constraints. Grosz imagines an alternative view of freedom that is not defined negatively in terms of what an individual is free from (i.e., freedom from restrictions on marriage, freedom from patriarchal control, freedom from religious oppression, or freedom from state control of the media), but rather positively in terms of capacity for action. In this view, we would not ask whether an individual (or a family) is free as if freedom were a property or inherent characteristic, but rather ask about the degree of autonomy of particular acts, recognizing that the capacity for action arises from relations between bodies. In this essay I aim to show how popular discourse about American social policy tends to align with a conception of freedom that assumes today's families form and maintain themselves according to the ideological or philosophical commitments of the adults directly involved (that is, "free choice"), while minimizing or ignoring factors that can limit or facilitate the action of the component individuals. While this distinction may seem fuzzy at times, what I want to emphasize is how even when family formation is assumed to be a freely made philosophical choice, the range of choices in play can actually be quite limited. In this case, "choice" often serves as a terministic screen that assumes a preselected array of options are the only possible options. In contrast, Grosz's conception of freedom shifts the focus to what a body is capable of and how its relations with other bodies can best facilitate the actualization of that capacity. When popular discourse about social policy—for all its preoccupation with "free choice"—takes for granted a limited array of options, it is problematic in two ways. First, it limits our collective imagination in developing updated social policies more suited to our current situation, and, secondly, it limits individuals from experiencing the full range of expression and transformation of which they are capable.

One specific example of this discursive tendency took place during the 2012 Presidential primaries when the co-hosts on *The View*, ABC's daytime talk show, discussed Presidential candidate Rick Santorum's response to criticism for stating in his book that feminism undermined families and convinced women that (paid) work is more fulfilling than homemaking. Co-host Barbara Walters conceded (surprisingly, she admitted) that Santorum accurately characterized the women's movement as it once was, giving particular credit to Betty Friedan's *The Feminine Mystique* for condescension toward women who were housewives. Although co-host Joy Behar took issue with Walters' representation of the women's movement, both Walters and Behar agreed that today there is more emphasis on choice—that the message of feminism today is that women can choose whether to have a career or be a housewife. While the two co-hosts differ from Santorum in their celebration of the advances women have made, their arguments align with his in so far as they also frame women's family roles in terms of affective or ideological choice. In the process, they problematically reduce women's presence in the paid workforce to a matter of personal preference as if working at a job or in the home are options freely available to all women. In the process, these two options are also set up as dualities, as the only conceivable options that might be considered.

These assumptions were disrupted in the on-air discussion by co-host Sherri Shepherd when she said, "Well, I come from a place where it wasn't even a matter of feminism—my mom had to work so we could eat." Co-host Whoopi Goldberg expanded on the role of economics in shaping the range of choices available to some women, saying that her problem with feminists was that they "were not representing the women who had no choice and who had to go out and work. They weren't speaking to them, because that wasn't what they were talking about." Shepherd and Goldberg bring up an important dimension of this issue—how race and social class intersect with gender to create a simultaneity of oppressions (Crenshaw). Their perspectives demonstrate the limits of individual choice in accounting for the occupational pursuits of many women in recent decades.

The co-hosts' brief four-minute discussion distills a variety of perspectives on feminism: Walters' memory of second wave feminism of the 1960s, Behar's conception of (neo)liberal feminism, and Shepherd and Goldberg's accounts of those women often overlooked by white middle-class feminisms. Yet, despite the range of views, this discussion demonstrates how key assumptions, shared by those on both the political right and left, the religious and the secular, are threaded through dominant affective rhetorics about family. Alternative accounts that highlight the significance of material concerns such as social class, race, and economics are often represented as if they are merely infrequent aberrations from the norm.

In many ways, these affective, ideological rhetorics about family are unremarkable because they are so common, so everyday. The arguments forwarded by Santorum, Walters, and Behar are just a few examples of related discourses that circulate in on- and off-line sites among pundits and commentators, mommy blogs, political candidates, and in popular magazines. However, limiting our analysis to this one discussion and its particular speakers, text, audience, context, exigencies, and contingencies as though they comprise a discrete rhetorical situation could not tell us much about how these arguments have evolved to become normalized as well as how they engage with "prior and ongoing structures of feeling that shape the social field" (Edbauer 10). In other words, an ecological framework that situates public rhetorics in terms of their history and fluidity can help us better understand how this debate discussed on *The View* has become rhetorical in the context of global capitalism. Its rhetorical power lies in the interactions and shifts between various speakers, audiences, and texts, cultivating and being cultivated by the accumulation of its "processes and encounters" (Edbauer 13).

TRACING THE RHETORICAL EVOLUTION OF WOMEN'S WORK

Understanding the normalizing power of these rhetorics, then, requires observing where and how they surface and with what ideologies and structures of feeling they engage. What have come to be known as the "mommy wars" over the past few decades involve an ongoing discussion about whether stay-at-home-mothers or employed mothers are making the best choices for their children, themselves, and society. Typically, the discussion is framed in terms that suggest that the interests of children, mothers, and society are inherently at odds. Phyllis Schlafly is often credited with leading the conservative backlash in the 1970s against the women's movement generally and in resisting the Equal Rights Amendment (ERA) particularly. Empowered by her years of experience in conservative activism, a law degree, and household help for her five children, Schlafly popularized the idea that mothers' rightful place is in the home

(Daum). While second-wave feminists championed women's access to more lucrative white-collar jobs, Schlafly lectured that women who eschewed careers in favor of homemaking were morally superior.

Eventually, socially conservative Protestant voices took up the arguments that Schlafly, a Catholic, popularized. Organizations such as Focus on the Family, founded by evangelical child psychologist James Dobson, have held the position that mothers should be in the home ("Please Explain Why"). They offer a caveat for single mothers and mothers who must work for financial reasons—as if these women were statistical exceptions to the norm and do not represent the significant number of American households where all adults are employed. Their statement emphasizes the moral influence that stay-at-home mothers have over their children that working mothers do not, implying that homemakers occupy a higher moral ground.

In the closing decades of the twenty-first century these ideas manifested themselves in American social policy such as the 1996 *Personal Responsibility and Work Opportunity Reconciliation Act* (PRA). Prescribing sweeping welfare reform, the Act opens with the lines, "Marriage is the cornerstone of society," recommending marriage—not living wage jobs nor gender and racial equity—as the solution to poverty (Dingo 499). Such social policies, framed in moralistic terms, served to further stratify motherhood: while middle-class mothers were being urged by social conservatives to stay home as primary care-givers, impoverished mothers' care-giving labor was effectively erased when many were forced into low-wage, service-sector jobs that have increasingly replaced industrial jobs since 1980. The PRA disregards the reality that these wages do not come close to covering all the expenses of housing, transportation, childcare, and the many other costs of rearing a family. Rather, by dramatically reducing poor single parents' (usually mothers') access to federal benefits, the PRA limits the options to two: cast yourself onto the mercies of market forces or get married and become "more integrated into patriarchal structures" (Dingo 495). Furthermore, in its references to "personal responsibility" and its privileging of the heterosexual nuclear family as the ideal to which poor mothers should aspire, this legislation associates poverty with the moral failure of the individuals in its grip.

"Mommy Wars" in the Twenty-first Century: All About Choice

Santorum's book discussed on *The View* echoes the logics of PRA and the culture wars when he argues that the solution to poverty lies in stronger families via more barriers to divorce and more fatherhood training programs. Yet, despite the fact that the PRA approach to alleviating poverty is premised on greatly narrowing mothers' workforce participation options, Santorum responded to criticism of his statements about working mothers by claiming that what he was really advocating was "affirmation of whatever decision women decide to make" (Knowlton). Santorum's retreat to the "free choice" framing of mothers' paid work may at face value appear to be backtracking or pandering to a more progressive audience; however, it also reflects a dynamic relationship between the language of social conservatism and austerity policies of late capitalism. Socially conservative arguments like these lend capitalism a moralistic justification for demolishing social safety nets, yet as families find themselves negatively affected by those policies, social conservatives point to "external scapegoats—most notably, feminists, gays, and lesbians" rather than address the detrimental effects of free market capitalism (Lassiter 28).

This "choice" mothers in late capitalism face to either join the paid labor force or care for their children at home (often referred to as the "mommy wars") was reframed for the twenty-first century in Lisa Belkin's 2003 *New York Times* article, "The Opt-Out Generation." Belkin's article celebrates upper-middle income women who were leaving lucrative, professional careers to stay home with their children. Although Belkin describes the crushing work-life pressures that came with these demanding jobs, prompting these mothers to stay home, her disproportional focus on mothers in upper income brackets is troublesome given that their affluence is shared by only eight percent of American women (Williams, Manvell, and Bornstein 2). Nevertheless, the article speaks of "many" and "most" mothers, failing to acknowledge the relatively small proportion of women she was describing while generalizing their situations to all mothers. Not only does Belkin's article elide how welfare reform was simultaneously forcing less well-off mothers into the workforce, but also fails to tell the bigger story—that an even greater number of working-class married mothers were staying home because they could no longer afford the rising costs of child care (Linn). Belkin's article triggered a new wave of "opt-out" news stories and books that essentially extolled affluent mothers' resignation to what was framed as their innately feminine biology, choosing a return to traditional gender roles (Williams, Manvell, and Bornstein).

Yet, Belkin's narrative did not go unchallenged. Books such as Miriam Peskowitz's *The Truth Behind the Mommy Wars: Who Decides What Makes a Good Mother?* and *Mommy Wars: Stay-at-Home and Career Moms Face Off on Their Choices, Their Lives, Their Families* by Leslie Morgan Steiner were published in 2005 and 2006 respectively. Writers such as these complicate Belkin's simplistic framing of opting out as an empowered choice by arguing that these choices were not made in a vacuum and that not all mothers share the same range of options. They note ways in which education costs, workplace demands, and expectations for "good" parenting have all ratcheted up in recent decades, squeezing families—especially dual income families—in the process (Blair-Loy).

Additionally, a Center for Worklife Law study surveyed the opt-out narrative in 119 news stories between 1980 and 2006. The researchers argue that looking beyond the personal anecdotes that many of these stories rely on as evidence actually shows that "most mothers do not opt out; they are pushed out by workplace inflexibility, the lack of family supports, and workplace bias against mothers" (Williams, Manvell, and Bornstein 7). The researchers fault the opt-out narrative for "send[ing] the reassuring message that nothing needs to change" in social policy even though there have been dramatic changes both in the *workplace* and the *workforce* in recent decades (10). Some of these workplace changes include the demand for longer work hours for professional/managerial positions—not to mention the off-shoring of manufacturing and technology jobs that have been replaced by lower-wage service-sector jobs. At the same time, the workforce is not primarily comprised of male bread winners supporting nuclear families in households where mothers devote themselves full-time to housekeeping, childcare, food preparation, the family social calendar, shopping, and a myriad of other duties claiming their unpaid labor. Rather, seventy percent of American children now live in households where all adults are employed (Kornbluh, Heymann 4). Therefore, when employers' expectations of their employees continue to be structured on the assumption that the ideal worker will always be available thanks to a spouse at home managing all personal affairs, the pressure will be especially severe on families without that unpaid spouse. Thus, opt-out rhetoric distracts from the tension that results when fathers (not to mention mothers) in professional/managerial jobs are working more hours than ever due to increasingly inflexible workplace demands (fifty-plus hours per week), leaving less time for their involvement at home. In these situations, mothers are left with three undesirable options: "(1) have a great career and never see your children awake; (2) take a dead-end, underpaid part-time position; or (3) drop out and face economic vulnerability for your children and yourself" (Williams, Manvell, and Bornstein 37). Since less than a third of the articles surveyed in the study even acknowledge that the range of choices mothers face are problematic, the writers of the report hoped to provide journalists with new story lines that better reflected the reality for many Americans.

Yet, despite these evidence-based calls to consider the demographic and economic variability in which the so-called "mommy wars" take place, the opt-out or "free choice" narrative persists in popular media.

In 2011, *The Economist* magazine hosted an online debate on whether or not "a woman's place is at work" ("Economist Debates"). In response to the notion that "for most women work is a matter of economic necessity, not choice," the opposition argued that the five million women in America who are in the home as full-time mothers have freely chosen to be there. This argument was based on the belief that men and women choose different career paths because of innate differences and not because of institutional pressures as the statistical data referenced above show. The terms of the debate were reflected in 152 reader comments where many seemed to read the proposal as a mandate (i.e., "Women *must* work.") and not as a normative ideal (e.g., "Since women merit workplace inclusions, their rights deserve full consideration."). However, a significant number also challenge the narrative of "free choice," pointing to their own experiences as well as the privileged position of those who have a choice to make in the first place (i.e., those sufficiently well-off to make paid work an option rather than a necessity).

More recently Sheryl Sandberg, Chief Operating Officer of Facebook, in her speeches and her book, *Lean In: Women, Work, and the Will to Lead*, urges women in the workforce to pursue professional success by making "better" choices in the partners they marry, in their time management, and in their level of commitment to their careers. Her message implies that what holds women back from high-level positions is simply their own behavior rather than increasing workplace and parenting demands. Applauding the opposite response to excessive workplace demands, *New York* magazine's 2013 article, "The Retro Wife: Feminists Who Say They're Having It All—By Choosing To Stay Home," frames mothers' return to traditional gender roles as a hip, empowered choice when faced with the daunting pressures that accompany two-career households with children. One commenter (Jane_Vassar) offers a dissenting take on how her choices were constrained. She remembers the anti-family corporate policies of the 1980s as the reason mothers returned to the workforce a mere six weeks after giving birth. She saw these kinds of policies as forcing her to choose between being an ideal worker and an involved mother; she chose to go home. As Williams, Manvell, and Bornstein point out, this is usually where the opt-out narrative ends with a mother happily at home. Its consideration of the pros and cons is usually limited to the short term and doesn't take into account the long-term implications of lost wages, retirement preparation, and the reality that many American marriages end in divorce. However, this particular commenter tells the rest of the (typical) story. Twelve years after going home, she and her husband divorced, prompting her unplanned return to the workforce twelve years after leaving it. This story is not at all unique although opt-out narratives often fail to include it. When mothers are forced out of well-paying jobs, they may get the "hugs and kisses" the opt-out narratives celebrate, but they and their children are also likely to experience serious financial vulnerability.

Yet, this vulnerability does not concern bloggers like Jessica Wakeman who self-identifies as a feminist but says she finds herself nodding along to "The Retro Wife." She too plans to take time off when she has her future children, resisting unidentified feminists' insistence that she prove her commitment to her career. If she or anyone else wants to take on traditional roles, she says, "Feminists need to deal with it." Here again, commitment to one's career and corporate workplace pressures are simplistically conflated in a celebration of self-determination with little thought of the larger environmental factors that constrain lives and that, conversely, individuals' choices affect. Readers responded positively to Wakeman's article with comments such as "Amen Jessica! Doing what's best for YOU is feminism!" When some commenters point out the potential long-term implications of leaving the workforce even for a few years, Wakeman and other readers discount them as "underestimating the abilities of Jessica and other intelligent women to prepare for the future." Of course, in an era when change is the only thing workers can count on, this kind of advice has limited value since it is difficult to plan years in advance for an unpredictable job market.

Perhaps the pushback by comments like these does indicate a grow-ing sense that the individualistic terms of the debate are problematic. Dissatisfaction with the very idea of the "mommy wars" was evident in responses to a May 2012 *Time* magazine cover that featured a mother breastfeeding her preschooler son, accompanied by the question "Are you mom enough?" The article reaches beyond the typical dualistic focus on work to engage with the issue of prolonged breastfeeding as a feature of attachment parenting, a childrearing philosophy that, fully implemented, makes employment outside the home virtually impossible for mothers (Pickert). Bloggers and journalists responded by critiquing the provocative image, agreeing that the cover was a crass attempt at selling magazines, and that parents should rather support each other in their individual parenting choices. A writer at Spiked.com pointed out that *Time* did not create the "mommy wars" but is exploiting tensions about parenting that date back to the 1970s when mothers entered the workforce in record numbers (McDermott). Despite thoughtfully con-textualizing these tensions in the economic and cultural norms of late capitalism, McDermott's conclusion is an individualistic call for parents to have more confidence in their own judgments as well as those of other parents. A similar call by a Babble.com columnist elicited much enthu-siastic agreement in the comments—"What a needlessly judgmental and divisive headline. We are 'mom enough' no matter what parenting philosophy we use" and "Agreed. Let's stand together. Not against each other" (Stone). While these responses are admirably pluralistic, their em-phasis on individual choice risks eliding conversations about the condi-tions in which those choices are made. They exemplify what Wendy Brown calls the "model neo-liberal citizen . . . who strategizes for her/ himself among various social, political and economic options, not one who strives with others to alter or organize these options." Thus, the idea of non-judgment may dial down the so-called "mommy wars," but as a comprehensive solution this approach doesn't change anything ex-cept to further isolate mothers and fathers in their work-life situations as self-care entrepreneurs, model neoliberal citizens. Extending this logic to social policies about work-life, then, would be to say that citizens should accept with equanimity workplace speed-ups, flattened wages, and evis-ceration of the social safety net to become self-sufficient entrepreneurs who limit their political involvement to voting for party-determined op-tions A or B at the ballot box.

As columnists and commenters point out, the circulation of the "mommy wars" and opt-out-out narratives seems to be more a matter of marketing gimmicks than substantive discussion or debate. Not only does it serve commercial interests as a way of propping up print-based media for outlets like *Time* magazine and as a way of attracting viewers to online sites, but it is also useful for politicians like Santorum interested in goading on or re-igniting the culture wars and useful for employers such as Sandberg who are interested in maximizing employees' commitment to their jobs. Thus, these narratives haven't solved problems for families over the past three decades because they don't exist for the interests of families. In fact, the re-circulation of these narratives hinders the problem-solving necessary to find solutions for families dealing with the very real professional, economic, and cultural pressures of the day. Even attempts to resist these arguments tend to unintentionally re-circulate problematic assumptions when they frame the issue as primarily a matter of choices made by inherently free agents. Because if we all already possess unhindered agency, there are no structural policy changes needed.

KAIROTIC RHETORICAL ENTANGLEMENTS

Whether these arguments take on religious, secular, moralistic, feminist, conservative, liberal, sentimental, or other ideological casts, their very "everyday-ness" makes them noteworthy because as everyday rhetorics in "heavy rotation," they are vehicles of social and cultural reproduction (Edwards, Hallenbeck). In the context of late capitalism, their rhetorical value (persuasive power) lies in their circulation and repetition rather than in their historical truth, "energiz[ing] our habituated movements as well as our commonsensical beliefs" (Chaput 8, 14,). Thus, banal, ordinary discourses are key indicators of the ideological assumptions and taken-for-granted norms that "haunt" our rhetorics (Rickert). The circulation of everyday rhetorics matter because of their subtle, but persistent effect in priming audiences and thus increasing the chances for persuasion to occur (Söderlund). Thus, retrospectively, their circulation can also reflect how receptive audiences have been cultivated for future rhetorical action (Rivers, Seas).

While the chronological timeframe of these circulating rhetorics is clearly relevant—late capitalism, the 2008 housing boom and bust, the 2012 election cycle—the element of timing is also key. *Kairos*, the Greek word for the ancient concept of *rhetorical timing* suggests a singular moment in which an argument is most likely to be persuasive. However, given the futility of attempting to pinpoint the moment a circulating rhetoric becomes persuasive, rhetoric scholars such as J. Blake Scott, Thomas Rickert, and Lars Söderlund have re-imagined kairos for a net-worked world of mediated texts, shifting arguments, and unintended audiences. Their revision of the concept of *kairos*—which is consonant with the relational ontologies that new materialists such as Barad, Grosz, and Jane Bennet discuss—shifts analysis *away from* questions that center on the inherent agency of an individual (speaker) and *toward* relations within the individual's (nonhuman) context. This technologically rich context produces circulating, repeated messages that flow persuasively between the fluctuating, amorphous positions of speaker and audience. The unpredictable movements of texts are not only due to the actions of humans, but now are also influenced by online search algorithms and other nonhuman actors such as the ads social media users see that are not entirely directly controlled by any one human agent, but by com-plex calculations that attempt to predict users' interests based on their past actions to influence future behavior. In this context, for example, "mommy war" arguments can circulate easily as click-bait, bearing pro-vocative titles that deliver little in the way of substance.

It is this (potential) lack of human control over rhetorics that prompts Scott to call rhetoricians to consider such complex exigencies by pro-posing a conception of kairos as "something distributed across rhetor-ical-cultural networks rather than within discrete rhetorical situations" (134). Scott argues that the opportune timing of an argument is not a one-time, predictable event but the result of converging elements that to-gether create an environment conducive to persuasion. According to this view, then, persuasion results less from a well-crafted argument than it does from a receptive audience that has been cultivated as a consequence of the relations between human and nonhuman agents. Thus, over the past decades, "mommy war" headlines have become part of the environ-ment in which American audiences have conceptualized (or ignored, as the case may be) social policymaking.

Fundamental to cultivating kairotic moments and receptive audienc-es is repetition, defined as "a constant, subtle process of influence, and *the kairotic moments of persuasion that we perceive are catalyzed by processes of repetition that prepare audiences to respond to certain forms of discourse*" (Söderlund 3; emphasis added). In other words, recurring, everyday ar-guments offer some indication of what resonates with audiences and what those audiences find persuasive. Furthermore, repetition's persuasive potential in "prepar[ing] audiences" is key to understanding how arguments originating in one context can "jump species" to be persuasive in geographically or ideologically distant places (to use Jenny Edbauer's metaphor). That is, the constant repetition of otherwise objectionable arguments often serves to normalize ideas even among unlikely audiences across the political spectrum. In the examples I use here, recurring arguments that frame paid labor as a purely affective or ideological choice serve to shut down critical thought and to normalize regressive ideas for audiences that identify as progressive. In this way repetition of these arguments creates kairotic moments in disparate but networked places where unlikely audiences are cultivated and mobilized for political action.

READING DISCOURSE THROUGH MATERIAL CONTEXTS

But if, according to a new materialist view, "society is simultaneously materially real and socially constructed," the rhetorical analysis above only tells part of the story (Coole and Frost 27). A more complete analysis needs to situate these rhetorics "within the fields of material forces and power relations that reproduce and circumscribe their existence and co-existence" (Coole and Frost 28). Similarly, Barad's analytical approach of diffractive reading is not done by "pointing out similarities between one place or event and another, but by understanding how those places or events are made through one another" (*Meeting* 246). Thus, "detailed, evidence-based knowledge of domestic and international politics and of shifting geopolitical relations," offers greater insight into how and when these relations constrain action or facilitate it (Coole and Frost 29). In line with this approach, a new materialist analysis of rhetorics about family and work requires a consideration of the relations between broader economic, political, and global contexts in which they arise. The work of historians, economists, family studies, and other scholars can contribute to this contextualizing, offering one explanation for their persistence over time and bringing to our awareness the relevant economic and geopolitical conditions and how they interact with emerging cultural and social narratives.

What follows are just a few of the historical, cultural, material and geopolitical factors whose interactions contribute to the rhetorical power of "mommy war" rhetorics as discussed by Rick Santorum, *The View* co-hosts, and the many commentators quoted above. These conditions play off each other, contributing to the cultivation of kairotic environments and receptive audiences where these ideas can circulate widely and influence social policy.

Historically, the prototypical "traditional" or nuclear family model of a male breadwinner and female homemaker as it is popularly conceived existed for a comparatively short period (Coontz 63). Prior to the Industrial Revolution, able-bodied adults and children of all genders typically contributed to the family's economic production. With the advent of factories that moved economic production out of the home, the concept of a housewife or stay-at-home-mother who supervised the family's consumption of goods became a symbol of prosperity (Gornick and Myers 26). Thus, the domestic ideal of a wife and mother at home reflected an aspiration to middle or upper-middle class status that eluded many. As child labor laws and compulsory school attendance laws removed children from the workforce throughout the early years of the twentieth century faster than women entered it and unions improved overall working conditions that included a living wage, the United States entered into a relatively short-lived period of approximately fifty years (from the 1920s through the 1960s) when the ideal of the male breadwinner was at its height (Coontz 57). Of course, as *The View* co-hosts Shepherd and Goldberg point out, not all US households realized the one-income ideal; impoverished families of all races have long relied on multiple breadwinners (or one breadwinner if only one was present) to survive. This historical context demonstrates that the often romanticized and moralized notion of a single-earner household is actually more of an aberration than the norm. Increasing urbanization and post-war affluence of the mid-twentieth century helped make this family structure possible for many white Americans. Developing alongside anti-communist sentiment, institutionalized racism, and selective upward mobility of the period, this patriarchal and classist family structure quickly became a cultural standard.

Thus, Santorum's statement about radical feminism rests on the inaccurate assumption that until the women's movement came along, homemaking was an inevitable and universal expectation for women. It is a rhetorically powerful statement since its assumptions about social norms align with Walters' narrative of the women's movement as liberating women from domesticity. Even though Walters celebrates the social change that Santorum laments, they share an underlying assumption about the history of domesticity in the United States that is not reflected in the historical record as pointed out here by historians and social scientists. Yet, the stakes of framing the issue in this way are more than a matter of historical correctness. In line with Elizabeth Grosz's new materialist reimagining of agency, this shared point of departure (or stasis) is an example of liberation conceived as what an individual is freed from (e.g., domesticity). As long as women's liberation is understood to be primarily about freedom from domesticity rather than about the full expression of one's capabilities, the associated discourse will necessarily be limiting.

Other material developments that are elided by the normative narrative of the nuclear family include those of the decades following the 1960's women's movement. With the growth of global markets came the off-shoring of American jobs, automation, and downsizing of companies as the jobs that had been capable of supporting entire households began to evaporate. In fact, in just the two decades following the mid-1970s, the buying power of working *men's* wages dropped significantly, an average of nearly one percent per year by some estimates (Gornick and Myers 29, Gordon 31, Nilsson 134). This decline in men's real wages correlates with women's increased participation in the paid workforce (Coontz 57). Consequently, just as the Industrial Revolution was responsible for championing women's exclusion from the workforce, global capitalism forced more women back into the paid workforce just to maintain their households' standard of living. In fact, economic conditions driven by global capitalism have made two incomes a necessity for many couples with children and the corresponding decrease in state-sponsored welfare benefits have made paid work an absolute necessity for single mothers.

At the same time, the late twentieth-century conservative backlash against the 1960's Civil Rights and women's movements that villainized middle-class mothers for working and poor mothers for not working framed its arguments in moral terms. The emphasis on marriage in the welfare reforms of 1996 (*Personal Responsibility and Work Opportunity Reconciliation Act*) drew its rhetorical and political power from the stigma of single parenthood that suggests a deviation from the nuclear family structure reflects a moral deficit. In the context of neoliberalism and its accompanying policies that seek to relieve the state of responsibility for the quality of life of its citizens, these narratives and policies together construct an environment where austerity can flourish. An individual or a family's failure to thrive in this environment can be explained by a narrative of moral weakness and poor choices without giving due credit to the corresponding forces that limit those choices. Similarly, women's choices can also be framed in moralistic or ideological terms, side-stepping a more robust critique of the cultural and economic forces that also influence family structures.

Therefore, when Walters and Behar, two of *The View*'s co-hosts, emphasized the role of the women's movement in motivating women to leave hearth and home for the paid workforce over the past four decades, their celebration unintentionally reinforced the rhetorical power of social conservatives' arguments that charge feminism with destabilizing families because of women's presence in the workplace. Together these arguments from the political right and the left that frame women's paid work as an ideological choice obscure the effect of material factors such as race, social class, economic recession, outsourcing of jobs, and wage stagnation in shaping the personnel demands of the United States workplace.

A new materialist view allows us to go beyond a more conventional Marxist critique that emphasizes the domination of these economic factors to also explore the ways that these narratives and economic realities are entangled and co-created. Hence the media networks that facilitate the circulation of these rhetorics are important to study since they are hospitable environments for sound-bites, one-liners, and memes that are "haunted" by logics that draw on capitalist values of individualism, self-determination, and personal responsibility. Furthermore, the repetition of these logics that reduce social and family issues to matters of affect, desire, or ideology cultivate kairotic moments for regressive policies that challenge the rights gained by women, minorities, LGBTQ communities, and others. The challenge for progressive activists is to avoid inadvertently reinforcing the assumptions of the policies they protest in their own arguments.

Often challenges to these assumptions—such as challenges posed by Goldberg and Shepherd on *The View* or by writers who dispute the claims of "The Opt-Out Generation"—are underemphasized or ignored, perhaps because they do not fit easily into existing political and affective frameworks. However, there is some suggestion that the tide may be turning. More recent articles in publications like *The Atlantic*, *Huffington Post*, and *Salon* about the pressures families face suggest general audiences may be more receptive to rethinking this concept than they have been in past years. In 2013, Judith Warner's article, "The Opt-Out Generation Wants Back In" appeared in *The New York Times*, describing the many professional barriers and out-right dead-ends experienced by mothers attempting to return to the professional/managerial positions they left a decade ago. Despite the acclaim heaped by many on these women for their seemingly selfless choice to stay home, they now find themselves penalized and their families made financially vulnerable as a result. The financial hardship is even greater when they unexpectedly find themselves, as many do, sole breadwinners due to divorce, death, or layoffs. The same year, *CNBC* posted a story that discusses why a much larger number of lower-income mothers who prefer to work are staying home because the jobs for which they are eligible would not cover the cost of childcare (Linn). In yet another 2013 article, *Parents* magazine questioned whether the "mommy wars" even exist, citing a survey of five hundred parents across the nation in which many respondents reported that although they believe the "mommy wars" are real, few had actually experienced any first-hand evidence of them ("Do Mommy Wars Exist?"). "If you read anything enough times," the writer notes, "you start to believe it," suggesting that this is a self-perpetuating narrative.

These challenges to "mommy war" rhetoric demonstrate how neoliberal rationality—despite its pervasiveness in organizing economic, political, and social structures in the context of global capitalism—is neither hegemonic, monolithic, nor universal (Gibson-Graham, Brown, Chaput). As the repetition of these kinds of challenges show, resistance is possible even if it is not successful in reaching its goal of political action. Put another way, the unpredictability of rhetorical ecologies is such that repetition alone does not guarantee persuasion, especially if the environment is unreceptive to those arguments (Seas). Arguments like these will not go viral, setting the stage for policy-making, as long as the social environment is not conducive to its spread. In the context of global capitalism, the "[a]ffective energy [that] precedes our conscious decisions, cajoling us into habituated movements that are valorized through repetition" such as the neoliberal values of individualism and self-care promote an environment in which the public imagination is inept at constructing arguments that challenge the discourses of self-determination and personal entrepreneurship (Chaput 15; Brown).

Thus, these popular critiques of the "mommy wars" reflect an impasse. Granted, they do acknowledge that viable choices are limited for many parents in the US. They acknowledge the socio-economic component to these choices. They acknowledge the profit-motives of corporate media in popularizing these headlines. They even acknowledge that social policy needs to change for more parents to have a more meaningful range of options open to them such as are available to families in many European countries. And yet in line with neoliberal logics, the proposed solutions are no more substantive than mere reminders to let everyone make their own choices. While on the surface this might appear to be a call for greater autonomy, this impoverished solution's failure to promote the kind of coordinated activism necessary to bring about substantive change demonstrates Grosz's concern that when freedom is only defined in terms of "that which is bestowed on us by others," it actually undermines autonomy by assuming passivity and acceptance of pre-determined options (153). This conception of freedom "remains tied to the options or alternatives provided by the present and its prevailing and admittedly limiting forces, instead of accessing and opening up the present to the invention of the new" (141). The ineffectiveness of this approach as an activist strategy is demonstrated by the virtual silence of legislators and policy makers in addressing work-life issues. In other words, this approach has not yet been successful in cultivating a kairotic environment where substantive change and broader array of options can develop and take root in public discourse and policy-making.

Furthermore, systemic problems require systemic solutions; just as individual workers' choices did not create the twenty-first-century workplace, they cannot reverse its ill effects in isolation from each other either. If freedom is not, as Grosz argues, "a transcendent quality inherent in subjects but is immanent in the relations that the living has with the material world, including other forms of life" then the power to cultivate receptive environments and audiences grows from connections, networks, and communities, not out of isolated bodies (148). In other words, a kairotic argument is dependent on the presence of material apparatuses that disseminate it and propel it forward to become persuasive. Thus, changing this narrative requires attention to the human, mechanized, cultural, and economic bodies that make up the networks in which it circulates. Not only are discourse and materiality deeply entangled, but effectiveness in changing one requires careful analysis of the other.

Thus, networked analysis that reads objects of study through multiple lenses, exploring connections between the primarily discursive work of one humanities field, rhetoric, to the material contributions of others can produce new knowledge about our world in the context of digital networks and the atomized power of late capitalism. Not only does it provide a way to explore dynamic relationships between academic fields and every day phenomena, but helps us imagine new possibilities in addressing the challenges of the twenty-first century in the humanities, in the academy and beyond.

ACKNOWLEDGMENTS

I want to thank Rebecca Dingo, Bonita Selting, and Derrick Clark for their valuable comments and critiques of earlier versions of this chapter.

WORKS CITED

Barad, Karen. "Matter Feels, Converses, Suffers, Desires, Yearns, and Remembers." *New Materialism: Interviews & Cartographies*, edited by Rick Dolphijn and Iris van der Tuin, Open Humanities, 2012, quod.lib.umich.edu/o/ohp/11515701.0001.001/1:4.3/--new-materialism-interviews-cartographies?rgn=div2;view=fulltext. Accessed 26 Jul. 2016.

—. *Meeting the Universe Halfway: Quantum Physics and the Entanglement of Matter and Meaning.* Duke UP, 2007.

Belkin, Lisa. "The Opt-Out Revolution." *New York Times*, 26 Oct. 2003, www.nytimes.com/2003/10/26/magazine/the-opt-out-revolution.html. Accessed 5 Jan. 2014.

Blair-Loy, Mary. *Competing Devotions: Career and Family Among Women Executives.* Harvard UP, 2003.

Borrego, Maura, and Lynita K. Newswander. "Characteristics of Successful Cross-disciplinary Engineering Education Collaborations." *Journal of Engineering* Education, vol. 97, no. 2, 2008, pp. 123–34. .

Brown, Wendy. "Neo-Liberalism and the End of Liberal Democracy." *Theory & Event*, vol. 7, no. 1, 2003, n. pag. muse.jhu.edu/article/48659f.

Chaput, Catherine. "Rhetorical Circulation in Late Capitalism: Neoliberalism and the Overdetermination of Affective Energy." *Philosophy and Rhetoric*, vol. 43, no. 1, 2010, pp. 1–25. .

Coole, Diana H., and Susan H. Frost. "Introduction." *New Materialisms: Ontology, Agency, and Politics*, edited by Diana Coole and Samantha Frost, Duke UP, 2010, pp. 1–46.

Coontz, Stephanie. *The Way We Really Are: Coming to Terms with America's Changing Families.* Basic Books, 1998.

Crenshaw, Kimberle. "Demarginalizing the Intersection of Race and Sex: A Black Feminist Critique of Antidiscrimination Doctrine, Feminist Theory and Antiracist Politics." *University of Chicago Legal Forum 1989*, U of Chicago, 1989, p. 139.

Daum, Meghan. "Phyllis Schlafly: Back on the Attack." *Los Angeles Times* 31 Mar. 2011, articles.latimes.com/2011/mar/31/opinion/la-oe-daum-column-schlafly-20110331. Accessed 5 Jan. 2014.

Dingo, Rebecca. "Linking Transnational Logics: A Feminist Rhetorical Analysis of Public Policy Networks." *College English*, vol. 70, no. 5, 2008, pp. 490–505. .

Edbauer, Jenny. "Unframing Models of Public Distribution: From Rhetorical Situation to Rhetorical Ecologies." *Rhetoric Society Quarterly*, vol. 35, no. 4, 2005, pp. 5–24.

"Economist Debates: Women & Work." *The Economist*. N. p., 7 Dec. 2011, www.economist.com/debate/overview/219. Accessed 6 Jan. 2014.

Edwards, Jason. "The Materialism of Historical Materialism." *New Materialisms: Ontology, Agency, and Politics*, edited by Diana Coole and Samantha Frost, Duke UP, 2010, pp. 281–98.

Freeman, Richard B. *America Works: The Exceptional U. S. Labor Market*. Russell Sage Foundation, 2007.

Frost, Susan H., and Paul M. Jean. "Bridging the Disciplines: Interdisciplinary Discourse and Faculty Scholarship." *The Journal of Higher Education*, vol. 74, no. 2, 2003, pp. 119–49.

Gibson-Graham, J. K. *The End of Capitalism (as We Knew It): A Feminist Critique of Political Economy*. U of Minnesota P, 2006.

Gordon, David. *Fat and Mean: The Corporate Squeeze of Working Americans and the Myth of Managerial "Downsizing."* Martin Kessler, 1996.

Gornick, Janet C., and Marcia Meyers. *Families That Work: Policies for Reconciling Parenthood and Employment*. Russell Sage Foundation, 2003.

Gries, Laurie E. "Iconographic Tracking: A Digital Research Method for Visual Rhetoric and Circulation Studies." *Computers and Composition*, vol. 30, no. 4, 2013, pp. 332–48, doi.org/10.1016/j.compcom.2013.10.006.

Grimm, Nancy Maloney. "Review of Writing Centers and Writing Across the Curriculum Programs: Building Interdisciplinary Partnerships." *Technical Communication Quarterly*, vol. 11, no. 4, 2002, pp. 476–78.

Grosz, Elizabeth. "Feminism, Materialism, and Freedom." *New Materialisms: Ontology, Agency, and Politics*, edited by Diana Coole and Samantha Frost, Duke UP, 2010, pp. 139–57.

Hallenbeck, Sarah. "Toward a Posthuman Perspective: Feminist Rhetorical Methodologies and Everyday Practices." *Advances in the History of Rhetoric*, vol. 15, no. 1, 2012, pp. 9–27.

Heymann, Jody. *The Widening Gap: Why America's Working Families Are in Jeopardy and What Can Be Done About It*. Basic, 2000.

Knowlton, Brian. "Santorum Faces Questions on Women in Work Force." *The New York Times*, 12 Feb. 2012, www.nytimes.com/2012/02/13/us/politics/santorum-faces-questions-on-women-in-work-force.html. Accessed 5 Jan. 2014.

Kornbluh, Karen. "The Parent Trap." *The Atlantic Monthly*, Jan./Feb. 2003, pp. 111–14.

Lassiter, Matthew D. "Inventing Family Values." *Rightward Bound: Making America Conservative in the 1970s*, edited by Bruce J. Schulman and Julian E. Zelizer, Harvard UP, 2008, pp. 13–28.

Latour, Bruno. *Pandora's Hope: Essays on the Reality of Science Studies*. Harvard U P, 1999.

Linn, Allison. "Opt Out or Left Out? The Economics of Stay-at-Home Moms." *NBC News*, 12 May 2013, www.nbcnews.com/businessmain/opt-out-or-left-out-economics-stay-home-moms-1C9881635. Accessed 5 Jan. 2014.

McDermott, Nancy. "Time Magazine Did Not Invent the Mommy Wars." *Spiked*, 21 May 2012, www.spiked-online.com/newsite/article/12464. Accessed 6 Jan. 2014.

Miller, Lisa. "The Retro Wife: Feminists Who Say They're Having It All—By Choosing to Stay Home." *New York Magazine*, 17 Mar. 2013, nymag.com/news/features/retro-wife-2013-3/. Accessed 6 Jan. 2014.

Miller, Thaddeus et al., "Epistemological Pluralism: Reorganizing Interdisciplinary Research." *Ecology and Society*, vol. 13, no. 2, 2008, p. 46.

Nilsson, Eric A. "Trends in Compensation for Production Workers: 1948–1995." *Review of Radical Political* Economics, vol. 31, no. 4, 1999, pp. 133–63.

O'Connor, Gail. "Do Mommy Wars Exist?" *Parents Magazine*, Aug. 2013, www.parents.com/parenting/moms/do-mommy-wars-exist/. Accessed 6 Jan. 2014.

Personal Responsibility and Work Opportunity Reconciliation Act of 1996. Congress. 104th Congress. 2nd Session. H. R. 3734, 21 Aug. 1996, pp. 1–251, aspe.hhs.gov/report/personal-responsibility-and-work-opportunity-reconciliation-act-1996. Accessed 1 July 2010.

Peskowitz, Miriam. *The Truth Behind the Mommy Wars: Who Decides What Makes a Good Mother?* Seal Press, 2005.

Pickert, Kate. "The Man Who Remade Motherhood." *Time Magazine*, 21 May 2012, n. pag.

"Please Explain Why You Emphasize Mothers Being at Home with Their Kids Rather Than in the Workforce. Do You Have Any Words for Moms Who Work Outside the Home?" *Focus on the Family*, 15 Nov. 2013, www.focusonthefamily.com/. Accessed 5 Jan. 2014.

Rickert, Thomas. "In the House of Doing: Rhetoric and the Kairos of Ambience." *JAC*, vol. 24, no. 4, 2004, pp. 901–27.

Rivers, Nathaniel A. "Rhetorics of (Non)Symbolic Cultivation." *Ecology, Writing Theory, and New Media: Writing Ecology*, edited by Sidney I. Dobrin, Routledge, 2012, pp. 51–66.

Rivers, Nathaniel, Jenny Bay, Derek Mueller, and Laurie Gries. "Networked Relations: New Materialist Contributions to the Digital Humanities." University of Kentucky Networked Humanities Conference, 16 Feb. 2013,

Whitehall Classroom Building, Lexington, KY. Conference Panel Presentation.

Sandberg, Sheryl. *Lean In: Women, Work, and the Will to Lead*. First edition. Alfred A. Knopf, 2013.

Scott, J. Blake. "Kairos as Indeterminate Risk Management: The Pharmaceutical Industry's Response to Bioterrorism." *Quarterly Journal of* Speech, vol. 92, no. 2, 2006, pp. 115–43.

Seas, Kristen. "Writing Ecologies, Rhetorical Epidemics." *Ecology, Writing Theory, and New Media: Writing Ecology*, edited by Sidney I. Dobrin, Routledge, 2012, pp. 51–66.

Söderlund, Lars Erik. "Catalyzing Persuasion: Toward a Theory of Kairos and Repetition." Dissertation, Purdue University, West Lafayette, IN. 2011, docs.lib.purdue.edu/dissertations/AAI3481153/.

Steiner, Leslie Morgan. *Mommy Wars: Stay-at-Home and Career Moms Face Off on Their Choices, Their Lives, Their Families*. Random House, 2006.

Stone, Katherine. "It's TIME To Stop Fighting the Mommy Wars." *Babble*, 10 May 2012, n. pag, web.archive.org/web/20130530140942/http://www.babble.com:80/mom/its-time-to-stop-fighting-the-mommy-wars/. Accessed 6 Jan. 2014.

The View. Hot Topics: The Effects of Feminism. ABC. KMIZ, Columbia, MO, 13 Feb. 2012.

Torrant, Julie P. *The Material Family*. Sense, 2011.

Wakefield, Jessica. "Breaking News: You Can Be a Feminist and a Stay-at-Home Mom." *The Frisky*, 19 Mar. 2013, n. pag, www.thefrisky.com/2013-03-19/breaking-news-you-can-be-a-feminist-and-a-stay-at-home-mom/. Accessed 6 Jan. 2014.

Warner, Judith. "The Opt-Out Generation Wants Back In." *The New York Times*, 7 Aug. 2013, www.nytimes.com/2013/08/11/magazine/the-opt-out-generation-wants-back-in.html. Accessed 6 Jan. 2014.

Williams, Joan C., Jessica Manvell, and Stephanie Bornstein. "'Opt Out' or Pushed Out?: How the Press Covers Work/Family Conflict." 2006. Accessed 5 Jan. 2014.

16 Provocation: "Even if it's just Writing Letters": Networking Japanese Americans in World War II

Kathleen Blake Yancey

> [T]he postal revolution [in the 19th century] amounted to a complex conversion of an already powerful state institution into a network of popular exchange and sociability. This involved not only the radical opening up of the network to mass participation . . . but also a fundamental redefinition of the basic function of the post. Whereas an earlier generation of Americans had experienced the post as a kind of broadcast medium, postal users in the antebellum era joined a far more interactive network, employing the older bureaucratic apparatus for a new set of recognizably modern purposes. (Henkin, 42)

Born and raised in San Pedro, California, Mary Makahara, a twenty-one-year-old Japanese American, was first removed, in 1942, to an assembly center before being moved again to an internment camp. In Mary's case, the first camp was at Santa Anita Raceway, where horse stalls were re-named as residences, Mary and her family living at Avenue 8, Barrack 48, Room Number 11. As she moved, Mary began a diary, its title—"The Bordered World"—reflecting her new reality, with a specific purpose: "Daily diary of how I think and feel." But how she would think and feel in terms of what she would compose was circumscribed by her own philosophy: "may I never put in writing that which would hurt, humiliate, look down, blame, or show dislike for any person, nation, race, relation, or station in life."

The diary itself—the physical diary—is nondescript. It's a composition-book-turned diary, handwritten, a draft, as it were, with drawings; headers for each day; sidebar comments adorning headers; and many cross-outs and corrections and revisions, especially at the end when Mary struggles with the racism and discrimination she, her family, and her friends are experiencing. Like most diaries, it includes a mix of daily accounts of life, personal observation, and reflections on the world at that moment; unlike most diaries, it emphasizes her sense of writing and the role it plays in her life. Mary shows us the tenor of the time with telling detail, for instance, when she describes the family's departure from San Pedro: "Curious onlookers, passerbys, workmen, house-wife, school-children would all stare at us as we went on our way. Some even waved good-bye. One little boy said, 'Wish I had a machine gun.'" She uses revision to show us her sense of humor: "The line is slowly moving, but there is still over a hundred in front of me. (Pardon me, the line hasn't begun to move yet)." She uses the space of the diary to reflect upon shared experiences: working as a nurse's aide in the camp's ad hoc medical center, for example, she encounters a child whose situation prompts this analysis:

> At the hospital there was . . . a darling boy. He was completely Caucasian, with sort of an English accent. His last name, however, was Japanese. I only hope that the outside world will be good to him when he grows older. It will probably be "tough going" for him when it comes to jobs and marriage . . . but by that time perhaps people will be more broad-minded on those issues.

At the center of Mary's life, however, is writing. In part, she values writing because it provides an opportunity to think: "It feels good to be alone to write, to think, to reminisce." In part, she values writing because it provides a mechanism for recording her experience at Santa Anita, both verbally and visually. Deprived of a camera—on December 27, 1941, the federal government had ordered all suspected "enemy aliens" in the Western US to surrender short wave radios and cameras—

Mary illustrates her diary with drawings of the windows that must now be blacked out of the hospital where she volunteers. In part, Mary values writing because writing enacts her network of relationships and keeps her connected to her past: "And—gee-there really was mail. Gosh! I was so happy . . . I was just overcome. Letters can really bring happiness. It makes you ~~realize~~ think how happy then a soldier must become when he receives letters at some camp hundreds of miles from his home." That network—created by her departure from San Pedro, represented in letters from her friends from the recent past delivered to the camp by the US postal network—is Mary's first network, the social group that may once have been geographically located, but is now in transit. It is that network she calls on to sustain her when she begins life in Santa Anita.

Mary cannot stay in Santa Anita, however: like other Japanese Americans, she received orders to move to a more permanent site, in her case Jerome, Arkansas. Just before the move, the diary—previously replete with detail, observation, reflection—goes quiet before concluding with only two more entries, a period I think of as the time of empty pages. One of the last entries preceding the empty pages reports a friend's experience in applying to nursing school. A qualified candidate, Susie Matsumura, encounters a rejection from each of the twenty institutions to which she had applied, from hospitals like Lutheran Hospital in Sioux City and Mercy in Denver, schools like St Joseph College of Nursing. As often as not, the reason for the rejection was clearly explained: the institution is afraid that the public will not accept care provided by a person of Japanese ancestry. Mary's indignation is ignited. It is writing, she says, that can provide a form of resistance and redress: "Even if it's just writing letters, I'll write them—as I've never written before, letters that might inspire and encourage." There had been other insults small and large—meals were institutional and European; Japanese American health professionals staffing the ad hoc clinic were treated disdainfully—but it's the straightforward rejection of her friend that prompts silence from the diarist who so loved writing.

During the time of the empty pages, we don't know exactly what happened to Mary. We do know that it was during this time that she creates a new network, a network of letter writers she calls The Crusaders. As she explains retrospectively,

> While waiting to be relocated to the internment camps, I wanted to do something to help the war effort and our boys in the service. . . . I thought it would be a good idea to write to them.

> The group called itself the "Crusaders." We became more active, and my [Sunday school] class began to grow in size as the older teenage girls whose brothers were in the Army wanted to join the Crusaders. (Kochiyama 13)

This effort was no small enterprise, though it began as one, with only five Sunday school girls writing to an even fewer number of Japanese American soldiers—two. As the class was disassembled, girls scattering to different internment camps across the west and midwest, the Crusaders continued, initially writing on penny postcards to save postage since at a penny apiece, the postage for the cards was lower than for letters. The network expanded: more soldiers wanted to correspond with the Crusaders, who invited other young women, new Crusaders and Junior Crusaders, pre-teens who performed clerical tasks, into the Crusader network. Given the expansion, more funding was needed, and residents of the internment camps made contributions to support this network. As Ruth Ishizaki, one of the Crusaders, explains, "As the people in the camp caught on to what the Crusaders were doing, many of the incarcerated started to donate their scarce tiny sums of money for postage stamps and postcards to help out." Likewise, they contributed greeting cards that could be sent to the soldiers at holidays, and the soldiers themselves contributed parts of their salaries so that a short postcard could be replaced by a more substantial letter: "We gradually received a lot of support, especially from the 232nd Engineers (part of the 442nd) soldiers who started sending money to us from the front lines! We then changed from postcards to regular paper and envelopes that only required two-cent stamps." The soldiers sent their own correspondence as well—postcards from Europe, notes of thanks, greeting cards. Eventually, the mailing list included five thousand soldiers, nearly all—but not all—Japanese American soldiers. Eventually, the letters became newsletters, what one of the Crusaders called a "mixed-up letter," filled with news, encouragement, poetry, and drawings. Eventually, many in the internment camps became Crusaders, including "the nameless church secretaries and stenographers who cut the stencils and ran them off on monograph machine" (Ishizaki).

The Crusader network, initiated in a Sunday school class by a twenty-one-year-old teacher and four of her pupils, created ties among people who mostly did not know each other and who mostly had not met; that network facilitated an articulation of the collective experience of Japanese Americans during World War II. The first Crusaders met each other through a forced internment camp experience. The young women wanted to act; they understood writing as action; and we know from Mary's diary that her first network gave her strength and that she saw in her own response to letters how welcome a letter would be to a soldier overseas. But creating this network was a political act: through their writings, they believed, these young women calling themselves Crusaders could draw on the US and US military postal service to provide support to Japanese American men fighting for the very country interning them—the letter-writing sisters, wives and cousins at home.

David Henkin argues that the nineteenth century postal service, a bureaucratic apparatus, served many different purposes and fostered interaction: in the case of the Crusaders, the US postal service, somewhat ironically, supported the creation of a new group of Japanese Americans, many of whom were the very people its government was discriminating against. In that sense, the Crusaders are a more modern instance and an extension of Henkin's network theory. At the same time, the Crusaders' network anticipates our current—seemingly ubiquitous, often ahistorical—understanding of ICT-driven networks, which according to Vincent Miller, share five characteristics: (1) "they are a-spatial"; (2) they are "based on choice"; (3) they "are a product of instrumentalism"; (4) the ties are "tenuous"; and (5) they are "open-ended" (200–201). Or: the Crusaders.

WORKS CITED

Henkin, David. *The Postal Age: The Emergence of Modern Communications in Nineteenth-Century.* U. of Chicago P, 2007.

Ishizaki, Ruth. "My Life as a Crusader." *Japanese American Museum of San Jose,* 2009, www.jamsj.org/newsletter/summer09/ruth.html

Kochiyama, Yuri Nakahara. *Passing It On—A Memoir.* UCLA Asian American Studies Center Press, 2004.

Miller, Vincent. *Understanding Digital Culture.* Sage, 2011.

Nakahara, Mary. "The Bordered World, V. I." National Japanese American Museum. Los Angeles, CA.

NETWORKED PROCESSES

17 Elaborating a Network: Rhetoric's Relationship with Psychology's Elaboration Likelihood Model and the Promise and Risks of Expanding It

Lars Söderlund

The Elaboration Likelihood Model (ELM) is a theory of persuasion from social psychology, and it is "one of the most researched theories of attitude change" in academia (Stephenson). This may come as a surprise to a scholar in rhetorical studies, who is unlikely to have heard of it. The ELM is primarily used in the fields of social psychology, consumer studies (especially advertising), health communication, and occasionally in the broader field of communication, but not in journals that specifically study the history and theory of rhetoric, such as *Rhetoric Review*, *Rhetoric Society Quarterly*, or *Quarterly Journal of Speech*. That the heavily-researched ELM rarely appears in rhetorical studies is strange, as both pursue the study of persuasion. And the reverse is also true: researchers in social psychology, consumer studies, and health communication who study the ELM are not in the habit of engaging with research from the field of rhetorical studies.

The goal of this chapter is to begin building a network between the humanities discipline of rhetorical studies and an area of study from the social sciences, the ELM, examining specifically how the ELM and aspects of rhetorical studies vary from each other and could inform each other's practices. My home discipline is rhetorical studies, and so I will discuss the ways in which the empirically focused ELM could inform rhetorical studies, which is generally focused on discursive analysis. I believe that a network between the fields could perhaps yield hybrid approaches to persuasion between the two areas of study and eventually raise the visibility of rhetorical studies among fields that engage with the ELM. Obviously, I cannot lay all of the necessary groundwork in this brief chapter, but I hope to lay out a vision of networked cooperation between the two paradigms.

Because the field of rhetorical studies is so large, I will discuss what the ELM could add to a specific, emerging area of inquiry within rhetorical studies: circulation. Circulation is the way that texts and ideas propagate throughout culture, exercising influence on individuals as they do so. Scholars have investigated circulation by looking at specific texts (or what Michael Warner calls the punctual rhythms of circulation) and analyzing how other texts form their context, but the disadvantage of this approach is that there is no method for examining how deeply the texts influence individuals and thus how likely individuals are to participate in the texts' continued circulation (Warner 98). The ELM could provide a way of empirically studying the spectrum of engagement levels audiences may have with a circulating communication, because the ELM measures individuals' reactions to texts and the likelihood that they will think further about the text's message.

The ELM is a dual-route cognitive theory of "attitude change," which is a term ELM researchers use interchangeably with persuasion (as I will also do). Social Psychology has a significant history of attempting to reduce persuasion to a set of variables,[1] and the ELM organizes those vari-

---

1. Referencing the "variables" that the ELM studies without an exhaustive treatment of them may seem unsatisfying, but I am holding back the lengthy discussion required to fully explore the variables because it would be of limited use to the purpose of this chapter. I am confident that the present chapter's basic description of the ELM and its consistent folding in of example variables provides enough information about the ELM to understand its merits for rhetorical studies, but interested readers may appreciate knowing that the variables that the ELM (and Social Psychology in general) considers are separated into the categories of credibility (expertise, trustworthiness, attractiveness/likableness, power, speech of speech, demography, majority/minority status, similarity to receiver, and number of sources), message (issue relevance/importance, position/discrepancy, conclusion drawing, use of rhetorical questions, argument

ables into a coherent account of message processing ("Attitude Change" 325). Put simply, the ELM holds that discrete variables about a message's source, its content, its applicability to its recipient, and the situation in which a recipient is exposed to the message determine how much cognitive energy a recipient will spend thinking about (or "elaborating") a message. Situations with a high elaboration likelihood are those in which the recipient is willing and able to think about a message in depth, such as a doctor's office visit in which a physician explains simply to a patient why he needs to lower his blood pressure. In ELM language, the source, message, context, and recipient variables of such a situation all reflect that the message is likely to be "centrally processed," or carefully weighed by the receiver. The recipient has the desire and ability to think about the doctor's message about his blood pressure, and so it is likely that the patient will spend time thinking about the message after he hears it ("The Elaboration Likelihood Model" 41).

Because of the cognitive concentration involved, the ELM contends that central processing yields a longer-lasting attitude change than "peripheral processing," the alternative route that is followed when a receiver does not have the inclination or ability to weigh a message carefully. Peripheral processing yields attitude change through simpler heuristics, such as the number of arguments for an idea or whether the message comes from a trusted source. Thus, if the patient in the above example lacked the time or ability to think about his doctor's statement that his blood pressure was high, then the message would be peripherally processed and he might believe he has high blood pressure just because his doctor said so (or not at all, depending on his faith in his doctor). In fact, an example of an ELM experiment would be to change a select variable such as the time that a recipient has to process a message and then see how it affects the patient's acceptance of the message and its persistence in his mind over time. In similar experiments that ELM scholars have done, the lack of concerted thought in peripheral processing has been found to give peripheral processing only a tenuous effect on attitude

---

quality, argument quantity, positive versus negative framing of arguments, fear/threat appeals, emotion versus reason in messages, one- versus two-sided messages, and message organization), recipient (attitude accessibility, issue-relevant knowledge, gender, age, personality/skills, intelligence, self-esteem, self-monitoring, and need for cognition), and context variables (distraction, audience reactions, forewarning of position, forewarning of persuasive intent, anticipated discussion or interaction, message modality, mood, and repetition of the message) ("Attitude Change" 344–66).

change, one which could be replaced by future messages as easily as the first message was accepted (Petty and Caccioppo 13). For the peripheral-route blood pressure patient, it might only take a special on Oprah about how doctors overdiagnose high blood pressure for him to stop believing he has high blood pressure. The new message wipes out the old because the patient initially only processed the message using a peripheral cue (his level of trust in his doctor) which left him open to counter-messages providing different peripheral cues (perhaps his level of trust in famous people and the number of arguments per side, if Oprah had a panel of doctors saying high blood pressure is overdiagnosed).

Thus, we could say that the ELM is in fact a variable-driven method of studying the cognitive effects of the conditions of circulation, including both textual and extra-textual elements. The ELM could provide us with an experimental method of examining the contents and conditions that affect how texts are transmitted throughout a culture. Scholars have already used the ELM to study issues such as the affection and repulsion that prominent religious imagery in texts produce on readers (Dotson and Hyatt), the influence that electronic media have on group decision-change as compared to printed media (Di Blasio and Milani), and how one's personal involvement in ecological issues affects one's attitudes toward the environment (Noe and Hammitt). In these studies, the ELM lets researchers examine how these elements affect the likelihood that a circulating message will be meaningfully considered by one exposed to it, and allows researchers to use empirical research to test the magnitude of the effects. For example, Di Blasio and Milani found that discussions among groups carried out via a computer chat function appeared to yield more central route processing than discussions carried out face to face (808). In other words, decision-making over computer chat led to more information-intensive decision-making, with fewer changes in opinion throughout. This focus on the conditions of a message's transmission extends past our currently popular method of focusing on textual analysis to understand circulation, and expands our vocabulary for talking about how circulation functions. Specifically, the empirical attention to the conditions of communication (media, in the case of Di Blasio and Milani) could be of great use to rhetorical studies in general and circulation studies in particular.

I will also discuss the obstacles to bringing the ELM into rhetorical studies, especially in terms of the differences in the two fields' paradigms. Rhetorical studies tends to focus on the moment of persuasion, whereas the goal of the ELM is to identify the longevity of a message's influence. This difference in temporal foci is bound up with a difference in perspective: rhetorical studies tends to focus on the perspective of the writer doing the persuading, whereas the ELM focuses on a message's effects on an audience. These differences run deep, largely due to rhetorical studies' roots in classical rhetoric and the ELM's origins in experimental psychology, but I argue that they are not unbridgeable. In fact, circulation represents an example of rhetorical studies' interest in persuasive influence past the initial moment of an audience's exposure to a message, and I will argue that circulation is but one of the areas in which rhetorical studies could benefit from the ELM, and vice versa.

The ELM rose to prominence in the late 1970s because it organized the scattered research on the external variables of attitude change from the 50s and 60s into a flexible process of attitude change ("Attitude Change" 325). Rather than one type of attitude change resulting from one possible interaction with variables, as previous research had posited, the ELM is a dual-process model that postulates central and/or peripheral cognitive processing of information, with a continuum enveloping the two (Wegener and Petty 178). The theory revolves around the seven postulates that have been at the core of the ELM since its creation (Choi and Salmon 61):

1. People are motivated to hold correct attitudes.

2. Although people want to hold correct attitudes, the amount and nature of issue-relevant elaboration in which they are willing or able to engage to evaluate a message varies with individual and situational factors.

3. Variables can affect the amount and direction of attitude change by (a) serving as persuasive arguments, (b) serving as peripheral cues, and/or (c) affecting the extent or direction of issue and argument elaboration.

4. Variables affecting motivation and/or ability to process a message in a relatively objective manner can do so by either enhancing or reducing argument scrutiny.

5. Variables affecting message processing in a relatively biased manner can produce either a positive (favorable) or negative (unfa-

vorable) motivational and/or ability bias to the issue-relevant thoughts attempted.

6. As motivation and/or ability to process arguments is decreased, peripheral cues become relatively more important determinants of persuasion. Conversely, as argument scrutiny is increased, peripheral cues become relatively less important as determinants of persuasion.

7. Attitude changes that result mostly from processing issue-relevant arguments (central route) will show greater temporal persistence, greater prediction of behavior, and greater resistance to counterpersuasion than attitude changes that result mostly from peripheral cues. (Petty and Cacioppon 5)

For an individual to centrally process a message, that person must have the motivation and ability to do further processing after the initial exposure to the text. In central processing, the person compares the merits of the information to which they have been exposed with counterarguments on the topic, and as a result either changes their attitude about the issue wholly, in part, or not at all (Petty, Wheeler, and Bizer 138). Central processing has always been the ELM's focus and gold standard for attitude change, as more concerted effort in considering the (especially logical) value of information leads to a longer lasting attitude change, in ELM researchers' view (O'Shaughnessy and O'Shaughnessy 126).

The text is peripherally processed if it lacks any features relevant to the person's life or if an individual is unable to weigh the logical merits of an argument. This would happen if the topic under discussion is explained by advanced physics terms that the recipient is unfamiliar with, for example, or a recipient lacks the time in which to think further before being interrupted by additional cognitive duties. Because the receiver does not have the ability and motivation to process the message centrally, the message is peripherally processed. Peripheral processing of a message relies on simple cues or heuristics for deciding whether the information is worth changing the receiver's attitude. The receiver may be swayed by the number of arguments for a side, or the reputation of the person making the argument, or even the mechanisms found in classical conditioning studies, which the ELM classifies as part of peripheral processing ("Attitude Change" 338). Attitude change that comes from peripheral processing is quicker and less effortful (and less critical, in terms of the logical rigor of the information); but it can also be wiped away just as quickly by future peripherally processed information (Petty and Cacioppo 21).

The simple-sounding requirements for central processing are complicated by additional roles that variables can play.[2] In postulate five, we read that variables that increase or decrease an individual's likelihood to elaborate on a topic can also bias the person's thinking in a particular way. This includes situations in which a text has ramifications for oneself, as we can imagine in the example of an individual reading a newspaper article about whether their own job is important. Depending on the context, the experience of reading the article might encourage positive bias in their central processing or might discourage any central processing at all. If a postal worker reads a story about the continued relevance of the USPS, her personal stake in the enterprise could motivate her to believe the article and dig into its details (central processing), or to take its points as a given and skim it (peripheral processing).

The body of ELM research has also led to critical looks at the ELM. Specifically, the number of variables at play whenever an individual encounters a potentially persuasive situation is so high that it leads one to question the ELM as a model. Can any model hope to account for how all these variables work, much less predict the outcome of a scene of attitude change? Proponents of the ELM are quick to remind readers that the ELM is not meant to be a predictive model but an organizational one, creating a basic structure in which research can be done on attention and persuasion (Wegener and Petty 199). The focus is on productivity, and these postulates are designed to give a place and coherence to the specific research questions that researchers are interested in pursuing. Then empirical research can isolate the effects of variables at different points in the persuasion process and determine the nature and degree of their effects on the receiver's attitude. Indeed, many contemporary studies of the ELM are interested in how specific variables work in a given communication context, such as the influence of source credibility on the communication of public health information.[3]

---

2. The continuum of processing is additionally complicated by the potential of simultaneous processing at multiple levels of centrality-periphery, a prospect that the ELM never quite explains (Choi and Salmon 52). On the other hand, this potential is partly explained by the fact that the ELM calls itself an organizational rather than a cumulative or predictive model (Wegener and Petty 199).

3. In the research for this article, the author most readily found health communication to be the field of inquiry in which ELM theories are being utilized.

For example, a typical ELM article is Jones, Sinclair, and Couneya's "The Effects of Source Credibility and Message Framing on Exercise Intentions, Behaviors, and Attitudes," which studies the influence of Source Credibility and Message Framing variables on students' likelihood to exercise after exposure to pro-exercise messages from expert and non-expert sources. In their experiment, Jones et al., had students read accounts of the importance of exercise and then monitored whether the students followed up by exercising or not. The experimenters isolated Source Credibility and Message Framing as variables in their experiment plan and verified their success in doing so by questionnaires that the students filled out. The experiment did find that students who read accounts of the importance of exercise written by experts were more likely to actually exercise than students who received the same information written by a non-expert. Positive message framing from an expert source had a greater impact on the message receiver's behavior than negatively-framed messages from a non-expert (Jones, Sinclair, and Couneya 188).

This sort of study, in which established ELM variables are tested in particular situations, is common in social psychology and other fields that have embraced the ELM's focus on central processing, such as health communication. Such fields are interested in directly impacting the attitudes and practices of audience members through the cultivation of content, sources, and contexts for receipt that will allow the message to be carefully weighed by the receiver. The ELM is also popular in advertising and consumer sciences, however, which are more interested in the peripheral route to attitude change. For example, Dotson and Hyatt's "Religious Symbols as Peripheral Cues in Advertising," mentioned above, looks exclusively at the use of a cross in product advertisements and its attitude effect on people who view themselves as religious. They were surprised to find that people who identified as religious and had low involvement with the product (when they did not see it as relevant to themselves) had a less favorable feeling toward the product when the ad included a cross, but religious people who had an interest in the product were marginally more positive toward the product when the ad had a cross (63).

ELM studies have become intertwined enough with health communication studies that articles on the two appear in social psychology periodicals, public health journals, and communication journals. See Jones, Sinclair, and Couneya and Angst and Agarwal for examples.

The question of what the ELM has to offer rhetorical studies is bound up with the ways that they differ from each other. This is difficult to write about, as rhetorical studies is not nearly as unified in its methods or theories as the ELM is, but I will attempt to draw broad but accurate strokes. One major difference is the way that the two fields treat the elements of a persuasive event or message, including both aspects of the message itself, like logical rigor, and contextual aspects of the message's transmission, such as the audience's mood. The ELM considers the quality of information in a message to be its most potentially persuasive element, and this is the one that is examined in the central route to persuasion. Other aspects of a message's transmission, like its emotional content or the credibility of its source, affect persuasion in the peripheral route rather than the central one, as simpler mental heuristics in the place of logical argument. As long as the receiver has the ability to carefully analyze a message carefully, emotion and source credibility exert a lighter persuasive hold than the quality of the information. In rhetorical studies, however, source credibility, emotion, and argument quality are bound together in the overall effectiveness of persuasion. Although they may affect persuasion differently, they have not been explicitly parsed into separate categories of persuasion with different, quantified levels of hold on their audiences. They are often referred to as the "rhetorical triangle," a metaphor that suggests balance rather than hierarchy. Recent work in rhetorical studies have only deepened their interdependence, holding that *ethos* (source credibility) and *pathos* (emotion) are always bound up with *logos* (information quality) and that *ethos* and *pathos* contribute to and benefit from the force of *logos*'s persuasiveness rather than being simply extricable from it (see Gross and also Smith). A multi-step flow chart detailing the likelihood that *logos* be the primary driver of a message recipient's degree of persuasion, such as are often drawn in ELM articles, is foreign to rhetorical studies' holistic sense of persuasion.

That "sense of persuasion" is another difference between the two paradigms: rhetorical studies tend to focus on the sender of the message rather than the receiver, while the ELM focuses on the receiver rather than the sender. Aristotle's *Rhetoric*, after all, is still a foundational text of rhetorical studies and is explicitly a book to help orators succeed in their endeavors, in addition to understanding how persuasion works. This focus is echoed when looking through *The Rhetorical Tradition*, an anthology of writing on rhetorical studies from throughout history, often used in History of Rhetoric classes in rhetorical studies programs.

The excerpts in that book, from Gorgias in ancient Greece to Stanley Fish in the contemporary US, are focused on how rhetoric works from a rhetor's perspective, not that of the audience. Audiences are discussed in detail, but for the benefit of rhetors who must persuade those audiences. The Elaboration Likelihood Model, on the other hand, is explicitly focused on the effects an audience experiences from their reception of a message. Even the ELM name reflects this: the "elaboration likelihood" is found entirely in the receiver, brought on by a communication that was launched by a sender two layers removed from the theory's name. This reflects the empirical roots of the theory: just as accounts of scientific experiments are often written in third-person perspective, isolating the results of an experiment away from the individual contributions of scientists, the ELM strives to isolate the effects of variables away from any particular situation or sender (except where it can discover how aspects of a certain situation or sender work in general). For this reason, ELM studies are very unlikely to become preoccupied with "invention," the composition process that goes into a persuasive message, though it is a major term in rhetorical studies.

The timeline of persuasion also differs in rhetorical studies and the ELM. A key focus in rhetorical studies is *kairos,* or the moment of persuasion. This again is in keeping with the classical roots of rhetorical studies; *kairos* pre-dates Aristotle, but nevertheless he also mentions the kairotic encounter between rhetor and audience (Kinneavy 66). The focus of the ELM, though, is in the likelihood that the recipient will cognitively elaborate on the message after that moment has passed. It is here that we see why "attitude change" is used in the ELM; "persuasion" sounds like a final outcome, but "attitude change" sounds less so in that it can change back. "Attitude change" persists over time. It is also telling that when rhetorical studies discusses the moment after *kairos,* that discussion is not about continued persuasion but *metanoia,* the regret of not effectively seizing the moment (Myers 1). The moment has passed, and rhetoric has done its work; what is left is not relevant for rhetorical studies but still very relevant to the ELM.

These are significant differences. In general, rhetorical studies has a more holistic view of persuasion, not separated into types or degrees, and it holds that persuasion mostly occurs in the moment of transmission rather than afterwards. The ELM separates persuasive events' stimuli and their effects, holds that different stimuli yield different cognitive reactions and thus different degrees of persuasion, and this persuasion is perhaps most interesting for the extent that it lingers after exposure, including the degree of elaboration and the resistance it provides to counter-arguments.

But rather than see these differences as irreconcilable, I see them as potentially productive of cross-disciplinary discussions. Some elements can be more or less directly shared: the idea of degrees of persuasion could easily find a place in rhetorical studies, as could the idea of persuasion resisting counter-arguments or not. These ideas run counter to some of the assumptions of rhetorical studies, but that appears to be an issue of perspective. Perhaps in Ancient Greece the differential, long-term impact of rhetors' messages was not built into rhetorical paradigms, but that should not limit our present work, given the availability of new tools. The difference in treatment of persuasion variables is a deeper rift between the fields, but I can imagine rhetorical studies scholars collaborating on interesting theoretical work with ELM researchers on the connections that rhetorical studies has made between emotion and logic (again, as in the work of Gross and Smith) and possible ways of empirically testing such connections.

To consider what a hybrid rhetorical studies-ELM study might look like, I turn now to the specific topic of circulation. Circulation has somewhat recently been on the tips of many rhetorical theorists' tongues. *Rhetoric and Public Affairs* had a special issue on circulation in 2012, and many scholars have found it to be a useful interpretive lens for understanding how discourse forms public opinion as texts travel among people.[4] Linda Flower discussed circulation throughout her 2008 *Community Literacy and the Rhetoric of Public Engagement,* and defined it as "the movement and transformation of ideas, language, and attitudes in an ongoing discourse that gives the nod to what went before and anticipates a new response" (37). Her language there illustrates how circulation forms the discursive field that underlies any public rhetorical situation we study, and how circulation has been a key aid in rhetoric's investigation of communication networks.

Michael Warner's 2001 *Publics and Counterpublics* is the primary root of rhetoric's recent discussions of circulation, and in that book he holds that publics form merely by individuals paying attention to circulating discourses. Authors address texts to a public, ascribing to them certain norms and beliefs, and when audience members pay attention

---

4. See also Bennett, Tell, Lundberg, Finnegan and Kang, Asen, Olson, Ryder, Weisser, and Farmer, among others.

to the texts a public is formed (87). Accordingly, we can identify a public's norms and its relations to other publics and counterpublics in circulation's "punctual rhythms," which are specific moments of textual issuance and reception (95). For example, Warner recounts an eighteenth-century periodical in which the voice of the publication rebuffs a proto-feminist group's de-pruding event as "essentially unpublic" (110). In doing so, the publication strengthens its ideology of polite publicness and estranges the proto-feminist group's crusade against modesty from the public sphere represented by the periodical and its readership (110). This is not as simple a marginalization as banning someone from the public, or even as simple as taking away one's right to speak, but it is a specific power operation that curtails the public space for moving past female modesty. Thusly, circulation widens or narrows the possibilities for deliberation of specific issues in the public.

In keeping with this, the articles in the 2012 circulation issue of *Rhetoric and Public Affairs* analyze the circulatory impact of individual texts on larger issues like presidential oratory, neocolonialism, and nonfiction films, as well as looking at the general mechanism of circulation in specific publics. Jenny Edbauer Rice's 2005 "Unframing Public Models of Distribution: From Rhetorical Situation to Rhetorical Ecologies" takes this tack also, using public texts that assimilate the Keep Austin Weird slogan as indicators of the dynamics found in Austin's rhetorical ecology at that time (16). In all these cases, Warner's take on circulation has been useful in allowing rhetorical studies to focus on textual analysis to determine how circulation forms publics and disseminates specific ideas within them.

In such studies, we posit constituents' attention and attitude changes primarily by indicators in the discrete punctual rhythms, but with the ELM we could do much more. The ELM's theory of levels of persuasion could make the ELM a special aid to circulation studies, as adding (even basic) gradations of cognitive activity to our understanding of attention can lead us to new insights and questions about how circulation functions. Attention in circulation studies is treated about as statically as persuasion in rhetorical studies; people are paying attention or they are not, just as people are persuaded or they are not. Warner acknowledges that "between ideally alert publics and really distracted people there will always be a gap . . . because publics are only realized through active uptake," but he does not associate this difference with any significance in how publics operate (87). This is possibly due to the fact that such difference seems impossible to measure given the discursive analysis meth-odology of circulation studies (87). But the ELM's idea that attitudes change due to low cognitive processing (and attention) as well as high gives nuance to our idea that circulation provides its public with specific deliberative options. If we concur with the ELM's account that attitude changes derived from central processing have greater resistance to future rebuttals than peripheral processing, the ELM's way of studying attitude change would then provide us with a better sense of the comparative persistence that specific circulating texts of public discussion will have in the minds of individuals over time. The ELM is essentially a mechanism for theorizing and empirically recognizing the "active uptake" that War-ner mentioned above (we might say the ELM is a method for studying how actively the argument is taken up), and so with the right study we could potentially investigate the cognitive effects of this distraction on persuasion and public formation (87).

What would such a study look like? Obviously, we could import the ELM's method of studying the impact that certain conditions of a mes-sage's transmission have on receivers' propensity to think further on that message (the elaboration likelihood, which we would equate with the recipients' sustained attention), but that would simply be replicating the study of persuasion variables that the ELM has already been doing. I believe the more interesting approach would be to meld the methodolo-gies of the ELM and circulation, and create mixed-methods studies that would involve both empirical study of persuasion and discursive analysis.

I will now describe what such a study may look like. It will be a very loose description, not only because my own experience with empirical methodologies is scant, but also in order to suggest the flexibility that such a study would have in its specific deployment. I envision a multi-stage study of not just message exposure but exposure to and subsequent recirculation of a message. First, in keeping with previous ELM studies, participants could be exposed to a message. Perhaps it would be about global warming or some other ecological issue, one that people have dif-ferent opinions and different levels of familiarity with. The immedi-ate influence of the message (if any) on the participants could then be gauged. This would likely happen through pre- and post-tests, possibly done through indirect or proxy questions that get a sense of the per-son's opinions on the issue before and after exposure. Then, the subjects would be required to compose a message about the issue for a specific audience. Perhaps they would be required to write a letter or story about global warming for their local newspaper. At this point in the study, participants are being asked to participate actively in the circulation process. After completing their writing, the participants' perspective on the issue and their relationship to it could again be examined, and the study's researchers (in keeping with circulation studies) could analyze the writing the participants did for indications of circulating discourses, looking at the facets of the topic that the subject passed on in their writing from the message they had been exposed to, as well as any content notably left out. Did the writing bear the mark of the participants' initial opinion, or is there a perceptible change? Just as importantly, does any of the language of the message they were exposed to appear in their writing, any of the reasoning or data? Researchers could also analyze the paradigm that the subject took on in their writing, and what that paradigm shares with the message to which the subject had been exposed.

Such a study would thus involve both the ELM research method of measuring the outcomes of exposure and the circulation studies method of analyzing written discourses. It would begin the process of looking at the attitudinal and discursive effects of one's ongoing engagement with an issue, as opposed to one exposure on which ELM studies have been focused or the emphasis on punctual rhythms on which circulation studies has focused. The result would be research on the function of texts' production and transmission from both a qualitative, discursive perspective and a quantitative, situational-variable perspective.

CONCLUSION

The ELM can appear at first to be a giant step backward for rhetorical studies, echoing as it does many assumptions about the discrete parts of persuasion that we have not heard since the days of Lloyd Bitzer's essay on the rhetorical situation in 1986. I suggest instead that we view other fields' work on the ELM as a sort of alternate history of rhetorical studies, emerging from an empirically-focused field excited about finding the common elements in textual exchange and driven to derive communicational strategies from their findings. While we in rhetorical studies have enriched our understanding of speech acts by problematizing their discursive, social, and material construction, ELM studies have focused specifically on the describable cognitive processes in which audiences engage as they interact with texts. Coming to ELM studies now, we have the opportunity to build into our thinking the nuance that the ELM has found in texts' conscious influence.

In circulation studies, we can borrow the ELM's assertion that recipients of messages require the ability and the motivation to understand and circulate the message to which they are exposed. Knowing the ELM's theorized differences between central and peripheral processing, we can build insights into circulation about how resistant circulating ideas are to other ideas that conflict with them. This will allow us to discuss not just circulation but the hold that circulating messages have on individuals relative to their ability and motivation to consider messages. This hold should then affect the differential level of investment that individuals have to publics and counterpublics, given that we have a new language to describe the differential effects of attention and its influence.

In a broader sense, the ELM offers a challenge to rhetorical studies: can rhetorical studies scholars try on quantitative methodologies to look at issues of persuasion that they have heretofore examined using almost exclusively qualitative methods? Are scholars in rhetorical studies ready to muster the patience required to share their theories of rhetoric with researchers in psychology, consumer studies, health communications, and other fields, given all the work that will be required to reconcile field-specific assumptions and grapple with alternate methods of evidence-gathering? Obviously, this patience will also be required of the scholars in other fields that have studied the ELM. Can they work to find common ground with rhetorical studies, given how comparatively abstract rhetorical scholars' qualitative forms of proof can seem?

If we are able to build such networks, we will avoid the siloing of disciplines that is so common to contemporary academia while taking advantage of the decades of research our respective fields have generated and that we have ignored up to this point. To put it in ELM terms, these cross-disciplinary networks could increase the ability and inclination of researchers in ELM fields and rhetorical studies to read each other's work, which would yield more central processing of the research from both areas.

WORKS CITED

Abrams, Katie and Courtney Meyers. "From Opposite Corners: Comparing Persuasive Message Factors and Frames in Opposing Organizations' Websites." *Journal of Applied Communications*, vol. 96, no. 1, 2009, pp. 54–67.

Angst, Corey M., and Ritu Agarwal. "Adoption of Electronic Health Records in the Presence of Privacy Concerns: The Elaboration Likelihood Model and Individual Persuasion." *MIS* Quarterly, vol. 33, no. 2, 2009, pp. 339–70.

Asen, Robert. "Ideology, Materiality, and Counterpublicity: William E. Simon and the Rise of a Conservative Counterintelligentsia." *Quarterly Journal of Speech*, vol. 95, no. 3, 2009, pp. 263–88.

Bennett, Jeffrey A. "Passing, Protesting, and the Arts of Resistance: Infiltrating the Ritual Space of Blood Donation." *Quarterly Journal of Speech*, vol. 94, no. 1, 2008, pp. 23–43.

Bitzer, Lloyd. "The Rhetorical Situation." *Philosophy and Rhetoric*, vol. 25, 1992, pp. 1–14.

Choi, Sejung Marina, and Charles T. Salmon. "The Elaboration Likelihood Model of Persuasion After Two Decades: A Review of Criticisms and Contributions." *The Kentucky Journal of Communication*, vol. 22, no. 1, 2003, pp. 47–77.

Davis, Diane. *Inessential Solidarity: Rhetoric and Foreigner Relations*. Kindle ed., U of Pittsburgh P, 2010. MOBI

Edbauer, Jenny. "The New 'New': Making a Case for Critical Affect Studies." *Quarterly Journal of Speech*, vol. 94, no. 2, 2008, pp. 200–12.

—. "Unframing Models of Public Distribution: From Rhetorical Situation to Rhetorical Ecologies." *Rhetoric Society Quarterly*, vol. 35, no. 4, 2005, pp. 5–24.

Farmer, Frank. "Composition Studies as a Liminal Counterpublic." *JAC*, vol. 28, no. 3–4, 2008, pp. 620–34.

Finnegan, Cara A., and Jiyeon Kang. "'Sighting' the Public: Iconoclasm and Public Sphere Theory." *Quarterly Journal of Speech*, vol. 90, no. 4, 2004, pp. 377–402.

Flower, Linda. *Community Literacy and the Rhetoric of Public Engagement*. Southern Illinois UP, 2008.

Foubert, John. *The Men's and Women's Programs: Ending Rape through Peer Education*. Taylor and Francis, 2011.

Gross, Daniel. *The Secret History of Emotions: From Aristotle's Rhetoric to Modern Brain Science*. U of Chicago P, 2007.

Heller, Erik, and Charles S. Areni. "The Effects of Conditional Indicative Language on the Comprehension and Acceptance of Advertising Claims." *Journal of Marketing* Communications, vol. 10, no. 4, 2004, pp. 229–40.

Jones, Lee W., Robert C. Sinclair, and Kerry S. Courneya. "The Effects of Source Credibility and Message Framing on Exercise Intentions, Behaviors, and Attitudes: An Integration of the Elaboration Likelihood Model and Prospect Theory." *Journal of Applied Social Psychology*, vol. 33, no. 1, 2003, pp. 179–96.

Kinneavy, James. "Kairos in Classical and Modern Rhetorical Theory." *Rhetoric and Kairos*, edited by Phillip Sipiora and James S. Baumlin, 2002, pp. 58–76.

Lundberg, Christian. "Enjoying God's Death: *The Passion of the Christ* and the Practices of an Evangelical Public." *Quarterly Journal of Speech*, vol. 94, no. 2, 2009, pp. 387–411.

Myers, Kelly A. "*Metanoia* and the Transformation of Opportunity." *Rhetoric Society Quarterly*, vol. 41, no. 1, 2011, pp. 1–18.

O'Shaughnessy, John, and Nicholas Jackson O'Shaughnessy. *Persuasion in Advertising*. Routledge, 2004.

Olson, Christa J. "Performing Embodiable Topoi: Strategic Indigeneity and the Incorporation of Ecuadorian National Identity." *Quarterly Journal of Speech*, vol. 96, no. 3, 2010, pp. 300–23.

Petty, Richard E., Jamie Barden, and S. Christian Wheeler. "The Elaboration Likelihood Model of Persuasion: Developing Health Promotions for Sustained Behavioral Change." *Emerging Theories in Health Promotion Practice and Research*. 2nd Ed, edited by Ralph J. DiClemente, Richard A. Crosby, and Michelle Kegler, Wiley, 2009, pp. 185–214.

Petty, Richard, and John T. Cacioppo. *Communication and Persuasion: Central and Peripheral Routes to Attitude Change*. Springer-Verlag, 1986.

Petty, Richard, John T. Cacioppo, and Jeff A. Kasmer. "The Role of Affect in the Elaboration Likelihood Model of Persuasion." *Communication, Social Cognition, and Affect*, edited by Lewis Donohew, Howard E. Sypher, and E. Tory Higgins. Lawrence Erlbaum Associates, 1988, pp. 117–46.

Petty, Richard E., and Duane T. Wegener. "Attitude Change: Multiple Roles for Persuasion Variables." *The Handbook of Social Psychology*. 4th ed., edited by Daniel T. Gilbert, Susan T. Fiske, and Gardner Lindzey, vol. 1, Oxford UP, 1998, pp. 323–90.

—. "The Elaboration Likelihood Model: Current Status and Controversies." *Dual-Process Theories in Social Psychology*, edited by Shelly Chaiken and Yaacov Trope, Guilford Press, 1999, pp. 41–72.

Petty, Richard E., S. Christian Wheeler, and George Y. Bizer. "Attitude Functions and Persuasion: An Elaboration Likelihood Approach to Matched Versus Mismatched Messages." *Why We Evaluate: Functions of Attitudes*, edited by Gregory R Maio and James M. Olson, Lawrence Erlbaum, 2000, pp. 133–62.

Rickert, Thomas. *Ambient Rhetoric: The Attunements of Rhetorical Being*. U of Pittsburgh P, 2013.

—. "In the House of Doing: Rhetoric and the Kairos of Ambience." *JAC*, vol. 24, no. 2, 2004, 901–27.

Ryder, Phyllis Mentzell. "Multicultural Public Spheres and the Rhetorics of Democracy." *JAC*, vol. 27, no. 3–4, 2007, pp. 505–38.

Smith, P. Christopher. *The Hermeneutics of Original Argument: Demonstration, Dialectic, Rhetoric*. Northwestern UP, 1998.

Syverson, Margaret. *The Wealth of Reality: An Ecology of Composition*. Southern Illinois UP, 1994.

Tell, Dave. "The 'Shocking Story' of Emmett Till and the Politics of Public Confession." *Quarterly Journal of* Speech, vol. 94, no. 2, 2008, pp. 156–78.

Warner, Michael. *Publics and Counterpublics*. Zone Books, 2002.

Wegener, Duane T., and Richard Petty. "Understanding the Effects of Mood Through the Elaboration Likelihood and Flexible Correction Models." *Theories of Mood and Cognition: A User's Guidebook*, edited by Leonard L. Martin and Gerald L. Clore, Lawrence Erlbaum, 2001, pp. 177–210.

Weisser, Christian. "Subaltern Counterpublics and the Discourse of Protest." *JAC*, vol. 28, no. 3–4, 2008, pp. 608–20.

18 Provocation: Networked Humanities as a Creative Collaboration

Rudy McDaniel

C reative collaboration is the distinguishing characteristic of a functional networked humanities, though teamwork may occur differently in the humanities than in the sciences. For instance, collaborative processes have not traditionally been as common in the humanities during activities such as technology development, due to increasingly outdated but prevalent cultural beliefs such as "humanities scholars work alone." However, collaboration *is* routinely undertaken in traditional scholarly avenues such as the sharing of research and ideas (Palmer 356). Further, the ability to work collaboratively is a key learning outcome for those teaching the digital humanities (DH) (Burdick et al. 134). Collaboration is necessary because a network of individuals and ideas works best when those individuals and ideas are blended together for the sake of a common mission. Creativity is necessary not only for encouraging deeper and broader forms of collaboration, but also because this collaborative blending process requires invention, novel thinking, and the translation between domains.

Each of these characteristics have previously been used to help us conceptualize creativity, which is itself difficult to define. In fact, the very act of trying to define something might be considered uncreative; words impose boundaries, as do syntax and punctuation, and one might need to draw a picture, recite a poem, act out a play, dance, or sing a song to express creativity. Indeed, due to the restrictiveness of traditional assessments of creativity, some widely-used instruments such as the Test for Creative Thinking—Drawing Production (TCT-DP) uses drawing analysis rather than verbal responses to assess creativity (Urban 272). Creativity can also be difficult to study and recognize because inspiration often strikes at odd times and during moments outside the laboratory or office; Einstein is attributed with the well-known quote "creativity is the residue of time wasted," further testifying to its unpredictable timing and the importance of allowing creativity to emerge organically.

Creativity is also sometimes difficult to extricate from other related cognitive phenomena like imagination, curiosity, and learning, making it problematic to identify amongst other activities or characteristics. Imagination can be a great source of creativity, but it is possible for one to be creative without being imaginative. For example, As John Seely Brown argues, creativity in certain contexts can be overly mechanistic and constrained, especially when done in design scenarios to try and please clients or funding agencies; in these environments, it is imagination that is more valuable for moving toward new ideas (Chaplin, location 2433). Burdick et al. mention generative imagination and iterative, lateral thinking as core competencies for the DH, but do not mention creativity by name (132–33). And one of the foremost psychological experts on creativity, Mihaly Csikszentmihalyi, describes how creativity can be used to describe "at least three different phenomena" (24). These phenomena include a usage of the word to describe people who are unusual, but bright, thinkers; to describe people who experience the world in unusual ways and who are *personally* creative, but introspective; and to describe cultural innovators such as Edison, Picasso, or Einstein who changed our culture in some significant way through their thinking and work (Csikszentmihalyi 24). What is interesting about these slight variations is the absence or presence of external validation; for instance, do we need some external expert or authority to recognize creativity, or is this something we need only to internally recognize?

Creativity within teams is even more complicated due to the distributed and asynchronous demands of many team environments and the nature of creativity. However, creativity is not only important, but vital, for collaborative DH work. Novel ideas about fundraising and soliciting community support are important for the long-term maintenance and preservation of digital projects. Inventing new ways to parse primary source documents, and making findings relevant to increasingly disinterested public audiences, require unique ideas that are also appropriate and relevant for the task. And developing new digital projects, such as games and virtual reality simulations, requires expertise not only in humanities subject domains, but also in developing creative aesthetics and strategies for disseminating those projects to their intended audiences.

Despite these definitional and conceptual challenges with creativity, a working definition is still useful for framing ideas and helping to focus our thoughts in a productive fashion. Imaginative creativity means weaving the threads of disparate techniques and ideas into a cohesive fabric that extends ideas from both camps and leads to something original. A widely used definition of creativity is the "ability to produce work that is both novel (i.e., original, unexpected) and appropriate (i.e., useful, adaptive concerning task constraints)" (Sternberg and Lubart 3). Creative activities are often studied in relation to problem-solving in specific and applied contexts, such as engineering or writing, in terms of their utility for idea generation and invention. In fact, Zhang and Kitalong note the major techniques associated with creative problem-solving (e.g., brainstorming, lateral thinking, and problem/audience analysis) are also key to the process of rhetorical invention (201). On a broader scale, creativity takes multiple forms and is experiential, revealing itself through many human activities and contexts (e.g., "technological creativity [or invention], economic creativity [entrepreneurship], and artistic and cultural creativity") all of which are "deeply interrelated" and connected to one another through "cross-fertilization and mutual stimulation" (Florida 20).

Within the humanities—which include diverse academic fields such as English, history, languages, philosophy, and the fine and performing arts, among others—a desire to be creative and to engage with other creative people is often the siren call for those disciplinary experts who are willing to function in broader intellectual networks. Creativity is also a significant and necessary characteristic for enabling and sustaining interdisciplinary teamwork. The artist who collaborates with the English professor to complete a multimodal book arts project is creative not only in the mode of production, but also in the model of collaboration. To be a good interdisciplinary teammate on a DH project, one must imagine not only her own work, but also how that work engages and affords opportunities with ideas or techniques from another field. It may be necessary to suspend one's preexisting ideas about how research and practice are done when collaborating with someone trained to use other techniques.

It is not surprising, then, that along with teamwork, creativity and imagination are already deeply embedded within existing DH work practices. Matthew K. Gold mentions that the international group 4Humanities, created in 2010, argues that digital humanists have a responsibility to advocate for the humanities due to specialized knowledge about "making creative use of digital technology to advance humanities research and teaching." Burdick et al. agree, noting the need for the DH to change relationships between production and consumption and arguing for the need for novelty in thought and action, further explaining that "epistemological defamiliarization—the 'making strange'—is an important feature of modern critical thought" (135). In a call to action for future digital humanists, William Thomas III recounts the controversies of early historical quantification research and challenges digital historians to "dream up even more highly interpretive and imaginative digital creations" (66).

We currently find creativity and imagination at work within different layers of invention, design, production, and dissemination of networked humanities research. For example, consider some examples of a few of the many areas in which creativity is found within DH projects and practices:

- Creative juxtapositions of network content, such as using geographic information systems (GIS) to analyze or assist in visualizing historical records such as census data, social surveys, or other verbal texts in pursuit of answering historical questions (Knowles 2)

- Creative problem solving with electronic archives, such as determining how to link legacy documents with images of primary source materials and their digitized transcriptions, as was done in the *Transcribe Bentham* (Terras 177) or *Charles Brockden Brown* (Kamrath et al.) projects

- Creative philosophizing and theorizing of ideas, such as the Skype dialog between a philosopher and computer scientist in which a discussion unfolds about the possibilities and potential of a digital infrastructure for the humanities (D'Iorio and Barbera 61–87)

- Creative amalgamations of thought and practice that lead to new modes of textual production, such as the carousel book, which users layering, dioramas, and bookbinding techniques to create new possibilities for both art and print (Virginiabookarts)

• Creative data-mining approaches, such as mining large data sets of literature to figure out the prominence of different cities in literature, then applying visualization techniques to convey the results (Barbosa)

• Creative development of new tools and technologies for connecting ideas or sharing data, such as the Roy Rosenzweig Center for History and New Media's development of useful tools like Zotero and Omeka at George Mason University (Morton 952)

• Creative pedagogical strategies, such as the use of digital video to create narrative projects about generational identity in diverse student populations (Banmayor 189)

• Creative thinking about the dissemination and vetting of digital research, such as the development of open peer-review paradigms and essays considering how digital research is evaluated differently than print scholarship (Cavanagh 5)

• Creative policy making (e.g., advocacy for the need for new promotion and tenure criteria for digital texts, such as respecting the original medium in which work was produced [MLA], and considering new methods for grant review panels and connecting academic work with the public)

For these reasons, I propose a definition of networked humanities that rests heavily on the need for teamwork and for creativity in thought and practice: the networked humanities is a creative collaboration between scholars and/or practitioners that generates ideas, tools, procedures, and projects to advance knowledge and improve the human condition. The word "scholars" includes faculty members working in research and teaching positions, but also undergraduate and graduate students who support DH work in so many ways. Similarly, the word "practitioners" was also deliberately chosen, rather than the word "experts," to account for professionals that may be new to the field, but skilled in a particular technical area such as programming and graphic design, or a business skill, such as securing financial resources or developing the project management infrastructure for a new project. However, this term is also inclusive of the more seasoned, expert-level practitioners with many years of DH project work in their wheelhouses. Lastly, framing the goal or purpose of the networked humanities as advancing knowledge or improving the human condition is admittedly utopian at best and naïve at worst, but such positivity and a belief in the potential of DH scholarship to meaningfully impact society may be necessary for many participants to justify the extreme effort invested into such collaborations.

This proposed definition relies upon teamwork and the sharing of knowledge, but is open enough to allow for DH work to be done by teams of scholars, industry professionals, or hybrid teams composed of both. The networks built between them connect not only disciplines, but also research methods, technological frameworks, cultures, exigencies, and politics. Incompatibilities between these areas can introduce barriers that might inhibit progress and create tensions within the group. Overcoming these challenges to create good work requires not only teamwork, but also imagination, creativity, and the willingness to work together to solve problems and investigate novel and appropriate ideas for the good of the scholarship.

WORKS CITED

Barbosa, Edgard. "Books of Cities Infographic." 2013, www.behance.net/gallery/Books-of-Cities-Infographic/9188073. Accessed 20 June 2016.

Benmayor, Rina. "Digital Storytelling as a Signature Pedagogy for the New Humanities." *Arts and Humanities in Higher Education*, vol. 7, no. 2, 2008, pp. 188–204.

Burdick, Anne, et al. *Digital_Humanities*. MIT Press, 2012.

Cavanagh, Sheila. "Living in a Digital World: Rethinking Peer Review, Collaboration, and Open Access." *ABO: Interactive Journal for Women in the Arts, 1640–1830*, vol. 2, no. 1, 2013, pp. 1–13.

Chaplin, Heather. "Q&A: John Seely Brown on Why We Should Look Beyond Creativity to Cultivate Imagination." *Leading Thinkers: Digital Media & Learning*, edited by Ray, Barbara, Sarah Jackson and Christine Cupaiuolo, 2013. Kindle file.

Csikszentmihalyi, Mihaly. *Creativity: Flow and the Psychology of Discovery and Invention*. Harper Collins, 2009.

D'Iorio, Paolo, and Michele Barbera. "Scholarsource: A Digital Infrastructure for the Humanities." *Switching Codes. Thinking through New Technology in the Humanities and the Arts*, edited by Thomas Bartscherer and Roderick Coover, U of Chicago P, 2011, pp. 61–87.

Florida, Richard. *The Rise of the Creative Class: Revisited*. Basic books, 2012.

Gold, Matthew K. *Debates in the Digital Humanities*. U of Minnesota P, 2012.

Kamrath, Mark L., et al., "The Charles Brockden Brown Electronic Archive: Mapping Archival Access and Metadata." *Archive Journal*, vol. 4, 2014, www.archivejournal.net/issue/4/archives-remixed/the-charles-brockden-brown-electronic-archive-mapping-archival-access-and-metadata/. Accessed 20 June, 2016.

Knowles, Anne Kelly. "GIS and History." *Placing History: How Maps, Spatial Data, and GIS Are Changing Historical Scholarship*, edited by Anne Kelly Knowles, ESRI Press, 2008, pp. 1–13.

MLA. "Guidelines for Evaluating Work in Digital Humanities and Digital Media." MLA, 2016, www.mla.org/About-Us/Governance/Committees/Committee-Listings/Professional-Issues/Committee-on-Information-Technology/Guidelines-for-Evaluating-Work-in-Digital-Humanities-and-Digital-Media. Accessed 22 June, 2016.

Morton, Amanda. "Digital Tools: Zotero and Omeka." *Journal of American History*, vol. 98, no. 3, 2011, pp. 952–53.

Palmer, Carole L. "Thematic Research Collections." *A Companion to Digital Humanities*, edited by Susan Schriebman, Ray Siemens, and John Unsworth, Blackwell, 2004, pp. 348–65.

Sternberg, Robert J, and Todd I. Lubart. "The Concept of Creativity: Prospects and Paradigms." *Handbook of Creativity*, edited by Robert J. Sternberg, Cambridge UP, 1999, pp. 3–15.

Terras, Melissa. "Present, Not Voting: Digital Humanities in the Panopticon." *Understanding Digital Humanities*, edited by David M. Berry, Palgrave Macmillan, 2012, pp. 172–90.

Thomas III, William G. "Computing and the Historical Imagination." *A Companion to Digital Humanities*, edited by Susan Schriebman, Ray Siemens, and John Unsworth. Blackwell, 2004, pp. 56–68.

Urban, Klaus K. "Assessing Creativity: The Test for Creative Thinking-Drawing Production (TCT-DP)." *International Education Journal*, vol. 6, no. 2, 2005, pp. 272–80.

Virginia Arts of the Book Center: A Community of Artists Exploring Books, Paper, and Printmaking. "Summer Bookmaking Intensive—Carousel Book." virginiabookarts.org/event/summer-bookmaking-intensive-carousel-book/. Accessed 21 June 2016

Zhang, Yuejiao, and Karla Saari Kitalong. "Influences on Creativity in Technical Communication: Invention, Motivation, and Constraints." *Technical Communication* Quarterly, vol. 24, no. 3, 2015, pp. 199–216.

19 Hacking the Humanities

John Jones

The digital humanities is a provocation. This provocation does not come (exclusively) from the humanities work that goes by that name, but rather it is inherent in the name itself. The digital humanities is not a reminder to scholars that they should use digital tools; indeed, digital tools are nearly ubiquitous in the humanities (Parry 432). Despite this ubiquity, however, the humanities largely behaves as if digital tools have had no effect on its work. Instead, the provocation of the digital humanities is that it challenges scholars to acknowledge—beyond the mere adoption of digital tools—that the scope of and possibilities for their work have changed and, consequently, to discover what those possibilities might be.

A networked digital humanities presents a similar provocation. Like the digital, networks are pervasive. Indeed, it is common to describe networks by emphasizing how they permeate all structures: "grasp[ing] the importance of networks," Barabási writes, involves realizing that "everything is linked to everything else" (Barabási 7). Just as digital tools have become standard for scholarly research, networks infuse the academy and humanistic studies. But there is a significant difference between networks and the digital. Where digital technology is a fairly recent phenomenon, networks, from individual social networks to communication networks, have always been a part of human society (Castells, *Rise* xviii). For this reason, the humanities is already networked, but, as with other digital technology, the ubiquity of this networking has so far done little to alter humanities work. The provocation of a networked digital humanities, then, is this: What will a humanities influenced by digital networks be?

Provocations invite provocations in return. By acknowledging the pervasiveness of networking, humanists are challenged to understand the effects of networks on their work and to provide an account of those effects. A networked digital humanities pushes scholars to imagine how the practices of the humanities might be transformed by the unique features of digital networking, including both network phenomena and the network as an abstraction that enables new ways of thinking and acting in relation to the world. In this essay, I argue that a networked digital humanities should hack the humanities, drawing on the logic of networking to create new practices within the humanities. Hacking provides an opening for the humanities to adopt from networked culture new methods of thinking and new means of understanding humanities work. In his exploration of appropriation in digital images, Rice proposes that suggestion is a fundamentally networked digital practice (Rice, "Occupying" 370). Here I describe a different form of appropriation, one that does not simply create new images or new texts but new networks. In the following I will briefly describe my use of the terms *hacking* and *networks* and introduce three versions of digital humanities work that I contrast with this networked appropriation. I then describe how the tools of network analysis can be used to create networks and highlight a few humanities projects that are currently doing so.

WHAT IS HACKING?

The term *hacking* is intimately connected to networks and computing culture, and tracking the evolution of its usage over time provides a view of changing public perceptions of that culture. Stroupe defines hacking as "tricking a system" in order to use that system "to do something it's not designed to do" (Stroupe 424). Early uses of "hacker" simply referred to obsessive computer users ("Hacker"), and even as the term evolved to include breaching networks, it was understood that "hackers who hack for fun still abide by the ethic of doing no or little harm by their exploits" (Zittrain 53). For this reason, hackers originally had a benign reputation within programming and computer science communities. Recently, however, the term has taken on more negative connotations. Rather than seeing the hacker as innovator or thrill seeker, hackers are frequently portrayed as criminals who use networks illegally. Wikileaks founder

Julian Assange, for example, is routinely described as a former hacker (Coddington 382; Fenster 761) and the US government has tried to attach the label to NSA whistleblower Edward Snowden (Benac). Recently theorists have resurrected the positive connotations of the term, using "hacktivism" to describe a broad range of protest methods that utilize "digital tools" to bring about "social and cultural change" (Lindgren and Lundström 1002).

Here, I do not advocate a networked digital humanities as either benign tinkering, criminality, or activism. Rather, I draw from these uses a more general definition of the term. Hacking names a tension between expectations and possibilities. For example, within computer systems this tension is between the intended use of hardware or software and the possibilities such technologies enact. To date, the humanities has not allowed the possibilities of networks to alter its practices. One largely untapped method of utilizing the resources of network culture in humanities work is the creation of new networks, going beyond the analysis or manipulation of networks to make systems that were not networked subject to networked logics. Such hacking is fundamentally about (re) making non-networked systems so that they are amenable to instances of networked power, and in this essay I am suggesting that creating networks can be a humanistic practice that will provide a new understanding of humanities work within a networked context.

WHAT ARE NETWORKS?

Network is a broad term with many different uses, so before I address how humanists can create new networks I will briefly describe what I mean by my use of the term. Spinuzzi ("Reading") identifies three uses of network that are relevant to this argument: network analysis, sociotechnical networks, and networked organizations. All three are concerned with interrelations within systems, yet, as Spinuzzi concludes, of the three, "[t]wo are analyses, one is a phenomenon" ("Reading"). Where network analysis and sociotechnical networks are tools for analyzing connections in systems, networked organizations exhibit networked behaviors independent of any analysis. In the following paragraphs, I will briefly address the distinctions between these three uses in more depth.

Network analysis, or network-graph analysis as I will call it, is the frame within which Barabási can identify everything being connected to everything else (Barabási 7): the mathematical investigation of relations between nodes. Yet, as Spinuzzi notes, this analysis does not change the fundamental structure of these systems. An example of this form of analysis would be citation networks, the relationships defined by citations within academic publications. Whereas a network-graph analysis of citations can yield insights into relationships in academic publishing, academic publishing is not a networked phenomenon. Power within academic publishing remains essentially hierarchical, controlled by publishers, editors, and the processes of peer review. Even though citations can be described via network analysis and this analysis can tell us something about academic influence and its spread, the actual mechanisms of that influence are not network phenomena.

Spinuzzi describes sociotechnical networks as "material assemblages . . . that interrelate in relatively stable ways" and that are composed of both "humans and nonhumans" (Spinuzzi, *Network* 46). Where network-graph analysis uses mathematical tools such as modeling to reach its conclusions, sociotechnical network analysis relies on discursive tools for analyzing interrelations within these systems, particularly qualitative description. Following Latour, Rice writes that this analysis is a "process of figuring out agency, influence, connectivity, and other factors in a given moment or situation" (Rice, "Networked Assessment" 29). Latour describes networks as "a trace left behind by some moving agent" (Latour, *Reassembling* 132), and Rice adds that "describ[ing]" these traces will "reveal unknown relationships" (Rice, "Networked Assessment" 29) and thereby give an account of the network. Examples of this form of analysis—like *Aramis* (Latour, *Aramis*) or *Network* (Spinuzzi, *Network*), book-length studies of sociotechnical network systems—attempt to account for the various actors, objects, and interactions influencing those systems.

Networked organizations are distinct from both of these forms of network analysis, as they are particular phenomena that operate according to networked logics independent of the analytical tools used to examine them. The Internet itself is an example of such a phenomenon, the open architecture of which consists of decentralized connections between autonomous and semi-autonomous hubs (cf. Castells, *Rise* 6). In contrast, Apple's App Store relies on numerous networks to connect with users, including the Internet and the private networks of cellphone carriers, yet this network is not one of openness and many-to-many connection. Rather it is one where corporate control manages all connections. Even though this store might utilize network-like features, such as recommending applications based on other user behaviors, it is a hierarchy organizationally, as the ability to add new applications or modify existing ones is tightly controlled. Although I acknowledge the distinctions between these three uses of network, in the following I argue that the tools of network analysis can be used to create new networks and provide new ways of thinking about humanities work.

Three Practices of Digital Humanities

In recent years scholars have attempted to theorize digital humanities work to address the provocations suggested by the term (cf. Gold). Here, I wish to add to these theories, arguing that acts of network creation are digital, humanistic practices related to other forms of interpretation and appropriation yet distinct from them. To provide the ground for this argument, I will briefly describe Parry and Rice's approaches to digital humanities work.

Parry outlines two approaches to the digital humanities. In the first, he criticizes uses of the term that are merely additive: that is, work that is performed with digital tools but is otherwise indistinguishable from the traditional work of the humanities. Although he acknowledges that digital tools have "significantly altered" many "scholarly activities," he argues that "the digital has done little to alter the *structure* of the humanities" (Parry 432–33). As an alternative, he suggests interrogating the effects of digital technologies from a humanistic perspective, a practice he calls digital humanism (Parry 433–34).

Although Parry makes a distinction between these two approaches— a traditional humanities aided by computers and the humanistic study of digital tools—Rice suggests an underlying similarity between them, arguing that both rely on interpretation—attempts to reveal "coded meaning" within digital texts and digital technologies (Rice, "Occupying" 361). In addition to interpretive practices, Rice suggests that the digital humanities should appropriate the products of digital culture into something new. Following Barthes, he calls this digital appropriation "mythologizing the myth" (Rice, "Occupying" 361). He writes:

> we consume and produce myths (representations); our task is not to interpret them in order to uncover their deception, but to appropriate them into new logics and communicative methods (which may or may not result in further issues of deceptive

representation) so that the mythology is recognized as part of a lager communicative act. (Rice, "Occupying" 361)

For Rice, this appropriation is not simply a form of communication, it is a networked act, demonstrating a digital practice that relies on the networks of meaning that are suggested within a text (Rice, "Occupying" 366). I follow Rice in arguing that appropriation is a fundamental digital practice, one that is evident in remix and other digital communication, but here I suggest a different form of appropriation as the foundation of a networked digital humanities. Where Rice seeks to "re-mythologize the myth" of interpretation (Rice, "Occupying" 361–62), I will describe a practice of appropriation that relies on creating new networks.

CREATING NETWORKS

As I have described, the subjects of network-graph and sociotechnical network analysis are not necessarily networked phenomena; however, the products of those analyses can become networked phenomena, forming the basis for networks that appropriate existing systems, effectively hacking those systems to make them amenable to network logics. Castells writes that "networks' programming capacity . . . ultimately depends on the ability to generate, diffuse, and affect the discourses that frame human action," adding that these discourses are intimately connected to the means by which networks "organize socialized communication" (Castells, *Communication Power* 53). Although the humanities considers the mathematical, technical, and physical properties of networks, the primary vehicle of this hacking is discourse.

In a case of network-graph analysis, when graph theorists analyze academic citations, they create databases of these citations that must be carefully assembled and formatted to permit their analysis; indeed, the existence of these "academic citation databases" (Page et al. 2) helped initiate the field (Kas 7). Databases are inherently networked, in that they encode the relationships that exist between groups of data, and the creation of such a database is itself the creation of a network.

Similarly, descriptions of sociotechnical networks have aspired to database-like connections and, consequently, network status. As Latour states, "what is represented" by this analysis—that is, the system under study—is not necessarily itself a network (Latour, *Reassembling* 118); however, in tracing the system's connections, a sociotechnical network analysis reenacts these connections like "the passage of another vehicle," highlighting relations within the system (Latour, *Reassembling* 132). Such a passage, in capturing the network in writing, is specifically connected to the database, attempting to account for all features of the sociotechnical system and the relations between them in a text. In other contexts, such databased writing has been described as "writing with sets" (Brooke 85) or "the actualization of possible connections" in a text (Brooke 80). Databased texts replace the traditional objects of such writing—the singular subject, or "one unit of the set" (Ulmer 64)—with a multitude of connections. Even though this writing is only a database in the figurative sense, it applies a networked logic to an essentially linear form, aspiring to networked status.

HACKING THE HUMANITIES

In both network-graph analysis and sociotechnical networks the product of the analysis is itself a network, for these products rely on the creation of networked structures in the form of databases, either actual or conceptual. However, I am not arguing that the creation of such databases represents a hack in itself, a transgression of the boundary between what is expected and what is possible within the humanities. Such analyses are inherently interpretive, falling within the boundaries of the hermeneutic digital humanities described by Rice ("Occupying") and Parry. Humanities scholars should study networks hermeneutically, but hermeneutic study, as Rice argues, does not represent a new form of humanities work. One reason for this is that, even though the products of network-graph and sociotechnical analysis are networked, these networks tend to remain proprietary and private, characteristics that prevent them from becoming networked phenomena. Both a sociotechnical network analysis and a network-graph database lack the potential to become networked phenomena if they are fixed in a permanent form and closed to new networked connections. To allow these networks to affect the mission of the humanities—to be hacks—they have to possesses some measure of what Castells describes as expandability and reconfigurability (Castells, *Rise* xviii).

Networked phenomena have always existed, but pre-digital networks, such as individual social networks, were restricted in their expansion because there is a cognitive limit to the number of connections that an individual can maintain in a network (boyd 16). Similarly, expanding the physical infrastructure that maintained analog networked structures like the railroad or telegraph systems was both expensive and time-consuming. These limitations led to the network properties of these systems being constrained by their hierarchical gatekeepers and ensured that reconfigurations of those networks outside of those approved by the hierarchy were severely limited. Digital technologies have allowed networks to thrive in a new way by making it possible for them to be easily altered, from adding new nodes to adjusting the connections between them (Castells, *Rise* xviii). Where adding stations to a rail system is expensive and beyond the reach of most individuals, adding connections within a digital network is relatively simple. In short, the products of network-graph and sociotechnical network analysis fall short of true hacks of the humanities—creating new versions of humanities work via the potential of networked culture—if they do not possess some level of expandability and reconfigurability that allow for them to become networked phenomena.

Wikipedia is one of the most prominent and successful examples of such a hack. From its inception, Wikipedia was a humanities project (cf. Sanger). Like academic publishing, encyclopedias and the articles they contain can be easily modeled using network-graph analysis, but encyclopedias prior to Wikipedia were hierarchically controlled and organized. In contrast, Wikipedia was designed to be expandable and reconfigurable by any user who desired to do so. Now, the publicly editable encyclopedia boasts millions of articles in hundreds of languages and is consistently one of the most visited sites on the Web. The community that developed around the site evolved particular guidelines to handle submissions, and these guidelines served to program the resulting network so that it became a reliable alternative to traditional encyclopedias, albeit one with unique affordances that emerged from those community rules.

The Wikipedia project's challenge to the authority and expertise of traditional encyclopedias was an enormous affront to the industry (cf. "Fatally Flawed"), and this hack was mediated by the technical possibilities of networking—anyone with access to the Internet could add knowledge to the encyclopedia and that knowledge could be fact-checked, edited, and proofed by anyone else. For good or ill, Wikipedia not only changed expectations regarding the processes of knowledge curation, it altered the power relations between gatekeepers of knowledge online. In short, Wikipedia used the technical possibilities of digital networks to upend a powerfully entrenched feature of humanities information sharing and knowledge-keeping.

Few projects would aspire to be as disruptive as Wikipedia has been to the encyclopedia, but a number of current humanities projects hold the promise to alter how humanities work is conducted in a networked society. The Research Exchange Index (REx) <http://researchexchange.colostate.edu/> collects descriptions of research that it organizes into "searchable fields and categories," specifically focusing on research methodologies and design, rather than the products of that research. By creating a database of these research processes, REx attempts to capture information about research that is typically unavailable, obscured, or not acknowledged in humanities work. The goal of REx is to not only make this previously trapped information accessible by collecting and networking it, but also to use it to develop new practices in writing research, including allowing researchers to identify collaborators, identify trends in research, and discover new sources of research materials. Another project, Rhetoric.io <http://rhetoric.io/>, will publish actual research data rather than analyses of that data or descriptions. Such projects, by tapping into the resources of networked culture to share previously overlooked information, and by making themselves open to continual updating and alteration, have the potential to change how humanities research is produced, disseminated, and verified.

The products of sociotechnical network analysis—typically long-form texts—can also become amenable to such network processes. CommentPress <http://www.futureofthebook.org/commentpress>, which allows for specific commenting on long-form texts that encourage readers to participate in the creation of a book and comment on the final product (cf. Fitzpatrick 92–93), and wikis, which facilitate even more detailed levels of feedback and interaction, are examples of such projects. CommentPress allows for the continual updating and revision of long-form texts, thus permitting databased texts to become expandable and reconfigurable by a networked community. Each tool provides the infrastructure to allow a long-form text to be subjected to network logics, thus enabling sociotechnical network texts the potential for disruption that other networked phenomena represent.

It is one thing to posit that a Wikipedia-like network of humanities would work, but it is another to achieve Wikipedia-like success with such a project. Just as most humanities scholarship finds only a niche audience, if it finds an audience at all, most networked digital humanities projects would see little success. The goal of a networked digital humanities, however, is not (necessarily) to increase the popularity of the humanities but rather to make humanities work inclusive of the possibilities brought about by a networked society, creating new networks and making them subject to "new logics and communicative methods" (Rice, "Occupying" 361) that provide new understandings of both the object of inquiry and the work of the humanities in general.

Conclusion

I have argued that hacking represents the tension between a norm and the technical possibilities of a system, representing the transgression of that norm by utilizing unacknowledged or neglected features of the system to bypass it. If networks are to be a feature of the digital humanities, it is necessary to hack the humanities, to alter it by deploying the affordances of network culture to reimagine humanities work. Creating networks—through analysis or other means—that are expandable and reconfigurable, and thus network phenomena themselves, is one such method. In both network-graph and sociotechnical network analysis— whether or not the original system is networked—the product of the analysis is networked, either a database of connections or a networked tracing of the system. Such networked representations are appropriations of the systems they analyze and, if they are made to be expandable and reconfigurable, have the potential to become new networked phenomena. The discourses that constitute the retracings of networks are, in their attempts to capture network activity and follow the logic of databases, a challenge to conventional methods of making meaning and conducting scholarship within the humanities and digital humanities that have the potential to become hacks of the humanities by expanding its domain of study to include the possibilities of networked culture.

Works Cited

"Fatally Flawed: Refuting the Recent Study on Encyclopedic Accuracy by the Journal *Nature*." *Encyclopædia Britannica*. corporate.britannica.com/britannica_nature_response.pdf. Accessed 30 Sep. 2006.

"Graph Theory." *Wikipedia: The Free Encyclopedia*. en.wikipedia.org/wiki/Graph_theory. Accessed 2 July 2013.

"Hacker." *Oxford English dictionary online*. 2013, www.oed.com/. Accessed18 July 2013.

Barabási, Albert-László. *Linked: The New Science of Networks*. Perseus, 2002.

Benac, Nancy. "Obama Recasts Edward Snowden as 'Hacker' in Effort to Downplay Him." *The Huffington Post*, n.d., www.huffingtonpost.com/2013/06/28/obama-edward-snowden-hacker_n_3515562.html. Accessed July 3, 2013.

boyd, danah. "Facebook's Privacy Trainwreck: Exposure, Invasion, and Social Convergence." *Convergence*, vol. 14, no. 1, 2008, pp. 13–20.

Brooke, Collin Gifford. *Lingua Fracta: Toward a Rhetoric of New Media,"* edited by Gail Hawisher and Cynthia L. Selfe. Cresskill, NJ: Hampton P, 2009.

Castells, Manuel. *Communication Power*. Oxford UP, 2009.

—. *The Rise of the Network Society*. 1996. The Information Age, vol. 1. 2nd ed. Blackwell, 2010.

Coddington, Mark. "Defending a Paradigm by Patrolling a Boundary: Two Global Newspapers' Approach to Wikileaks." *Journalism & Mass Communication Quarterly*, vol. 89, no. 3, 2012, pp. 377–96.

Fenster, Mark. "Disclosure's Effects: Wikileaks and Transparency." *Iowa Law Review*, vol. 97, no. 3, 2012, pp. 753–807.

Fitzpatrick, Kathleen. *Planned Obsolescence: Publishing, Technology, and the Future of the Academy*. New York UP, 2011.

Gold, Matthew K., editor. *Debates in the Digital Humanities*. U of Minnesota P, 2012.

Kas, Miray. "Structures and Statistics of Citation Networks." Carnegie Mellon U, 2011.

Latour, Bruno. *Aramis, or, the Love of Technology*. Translated by Catherine Porter, Harvard UP, 1996.

—. *Reassembling the Social: An Introduction to Actor-Network-Theory*. Oxford UP, 2005.

Lindgren, Simon, and Ragnar Lundström. "Pirate Culture and Hacktivist Mobilization: The Cultural and Social Protocols of #Wikileaks on Twitter." *New Media & Society*, vol. 13, no. 6, 2011, pp. 999–1018.

Page, Larry, et al., "The PageRank Citation Ranking: Bringing Order to the Web." 1998, ilpubs.stanford.edu:8090/422/1/1999–66.pdf. Accessed Nov. 14, 2011.

Parry, Dave. "The Digital Humanities or a Digital Humanism." *Debates in the Digital Humanities*, edited by Matthew K. Gold, U of Minnesota P, 2012, pp. 429–37.

Rice, Jeff. "Networked Assessment." *Computers & Composition*, vol. 28, no. 1, 2011, pp. 28–39.

—. "Occupying the Digital Humanities." *College English*, vol. 75, no. 4, 2013, pp. 360–78.

Sanger, Larry. "The Early History of Nupedia and Wikipedia: A Memoir." *Open Sources 2.0: The Continuing Evolution*, edited by Chris DiBona, Danese Cooper, and Mark Stone, O'Reilly, 2006, pp. 307–38, *http://safari.oreilly.com/0596008023*.

Spinuzzi, Clay. *Network: Theorizing Knowledge Work in Telecommunications.* Cambridge UP, 2008.

—. "Reading: The Exploit." *Spinuzzi,* spinuzzi.blogspot.com/2012/03/reading-exploit.html. Accessed Jul 8, 2013.

Stroupe, Craig. "Hacking the Cool: The Shape of Writing Culture in the Space of New Media." *Computers & Composition,* vol. 24, no. 4, 2007, pp. 421–42.

Ulmer, Gregory L. *Teletheory: Grammatology in the Age of Video.* Routledge, 1989.

Zittrain, Jonathan. *The Future of the Internet: And How to Stop It.* Yale UP, 2008. futureoftheinternet.org/. Accessed Feb. 4, 2010

20 Three Theses for an Ontology of Networks

Levi R. Bryant

In this work I explore the *material* conditions for the possibility of societies and cultures. At the outset, it's important to note that societies and cultures have a variety of conditions, both discursive and material, so clearly I won't be able to address them all here. If I here emphasize *material* conditions, then this is because the material requirements for societies and cultures often go overlooked by the humanities and social sciences. Our tendency in the humanities is to focus on the discursive—on meaning, signs, norms, ideologies, and so on—largely ignoring the material requirements for social relations and cultural formations. We treat the social world as a text to be deciphered. This, of course, comes as no surprise given that those of us in the humanities work with texts and cultural artifacts as our primary evidences. Nor am I suggesting that the discursive is not an essential component of social relations and cultural formations. Rather, I want to claim that (1) without the material, discursive formations as we know them are not possible at all (which is different than claiming that the material *determines* discursive formations), and (2) that indifference to the material blinds us to important mechanisms of social power and control that can't be explained in terms of ideology, and therefore we are led to miss half of why people tolerate oppressive circumstances as well as valuable possibilities for strategic intervention to produce emancipatory change.

My thesis—and it's not particularly original, nor, I hope, difficult to discern after a moment's reflection—is that social relations and cultural formations are not possible without networks and that networks are *material*. When I evoke the term *material*, I do so in the literal sense descended from the Greek atomist Democritus. I mean nothing more than "physical stuff," whatever that might happen to be. Following Latour in his article "Can We Get Our Materialism Back, Please?" (Latour 2007), I am thus not using the term *materialism* in the sense that we encounter it in neo-Marxist and Foucaultian thought. By "neo-Marxist thought," I have in mind pre-Habermasian critical theory as exemplified in the work of Adorno and Horkheimer, as well as the cultural Marxism of the French Althusserian school. As Latour argues, "historical materialism" there has come to mean little more than analyzing cultural artifacts in terms of the reigning ideology of the time, which is to say, in terms of the *discursive*. The case is similar with Foucaultian analysis of practices. It is not that these thinkers are mistaken—I certainly consider myself to be working in their tradition—but that the sense of materiality they evoke fails to get at the a-signifying, non-discursive, brute materiality of nonhuman material things and the power they exercise in social assemblages. Fortunately, this tendency to overlook the material in favor of the discursive has begun to change through the work of thinkers such as Haraway, Latour, Deleuze, and Guattari; the new materialist feminists; media theorists such as Kittler, McLuhan, and Ong; assemblage theorists such as Manuel DeLanda; and the object-oriented ontologists. While it is by no means dominant within the academy, a new appreciation of materiality *as matter* and the power that matter exercises has begun to emerge within social and political thought.

Before proceeding to discuss the theses I will propose, it's important to note that the question of the possibility of societies and cultures is a question of entropy. Often, the first thing that comes to mind upon hearing the term *entropy* is the idea of heat death. Under this conception, entropy is the tendency of closed systems to dissipate energy necessary for work over time, eventually becoming unable to engage in any further operations. However, in information theory, entropy signifies something a bit different. As the sociologist and autopoietic systems theorist Niklas Luhmann puts it,

> . . . a system is entropic if information about one element does not permit inferences about others. The system is entropic for itself if in the process of reproduction, thus in the replacement of

elements that have passed away, any possible successive element is equally probable. In other words, in entropy connectivity is not straitened and time is not won by the fact that not everything comes into consideration. (Luhmann 1995, 49)

In information theory, entropy is a measure of probability. A system is highly entropic if, given one element, no inferences can be made to another element or it is possible for one element to be related to *any* other element. Somewhat counter-intuitively, information theorists say that highly entropic systems are characterized by maximal information. By contrast, a system has a low degree of entropy if, given one element, it is possible to make probable inferences to another element. For example, in the English language, there is a good probability that we will find the letters like "e," "i," "o," and so on following "b," while it is less probable that we'll encounter "z" following "b."

Based on the foregoing, we can thus see why the concept of *entropy* is important to the humanities and social and political thought. Take, for example, hermeneutics—especially what Ricoeur called "the hermeneutics of suspicion" (Ricoeur 1977, 32–36)—and semiotics. An interpretation is also a statement about the entropy of a text or cultural artifact. It is the claim that there's a high probability that a particular element—say, a sign—is related to another element. The case is the same with societies. A society or culture is characterized by differentiation, which is to say that we find class, religious, occupational, racial differentiations, and so on—distributions of a regular nature. Everyone knows this. Yet, what we're saying when we say this is that societies are low entropic systems. We're saying that given one element—say a person of a particular class— we can make probable inferences to how this element is related to other elements. In short, we're saying that societies and cultures are organized systems. This is another name for power. Power would be those operations that maintain the low entropic state of social systems. Alternatively, power is the mechanism by which a society reduces entropy.

The question, of course, is that of how this is possible? Why do societies and cultures not disintegrate into chaotic Brownian motion? How do they take on an order, a regularity, that maintains itself across time. As Althusser noted in his famous essay on ideology, " . . . in order to exist, every social formation must *reproduce* the conditions of its production at the same time as it produces, in order to be able to produce" (Althusser 86; emphasis added). In other words, societies and cultures are not something that are just there or given; rather, if they are to exist across time and space they must overcome entropy. Time: from moment to moment and across duration, societies and cultures must find a way to maintain the relations among elements of which they are composed. Space: across large geographical expanses, societies and cultures must find ways to copy, iterate, or reproduce patterns of relations between elements. This is true both of the patterned relations among elements in discursive formations (signs), and differentiated relations among human and nonhuman bodies at the level of physicality; what Deleuze and Guattari referred to as the planes of expression and content respectively (Deleuze and Guattari Chaps. 4–5). Time and space both pose problems of entropy to organized social assemblages, and the resolution of these problems will necessarily have a material component and will require operations or activities. While the discursive is clearly a necessary element in overcoming the entropy that threatens societies and cultures, the humanities and social and political thought have a tendency to ignore and overlook the role played by the sheer materiality of time and space, treating semiotic entities as if they can leap across time and space without any trouble.

With these remarks about entropy, time, and space firmly in mind, we can begin to explore some theses concerning the material conditions for the possibility of societies and cultures.

THESIS 1: People must relate for societies and cultures to form and exist.

Everyone, of course, knows this. Societies and cultures are networks. However, the point here is that relations aren't things that are simply there, but that they must be forged or produced. According to the OED, a network is "[a]ny netlike or complex system or collection of interrelated things, as topographical features, lines of transportation, or telecommunications routes" (OED 2003). Luhmann notes that in social systems, "[t]he connections among relations must . . . somehow be regulated" (Luhmann 23). This is the question of how social systems overcome entropy. A social system is not a system in which *every* element is related to *every other* element, but rather is a system in which elements are related in particular ways and in which relations unfold in a particular order in time or duration.

Moreover, Luhmann will go on to say that for complex systems such as societies, we encounter " . . . immanent contrasts in the immanent constraints in the elements' connective capacity, [such that] it is no longer possible at any moment to connect every element with every other element" (Luhmann 24). A society or culture in which all elements were related to all other elements would be one characterized by maximal entropy. In other words, it would be a system in which any other element had an equal probability of appearing temporally and spatially in relation to any other element. Such a society would be characterized by what Quentin Meillassoux has called "hyper-chaos" (Meillassoux 64). At the level of the plane of expression, all discursivity and language would be impossible because there would be an equal probability of any element being related to any other element. All interpretation would be impossible because there would be no ordering relations in texts, linguistic acts, and cultural artifacts. At the level of the plane of content or material bodies, there would be no differentiated relations between classes, gendered bodies, religious groups, ethnicities, occupations, and so on. Given that we see nothing like this except in extreme circumstances such as those in New Orleans following Hurricane Katrina, it follows that relations between elements in societies are selective.

However, the more important point is that *relations do not come for free*. The relations characteristic of societies and cultures are not diaphanous entities like Greek *daimons* or angels, able to leap over time and space without constraint, but are constrained by the physics that constrains all matter and information. While networks differ amongst themselves, networks are not a new type of society. All societies, everywhere and always, have been network societies. If there is something new in network theory, ecology, or assemblage theory, it is the attention it draws to the *materiality* of social relations. The paths through which people relate materially and discursively are material; and, in being material, must conquer the physics of time and space. If I were to name one thing repeatedly overlooked by the humanities and social sciences, it would be this. Just as Heidegger teaches us in his analysis of tools (Heidegger Div. 1, Chap. 3), our tendency is to overlook the materiality of the medium with which we work—Heidegger uses the example of the hammer—so as to attend to its meaning or discursive content. This leads us to treat the material entities of the world as a sort of prose to be interpreted in a manner not unlike that described by Foucault with the pre-Modern world (Foucault Chap. 2), ignoring the way in which a-signifying and non-discursive agencies serve as both conditions for social relations and contribute to the form that social relations take.

The materiality required for social relations and cultures is no small matter, for certain forms of life and relation will not be possible without certain material mediums. James Gleick, for example, notes that railroads required standard time to be feasible (Gleick 148). Without being able to precisely coordinate the times of trains, there would be endless crashes. Such coordination required a particular material medium that could convey information at a rate that exceeded the speed of trains: the telegraph. Similarly, the markets characteristic of contemporary global capitalism would not be possible without fiber-optic cables, satellites, the internet, and transatlantic cables, allowing distance to be surmounted in an almost instantaneous fashion. Contemporary capitalism is not just a set of ideological beliefs, nor merely a set of practices, but is also a material network that can only exist under very specific material conditions. Networks are like spider webs that capture us in their relations. Attempting to overturn something like capitalism through discursive critique alone—while necessary—misses the material networks that trap us in their grasp.

The foregoing leads to a second thesis:

THESIS 2: The form that societies and cultures take will partially be a function of the material medium through which social relations are forged.

In *De Rerum Natura*, Lucretius writes,

> . . . I now begin
> To teach you about images [simulacra], so called,
> A subject of most relevant importance.
> These images are like a skin, or film,
> Peeled from the body's surface, and they fly
> This way and that across the air . . . (Lucretius 120)

As a materialist, Lucretius faced the question of how bodies at different locations in space could interact with one another as in the case of a person perceiving a tree over yonder. For the materialist, perception is a deeply mysterious thing, for things must causally interact to affect one another, yet the object perceived is over there while we are over here. How can something that I don't directly touch affect my eyes, ears, and nose? Lucretius's ingenious solution was to argue that objects exude a sort of invisible bark or film—what he calls images or simulacra—that are material, yet very fine and that travel through the air and affect our various sense-organs. Like invisible ghosts flying through the air, Lucretius's world is a world pervaded by invisible waves proliferating in all directions. While we now know that Lucretius was wrong in the details, he was nonetheless right in spirit. It's not that things exude films that travel through the air, but rather light bounces off entities and that our vocal cords, tongue, lips, and teeth create vibrations that travel across space.

Now the important lesson to draw from Lucretius is that these simulacra are material entities that are bound by the physics of time and space. Information, for example, is not simply an iterable and incorporeal pattern, but is also a material entity that physically travels through space. The (current) upper limit for the speed at which information can be exchanged is 186,282 mps (though this will change if we build reliable quantum entanglement technology), but generally the rates are much lower depending whether we're talking about the speed of sound, or information conveyed by automobiles, airplanes, horseback, and so on. What we are talking about here is essentially the *speed* at which social and cultural *relations* can *occur* given the medium that a society uses to transport messages. In other words, relations aren't something that are simply *there*, but are things that must be continuously forged across time and space. Forging relations requires *media* understood in the most material, non-discursive sense possible.

While the material medium through which relations are forged and maintained does not *determine* the form a society and culture will take, it does play a significant role in what is possible for a society and culture. As McLuhan has taught us, media both afford and constrain relations (McLuhan and McLuhan 98–99). In *Understanding Media*, he gives the nice example of electric light (McLuhan 8). Electric light *affords* a new form of social relation. With it, night is no longer menacing and dangerous, but becomes the opportunity for a romantic evening stroll, nighttime baseball games become possible, it becomes possible to run factories and labor for twenty-four hours a day, and so on. The materiality of the medium opens new forms of social relation.

The materiality of media takes two forms. On the one hand, it takes the form of mediums of transport: sound-waves, roads, rivers, air travel, fiber optic cables, satellites, and so on. The historian Braudel, for example, talks about how the development of markets and capitalism was impeded by the absence of roads allowing separated cities and villages to interact in a timely fashion (Braudel 415–429). The presence of roads affords certain possibilities, while the presence of overgrown wild lands, mountain ranges, deserts, jungles, oceans, and turbulent rivers constrain relations. In other words, the mediums that inhabit networks are not simply technological, but also include natural and geographical features. Just as technologies contribute to what relations are forged, so too do geographical features such as ocean currents contribute to what comes to be related to what (for the role played by ocean currents in where cities came to be located, cf. Delanda 2000). All of these mediums, in their sheer materiality, play a role in what can feasibly be related to what in space, and in the various temporalities characteristic of different cultures. Insofar as that which affords and constrains relations is a form of power, we should expand our understanding of power to include not only embodied and discursive practices, but also a-signifying differences contributed by features of transportation and communication technology as well as geography. Networks are composed of both technologies and natural entities.

The second form the materiality of media takes is that of forms of coding and inscription in their non-discursive dimension. As thinkers such as Havlock, Ong, and the ethnographer Vernant have shown us, the materiality of mediums makes a tremendous difference in what is thinkable; not by virtue of what they signify, but by virtue of what they *are*. It's difficult to imagine higher mathematics without Arabic numerals because of the ways in which Roman numerals constrain calculation. This isn't because Arabic and Roman numerals discursively *signify* different things—they don't—but because of what they are. Similarly, as Vernant notes, it's difficult to imagine enduring and universal laws without the intervention of *writing*, because inscription *itself* lends a durability to what it expresses that isn't found in speech, while also separating the expressed from the author (Derrida 313). In a similar vein, Benedict Anderson combines both forms of materiality, noting that nationalistic identities wouldn't have been possible without writing and the printing press, insofar as these media allowed geographically separated people to form shared identities or identifications, where otherwise geographical isolation would have led to distinct cultures (Anderson 2006).

I can only briefly state the third thesis without the commentary it deserves due to constraints of space, but it is a point that should always be borne in mind.

THESIS 3: All relations require energy to be produced and produce waste.

Insofar as relations don't come for free but must be *forged* and *maintained*, they require *work*. Insofar as they require work, they require *en-*

ergy; for no work takes place without energy. Energy takes the form of both calories required to sustain and power organic bodies—whether human or animal, for both belong to social assemblages—as well as all those forms of energy derived from the sun, whether in the form of solar power, geothermal power, organic matter such as wood, and fossil fuels. And, of course, the metabolism of energy inevitably produces waste.

I will thus conclude with two remarks. First, it is stunning that the humanities and social sciences barely have concepts of work and energy. We find them here and there as in the case of Marx's own thought—not so much that of his neo-Marxist heirs—as well as among philosophers of Will such as Schopenhauer and Nietzsche. But by and large it's as if we approach the world as if it were composed solely of the discursive and things. In this way, we miss huge swaths of power relations, for people do not tolerate oppressive social relations simply because they have mistaken beliefs, but also because they are dependent on certain sources of energy in the form of calories and fuels to live and function at all. We are as trapped by our dependence on energy as we are by our beliefs. Moreover, a failure to recognize the requirements of work and energy makes it difficult to see phenomena such as fatigue as genuine political issues. Second, it is with respect to this third thesis that the question of societies and cultures opens to questions of ecology and climate change. It is materialist network theory that provides us with the resources to begin thinking these issues. When I write at my computer and network on the highways of the internet, I am not simply trafficking in signs, but am also burning fossil fuels.

WORKS CITED

Althusser, Louis. "Ideology and Ideological State Apparatus (Notes Towards an Investigation)." *Lenin and Philosophy and Other Essays*, translated by Ben Brewster, Monthly Review Press, 2001, pp. 85—132.

Anderson, Benedict. *Imagined Communities.* Verso, 2006.

Braudel, Fernand. *The Structure of Everyday Life: Civilization & Capitalism: Volume I*, Harper & Row, 1981.

Foucault, Michel. *The Order of Things: An Archaeology of the Human Sciences.* Vintage Books, 1994.

Delanda, Manuel. *A Thousand Years of Nonlinear History.* MIT Press, 2000.

Deleuze, Gilles, and Guattari, Félix. *A Thousand Plateaus: Capitalism and Schizophrenia*, translated by Brian Massumi, U of Minnesota P, 1987.

Derrida, Jacques. "Signature Event Context." *Margins of Philosophy*, translated by Alan Bass, Chicago UP, 1982.

Gleick, James. *The Information: A History, A Theory, A Flood*. Vintage Books, 2012.

Havlock, Eric. *Preface to Plato*, Harvard UP, 1982.

Heidegger, Martin. *Being and Time*, translated by John Macquarrie and Edward Robinson, Harper Collins, 1962.

Latour, Bruno (2007), "Can We Get Our Materialism Back, Please?," *Isis*, vol. 98, pp. 138—142.

Lucretius. *The Way Things Are: The De Rerum Natura of Titus Lucretius Carus*, translated by Rolfe Humphries, Indiana UP, 1969.

"network, n." *OED Online*, Oxford UP, Sept. 2003.

Luhmann, Niklas. *Social Systems*. Translated by John Bednarz, Jr. and Dirk Baecker, Stanford UP, 1995.

McLuhan, Marshall. *Understanding Media: The Extensions of Man*. The MIT Press, 1994.

McLuhan, Marshall and Eric McLuhan. *Laws of Media: The New Science*. U of Toronto P, 1988.

Meillassoux, Quentin. *After Finitude: An Essay on the Necessity of Contingency*. Translated by Ray Brassier, Continuum, 2008.

Ong, Walter J. *Orality & Literacy: The Technologizing of the World*. Routledge, 2012.

Ricoeur, Paul. *Freud and Philosophy: An Essay on Interpretation*. Translated by Denis Savage, Yale UP, 1977.

Vernant, Jean-Pierre. *The Origins of Greek Thought*. Cornell UP, 1984.

21 Provocation: Networked Research, Networked Ethics

Neil Baird and Bradley Dilger

Scholarship in writing studies is more often turning to writing with data—empirical research—at the same time that a networked humanities is emerging. This complicates the ethical questions of empirical researchers who study writing through work with human subjects. When networks shift our understanding of agency, adding the inclusion of non-human elements and shades of grey from other sources, so too changes the very idea of participation at the heart of many ethical decisions. As Christina Haas wrote:

> When agency—and by extension consent and risks/benefit assessments—are understood in this more contingent, distributed, and distanced way, participation becomes much more complex. Rather than a fixed and readily identifiable quality, participation becomes a distributed accomplishment, one that exists along at least two intersecting dimensions: one from obligatory to discretionary, and one from immediate to extended.

Participation, informed consent, confidentiality, risks and benefits, and publication all change, potentially quite radically, when networks shape our inquiries. Meaning that of necessity research questions that invoke these and other seemingly discrete constructs—"What are the classroom practices, curricular elements, habits of mind, and cultural forces which influence writing transfer for students writing in the major?"—can become quite broad. Take the "classroom practices" of this research question, the principal focus of the research project we have conducted since late 2010: articulation agreements, the Common Core, and other forces have relevant classroom impacts. Are the people involved in state education our participants? Should they get a voice at the table as we conduct member checks with the students and faculty we've interviewed? When we explain teachers' decision-making, how do we acknowledge and include the individuals and organizations whose actions are interconnected through the networks we call "classrooms"? As the AOIR ethics working committee points out, even "human subject" inadequately characterizes participation, despite its role as the litmus test for oversight from the IRB. Given some of the experiences we've had in the study we mention above, in this short essay, we'll offer some depth about confidentiality, and follow with more on informed consent—the latter topic especially relevant given changes the federal government has proposed to the Common Rule which regulates human subject research.

To illustrate how networks impact confidentiality, we turn to Spinuzzi's four characteristics of networks as a heuristic, acknowledging there are other ways of theorizing networks. Spinuzzi argues networks are black-boxed and multiply-linked. That is, because networks hide their complexity, they are often difficult to see, and because networks are made up of innumerable parts, such linkages are nearly impossible to sever. For us, the selection of pseudonyms early in the study did not acknowledge the complexity of networks and failed to sever the multiple linkages protecting confidentiality. Shortly after our study began, participants Blake, Katrina, Scarlet, and Sophia began to show up on our Facebook feeds through the network of students and faculty we had created. We even received friend requests from Scarlet and Sophia that were difficult to decline because the student organizations and university organizations who extended the friend requests were important nodes in our own networks, both professional and personal, outside the context of our study. For example, we encountered Scarlet within her workplace network when she did some promotional work for the writing center. Through multiple extended interviews, we learned of the many networks Mitchell participated in, but we encountered him also within a network completely unrelated to school, a local cycling event for charity. Once we began presenting and publishing, would it be possible for someone to trace these networks to discover who our participants were?

The consequences for confidentiality of black-boxed, multiply linked networks are many, but two other characteristics help us understand how. Spinuzzi uses the metaphor of a fishing net to highlight the ways networks are transformative: "When you scoop a fish up in the net, the weight becomes *translated*: transformed, distributed, and redirected" (48). Our relationship with Mitchell transformed as we were "scooped" into this extra-curricular cycling network. In this network, we were no longer researcher and participant. Both of us were cyclists competing against each other. Since faculty and students interested in our work participated in this extra-curricular network, it was difficult to maintain confidentiality not only in the moment, but afterwards, as participants reflected on the event. In addition, what would be the consequences for confidentiality if Mitchell began to participate in our weekend breakfast ride group? Spinuzzi also notes networks are heterogeneous, meaning that networks "are assemblages of human and nonhumans." We had IRB approval to study one nonhuman aspect of Mitchell's networks: writing. However, in this extra-curricular network, the multi-media projects he designed around his cycling could potentially help us understand previously collected data. To what extent are we allowed to use such data in this way?

Turning to informed consent, we note several issues figure prominently in the Notice of Proposed Rulemaking (NPRM) published by the Office of Human Research Protections. (Respectively, these are the official statement of proposed changes to the Common Rule, and the federal agency directly responsible for oversight of research.) The many additions and changes made that address the increasing role of biospecimens speak to the very thorny question of agency for some medical research—a form of the extended distributed participation Haas references. Are cell cultures that live outside of a human body an extension of that body, a mini-body to be treated in the same way? Indeed, are these cells even "alive?" Much of the public commentary on the NPRM speaks to bioethical questions like these. But the NPRM also seems to make informed consent "more meaningful and transparent," noting that informed consent materials are often difficult to understand. There would be specific allowances for alternative forms of consent like videos or orally obtained consent, much like those David Wright proposed in "Redesigning Informed Consent Tools for Specific Research." The OHRP would offer templates, and a repository of approved consent forms would facilitate public review of research.

While many of these changes are sensible, they do not demonstrate a shift to thinking about participation as distributed. In fact, as the Conference on College Composition and Communication public comment on the NPRM pointed out, they avoid considering the issue by bracketing many types of research as "excluded"—that is, not research as defined by the Common Rule. Unfortunately, that includes a substantial amount of writing research, because of its qualitative approach and/or supposedly low risk. Specific consent exemptions for public health surveillance, data collection for national security purposes, and other purposes also simply waive aside a large amount of the distribution of agency, taking a hierarchical, not networked, approach to informed consent that simply exempts research from consideration. Reading the NPRM via Spinuzzi's four characteristics, the pushback against networks appears even stronger: reducing black-boxing by making archives of consent materials; denying the multiple links networks bring by maintaining a fixed, person-level approach to participation, and in some of the claims made about administering informed consent for multi-site research; acting against heterogeneity by offering templates and prescribing content and genre more directly; and denying the transformative nature of the network of research by suggesting research protections can successfully mitigate risk (also, we might add, by consistently portraying psychological risks as less serious than those typically associated with biomedical research).

As Haas points out, Jan Nespor and Susan Groenke have suggested networked visions of agency should impact research design. We might imagine participant recruitment and engagement as a process of network tracing, rather than the identification of a population based on easily defined demographic characteristics, including the work needed for making that tracing visible, then sketching possible actions forward from it. This should certainly include confidentiality and informed consent, so we offer some suggestions here in that regard.

We suggest that researchers should imagine confidentiality not as an either/or process, or assume, as many IRBs do, that it is both the default position of research and a panacea for risk mitigation. Indeed, as researchers trace networks of participation, confidentiality should be reconsidered throughout the research process, and both researcher and participants should jointly decide how to move forward when networks complicate confidentiality and identification.

Similarly, we might also assume that data will be diffused over time, rather than being protected from public eyes, and we might be better served to include thinking about this diffusion in participation design, rather than attempt to legislate it out of existence. Scholars influenced by action research have embraced the notion that researcher-participant relationships can be reciprocal without compromising the integrity of methods or results. Feminist writing research methods also approach data (not to mention confidentiality and identification) with this more nuanced and network-compatible approach.

Finally, we can more accurately represent our understanding of agency to include immediate and extended actors, as Haas puts it, in critical moments such as the development and presentation of informed consent. Indeed, we might explain the complexity of the commonplace "withdrawing from this study at any time," given that leaving the study is better understood along a continuum: perhaps the direct participation of one person is no longer possible, but the networks in which they move can remain engaged? Or the reverse?

None of this will be easy. More traditional (by which we mean experimental, quantitative, and clinical) research designs and methods that isolate and insulate researchers and participants retain a special place in scholarly circles and in the minds of policymakers. We risk being ignored if we reframe participation in a manner that creates too much grey area for those who value these traditional research frameworks. For us, this suggests action is needed from writing researchers who study networks, who believe the humanities should be networked, and who use empirical methods to study writing. We need to expand our engagement with policymakers and funding agencies, at both the local and national levels, explaining why thinking in terms of networks is essential for the humanities and beyond. Modeling distributed, network-aware research designs is the first step. The second is direct engagement with the ethical considerations we've only begun to sketch out here, not only in our journals, but in venues that expand our networks of research. Finally, though this is the most difficult, we need to address not only regulations like the Common Rule, but the underlying legislation which shapes those rules, our research, and our networks.

Works Cited

Conference on College Composition and Communication. "Public Comment on Proposed Rule: Federal Policy for the Protection of Human Subjects." 6 Jan. 2016, regulations.gov/document?D=HHS-OPHS-2015–0008–1889.

Department of Health and Human Services Office for Human Research Protections. "Notice of Proposed Rulemaking: Federal Policy for the Protection of Human Subjects." 8 Sept. 2015, regulations.gov/document?D=HHS-OPHS-2015–0008–0001.

Haas, Christina. "Ethical Dilemmas and Methodological Decision-Making in Writing Research." Dartmouth Seminar for Composition Research, 4 August 2011, Dartmouth College, Hanover.

Markham, Annette, and Elizabeth Buchanan. "Ethical Decision-Making and Internet Research: Recommendations from the AOIR Ethics Working Committee (Version 2.0)." December 2012, aoir.org/reports/ethics2.pdf.

Nespor, Jan, and Susan L. Groenke. "Ethics, Problem Framing, and Training in Qualitative Inquiry." *Qualitative Inquiry*, vol. 15, no. 6, June 2009, pp. 996–1012.

Spinuzzi, Clay. *Network: Theorizing Knowledge Work in Telecommunications.* Cambridge UP, 2008.

Wright, David. "Redesigning Informed Consent Tools for Specific Research." *Technical Communication Quarterly*, vol. 21, no. 1, 2012, pp. 145–67.

22 Afterword: Notes Toward a Liberated Network Language

Byron Hawk

In "Post-Digital Humanities" and elsewhere, David Berry questions the distinction between the analog and the digital, which is becoming so blurred that it will be difficult to find any cultural artifacts or processes that are untouched by the digital. This poses significant questions about the division between the humanities and the digital humanities, but opens a space for thinking about the networked humanities as a distinct and significant model that combines digital and material networks to provide a richer approach. In their Appendix to *The Exploit: A Theory of Networks*, "Notes for a Liberated Computer Language," Alexander Galloway and Eugene Thacker use a standard structure and categories for computer languages—data types, operators, control structures, and functions—to articulate a set of potential tactics for engaging and perhaps exploiting networks, which translates, without too much casuistic stretching, to the key elements of non-computer networks—objects, relations, situations, and actions:

- *Data Types*—things like text, image, video, or sound files that can be brought into a program and operated on and altered by the program translate to objects and their affordances.
- *Operators*—elements in a program that are used to establish relations such as AND, OR, >, <, or = correspond to types of relations between objects.
- *Control Structures*—blocks of code that dictate the flow of ac-

tions such as if A then B else C function as conditions of possibility that establish courses of action.

- *Functions*—sets of instructions that perform specific tasks in a program translate to particular actions enacted by particular circumstances that then feedback into the system.

This model of rhetorical situatedness derived from their computer language is ultimately a set of agencies, no isolated agents or autonomous actors, which is precisely how I read Bruno Latour's sense of networks. Networks for Latour are a series of actions and mediations that feedback and co-produce one another as the networks emerge. Much more than a set of static nodes and lines, networks are the emergent properties of movements and relations. If networks are emergent rather than static, then exploits—opportunities in the system to function otherwise—are always opening and closing. Galloway and Thacker's proposed computer language "liberates" it from computer networks and asks us to imagine how it might function in relation to material networks and how we might use them to hack networks of all kinds.

Computer programs can identify types of data and set the possible values for that type; the operations that can be done on those values; the meaning of the data; and how the values can be stored. Once brought into a program or network, a data type is ascribed these values, meanings, and affordances as a function of the network, even before the program is executed. Part of what control societies do is entangle objects and bodies in these kinds of networks. Galloway and Thacker write,

> If the body in disciplinary societies is predominantly anatomical and physiological (as in Foucault's analysis of the microphysics of the prison or hospital), in control societies, bodies are consonant with more distributed modes of individuation that enable their infinite variation (informatic records, databases, consumer profiles, genetic codes, identity chopping, workplace biometrics). (41)

The body, or object, cannot be isolated from these networks and their constant variation, distribution, and circulation.

In "The Berlin Key or How to do Words with Things," Latour gives a summation of his take on networks and an example of how ascribing meaning, values, and affordances plays out with the Berlin Key as such an object—a key particular to Berlin and its suburbs used to lock and unlock the outer doors on apartment buildings. The Berlin Key, for Latour, gives us an example of a thing co-producing and co-produced by such a network. Evoking Heidegger's thing that gathers Latour writes, "things do not exist without being full of people, and the more modern and complicated they are, the more people swarm through them" (10). Latour makes clear that the human-thing relation is not a dialectic of subject and object but a material-semiotic network, a movement of "circulations, sequences, transfers, translations, displacements, crystallizations, . . . many motions" (10). He imagines an archaeologist, digging up the key and attempting to sort out its use. Archaeologists are the closest to studying what modern philosophy calls an object—something isolated in the ground, detached from its original cultural, material, and social context of use. But as soon as the key is uncovered, it begins its gathering again. Other humanities fields never see objects in isolation this way. They automatically see human "plans, actions, behaviors, arrangements, habits, heuristics, abilities, collections of practices," some appearing more durable, some more transient (10). The archaeologist, however, is cut off from the (social) network that produced the object, but immediately begins "retro-engineering" its "chain of associations"— it again begins circulating from the hands of archaeologists through the classroom and the scientific literature (11). Once out of the ground, the object automatically becomes a thing again—gathering networks. The object becomes not only a thing but also a topology, one that exercises control not as an agent but as a series of agencies in a chain of emergent associations.

Tracing these associations is a matter of following transformations through operators and relations. Operators are elements in a program that are usually used to establish conditions, typically through relations such as AND, OR, >, <, or =. For example, IF ORDER_DATE > "12/31/2011" AND ORDER_DATE < "01/01/2013" THEN CONTINUE ELSE STOP. The operators in this example are: ">" (greater than), "AND," and "<" (less than). Some operators can have definitions for more than one kind of data, or can be converted or coerced to work with alternate types of data. This fluid situation between operators, relations, and data means that the generic node-edge model of a network breaks down. Nodes are slowed down edges; edges sped up nodes. Or as Galloway and Thacker put it,

> Nodes will be constructed as a by-product of the creation of
> edges, and edges will be a precondition for the inclusion of nodes
> in the network. . . . [N]odes are nothing but dilated edges, while

> edges are constricted, hyperkinetic nodes. Nodes may be com-
> posed of edges, while edges may be extended nodes. (99)

From this perspective, materiality is relations all the way down. But this doesn't negate the affordances of data types or objects. As products of edges or relations, nodes and their affordances co-produce new relations, and they do so precisely as a function of time: networks ultimately are "sets of *relations* existing in *time*" (33; emphasis added); networks are "only networks when they are 'live,' when they are enacted, embodied, or rendered *operational*" (62; emphasis added). And we see from Galloway and Thacker's "Liberated Computer Language" that operators are relations that "transform, decrease, assign, distinguish, combine, attach, increase" (161–62). Galloway and Thacker see isolated objects as increasingly difficult to locate because these operations produce the objects and continuously work on them.

Similarly, Latour sees isolated objects as problematic. For Latour, "there are only trajectories and dispatches, paths and trails. But we know that the elements, whatever they may be, are substituted and transformed. Association—AND—substitution—OR" (11). Provisional forms of humans and essences of matter emerge from these chains of association—these operators that establish the potential for relations. The essence of a jug, for Heidegger, is that it holds and pours water or wine. It has a capacity and potential for use, movement, and actions, and its essence is in this operation, this becoming or implosion of being and time. In performing these actions, holding and giving, the jug gathers humans who drink the wine, the language and symbolic systems that accompany the rituals, the rain and the sun from the sky that nourish the grapes of the earth—all of which perform an emergent set of relations. The Berlin Key itself has similar attributes or capacities that gather associations. The key has two identical bits on each end with identical symmetrical teeth. Each bit also has a groove in its opposite side, but always on the right side if it were facing outward. The specifications of the key bear a particular relation to the keyhole, which is also a-typical, with two slots that together form a 180-degree angle. On the street side of the door, the horizontal slot is to the right, with the groove on the outside of the slots. On the courtyard side of the door, the horizontal slot is to the left with the grooves on the inside. These values of the key and lock establish greater than, less than, and equal to sets of relation—if the key is greater than, less than, or equal to the keyhole, then its possible relations and effects are altered. Once the Berlin Key is unearthed, it becomes a thing, a node-edge that is circulating again, included in networks and becoming operational. And it is these operations that establish particular control structures.

If networks are the movements and relations of operations, then control structures make those relations work and operate in particular ways. In computer languages, control structures are blocks of code or containers that dictate the flow of actions through a series of function calls, instructions, and statements. The most simple is, if A then B else C. B and C will be included or excluded based on the condition of A. The if-then control structure is the most common, but there are many other types such as the jump or unconditional branch, the conditional branch, the loop—which is essentially a conditional branch, subroutines, coroutines, continuations, and the conditional halt—and lower-level flow controls such as interrupts and signals. For Galloway and Thacker, protocols are most generally the rules and standards of control structures that govern relationships within networks—"the horizontal, distributed control apparatus that guides both the technical and political formation of computer networks [and] biological systems" (28). Protocol is both a logic and an apparatus that distributes control through a system or network to "regulate flow, direct netspace, and connect life-forms" (30). DNA computing, for example, produces a network through molecules (nodes) and their sequences (edges) that is both an informational logic and a material apparatus. To solve a computational or informational problem, it produces multiple material networks, only one of which becomes the solution to the problem. The control mechanism is a process of producing multiplicity and selecting this one sub-network. What makes this protocological is that (a) there is no single problem-solving agent that determines the solution, and instead it "arises from a context of distributed regulation, . . . from an array of total possibilities" (53); and (b) the protocol produces an excess of potentialities or lines of flight. What we get from Latour's example is how this plays out in material networks even in what we'd consider to be disciplinary societies.

The imagined archaeologist, trying to discern the key's function, tries one end of the key in the door vertically, turns it 270 degrees counter-clockwise, and the door opens. But once it is inserted and the door is unlocked, the key can't be removed back out the front like typical keys. The only way to get the key back out is to lock the door again and remain on the outside. In Latour's exposition, the archaeologist mentally walks through the affordances of the key in relation to the door and the possible human uses for a lock and key in this particular situation, as a control structure, seeking to find the action or gesture that would make the control structure functional. The building, the courtyard, the wall, and the door make up a staggered series of boxes or blocks of code to control the flow of bodies and their values or properties as inside or outside the perimeter. But without being able to remove the key, the control structure isn't functional. Because the archaeologist is adept at understanding objects, she realizes that turning the key another 270 degrees to the opposite horizontal position allows her to slip the key through the other side of the door. But on the other side, she is still unable to remove the key. Once inside, she must turn the key another 270 degrees to lock the door, finally being able to remove it on the other side. But this isn't the end of the key's story. At ten o'clock the next morning, she tries the procedure again to find that she can only turn the key five degrees. The door remained permanently open without her being able to lock it. Only after ten o'clock at night would the procedure work again. Inhabitants of the apartment building, then, are forced to bolt the door at night but are unable to bolt the door during the day. But the archaeologist discovers that the *concierge* has a passkey—with no grooves, thinner profile, and one bit—which allows him to bolt and unbolt the door as he pleases. The keys and their affordances, along with sets of relations and operators, produce a material control structure for the flow of bodily action, prior to the advent of digital locks and codes that can now perform the same functions today ("The Berlin Key" 13–17).

Functions are sets of instructions that perform specific tasks in a program. A function is often coded so that it can be started (or called) several times and/or from several places during one execution of the program, and then branch back (*return*) to the next instruction in the main program after the *call* once the function's task is done. In different programming languages a function may be called a subroutine, procedure, method, or a subprogram. Distinctions and differences between functions and objects depend on the programming paradigm. Object-oriented programming, for example, is based on objects and methods (which are functions in or attached to the objects or object types, the verbs of an object that allow it to do things). Values, such as numerical weights, can also be passed to functions. And programs can contain functions within functions within functions. Galloway and Thacker's terms for functions in their "Liberated Computer Language" betray exploits in these structures: "backdoor, bitflip, crash, degrade, destroy, drift, fail, frees, invert,

jam, mutate, obfuscate, overclock, rebuild, et al.," (163–66). Just because
the protocol is also material, doesn't mean it is deterministic. The multiple solutions and their many paths of protocological control mean that
exploits are built into the system. Galloway and Thacker define these
exploits as an abstract machine:

- *Vector*: The exploit requires an organic and inorganic medium in
  which there exists some form of action or motion.
- *Flaw*: The exploit requires a set of vulnerabilities in a network that allow the vector to be logically accessible. These vulnerabilities are also
  the network's conditions for realization, it's becoming-unhuman.
- *Transgression*: The exploit creates a shift in the ontology of the
  network, in which the "failure" of the network is in fact a change
  in its topology (for example, from centralized to decentralized). (97)

Every protocol, then, is the condition for its own counter-protocol—regardless of how the network is programmed.

Latour, still playfully as most of this essay is written, imagines that
the archaeologist is impressed by the ways that the inventor of the key
as a *vector* "obliged all the inhabitants of Berlin to conform to a strict
collective discipline" and is preparing to write an article "in the style
of Foucault" (17). But then one of her Berliner colleagues exposes a
flaw, showing her a Berlin key from which he'd filed away the grooves,
making it a *concierge*'s passkey and providing him broader access to the
apartment building. Latour asks, "If we call the 'script' of the device its
'program of action,' what is the programme of action of such a key?" (17).
Translating the material capacities of the system into words, it becomes
a request rather than a demand: "Please bolt the door behind you during
the night and never during the day" (17). But the request is not simply
through the means of language and signs, or social relations established
through the *concierge* and the stream of legitimate and not so legit pass-
ers—everything from spouses and delivery persons to thieves. It is also
operating in material networks and a series of actions in a dance of control and access, mediated, in larger part, by the key. Such mediation
means something very particular to Latour. In many of his works he goes
to great pains to make the distinction between intermediaries and mediators. Intermediaries do nothing but "carry, transport, shift, incarnate,
express, reify, objectify, reflect" (18). The key, then, would only transmit
the meaning of the request, and provide a mirror of its social relations.
But mediators, of course, make the actions of these requests and relations

possible. "[T]he meaning is no longer simply transported by the medium but in part constituted, moved, recreated, modified, in short, expressed *and* betrayed" (19; emphasis added). The operations of the keys and the asymmetrical slots of the keyholes co-produce the actions of the network as a *transgression*. And in the process, the keys themselves can be transformed, filed down, lost, broken, passed around—betrayed through exploits in the system itself.

We could trace Latour's network back to an initial "programmer," whom Latour calls the "Prussian Locksmith," as the initial human designer or inspired inventor.[1] This humanist approach belies the fact that the programmer or designer, like the hacker or Berliner who files down a key, is simply an operative in the network, responding to and hacking its affordances and control structures to invent from its exploits, and being co-produced through these actions and mediations. The imagined Prussian Locksmith would have only been brought in after a whole set of exigencies and networks co-produced this possibility. Building owners likely relied on printed notices or the requests of concierges at first, but the doors remained open during the night or locked during the day. So, they had to extend the networks, not only to the Prussian Locksmith but also to mathematics, design drafts, architects, machinists, and the properties of various metals. The social, for Latour, cannot be constructed only from social relations: it needs material affordances. And meaning does not simply precede or antecede an intermediary as its means. The key, as mediator, becomes ends and means at once, that for all intents and purposes is an agency awash in agencies, a network built of flows and movements, actions and mediations. Like protocol, the key "serve[s] to provide that condition of possibility, and . . . the means of facilitating that condition" (Galloway and Thacker 61). The inclusion of the programmer and the key-lock system turns words and customs into a program of action through material networks.

But as the exploit makes clear, the fact that the program is now enacted through steel doesn't mean it produces a determination. Material mediation, for Latour, not only signals the network's alterity but also its fragility—a weakness that strong technological determinists often neglect to grant. It only takes an enterprising Berliner with a metal file to re-mediate (if I can use that term differently) the network, to materially change the key and continue its series of actions and mediations. Galloway and Thacker write:

> "User" is a term for any passive or "directed" experience with technology while "programmer" means any active or "undirected" experience with technology. Taken in this sense, anyone can be a programmer if he or she so chooses. If a person installs a game console modchip, he is programming his console. If she grows her own food, she is programming her biological intake. (143)

From this position, the exploit becomes a primary rhetorical tactic in control societies, even though the programmer is always a function of the system. In "For Public Distribution," Dale Smith and Jim Brown argue that the interplay of centralization and decentralization doesn't mean the systems are deterministic or open and democratic. On the one hand, Internet protocols make every node in the network both a sender and receiver capable of redistributing content at any time. This upsets centralization and hierarchical access because information is decentralized and can go viral. On the other hand, protocols can allow this information to be archived and contained by militaries, governments, and corporations. Mediating organizations like Google and even Wikileaks put additional controlling protocols in their systems on top of the grounding protocols of the Internet. Facebook and Google, for example, decentralize publication but centralize data collection. Smith and Brown note the complicated risks of rhetorically engaging these entanglements: Julian Assange is confined in the Ecuadorian embassy in London; Chelsea Manning faces prison for her participation in Wikileaks; and Edward Snowden is in exile in Russia. But exploiting protocols can feed back into the workings of civil societies and expose other exploits or co-produce events such as the Arab Spring. *The Exploit* shows the affinity between technical and biological networks and suggests rhetorical resources that the Networked Humanities could engage and deploy.

NOTE

1. Thanks to Jim Brown for suggesting that we look at the Appendix to *The Exploit* for our group presentation on the figure of "the programmer" at the University of South Carolina's Rhetorical Theory Conference in the Fall of 2013.

WORKS CITED

Berry, David. "Post-Digital Humanities: Computation and Cultural Critique in the Arts and Humanities." *EDUCAUSE Review*, May/June 2014, pp. 22–26.

Galloway, Alexander, and Eugene Thacker. *The Exploit: A Theory of Networks*. U of Minnesota P, 2007.

Latour, Bruno. "The Berlin Key or How to do Words with Things." *Matter, Materiality, and Modern Culture*, edited by Paul Graves-Brown, Routledge, 2000, pp. 10–21.

Smith, Dale, and James J. Brown. "For Public Distribution." *Rhetoric, Writing, and Circulation*, edited by Collin Brooke and Laurie Gries, Utah State UP, forthcoming.

Contributors

Neil P. Baird is an associate professor at Bowling Green State University. His essays have appeared in *WPA: Writing Program Administration*, *College Composition and Communication*, and *Enculturation*.

Jennifer L. Bay is an associate professor of English at Purdue University, where she teaches courses in rhetorical theory, professional writing, feminist rhetorics, and community engagement. Her work has appeared in journals such as *Technical Communication Quarterly*, *College English*, *JAC*, *Programmatic Perspectives*, as well as in edited collections.

Casey Boyle is an assistant professor at the University of Texas-Austin, where he directs the Digital Writing & Research Lab. His essays have appeared in *College English*, *Computers and Composition*, and *Rhetoric Society Quarterly*, and he is the author of *Rhetoric as a Posthuman Practice* (Ohio State University Press).

James J. Brown, Jr. is an associate professor at Rutgers University-Camden, where he is also Director of the Digital Studies Center. His book, *Ethical Programs: Hospitality and the Rhetorics of Software*, examines the rhetorical and ethical underpinnings of networked software.

Levi R. Bryant is a professor of Philosophy at Collin College in Frisco, Texas. He is the author of *Difference and Givenness: Deleuze's Transcendental Empiricism and the Ontology of Immanence*, *The Democracy of Objects*, and *Onto-Cartography: An Ontology of Machines and Media*. He has written widely on French theory, speculative realism, new materialism, and object-oriented ontology.

Naomi Clark is an assistant professor at Loras College where she directs the Writing Center and teaches courses in rhetoric and public writing. Her essay in this collection was written with the support of a dissertation fellowship from the American Association of University Women.

Bradley Dilger is an associate professor at Purdue University, where he serves as the writing program administrator. His essays have appeared in *College Composition and Communication*, *Writing Program Administration*, and several edited collections.

Kristie S. Fleckenstein is a professor of English and Director of the Graduate Program in Rhetoric and Composition at Florida State University. Her articles and book chapters have appeared in a variety of venues; in addition, she is the recipient of the 2005 CCCC Outstanding Book of the Year Award for *Embodied Literacies: Imageword and a Poetics of Teaching* (NCTE/SIUP, 2003), and the 2009 W. Ross Winterowd Award for Best Book in Composition Theory for *Vision, Rhetoric, and Social Action in the Composition Classroom* (SIUP, 2009).

Paul Gestwicki is a professor of computer science at Ball State University, where he teaches courses on advanced programming, human-computer interaction, and game design and development. He mentors multidisciplinary undergraduate teams in creating original, educational video games, working in collaboration with schools, museums, and libraries.

Tarez Samra Graban is associate professor of English at Florida State University, where she also leads an interdisciplinary reading group in the digital humanities. Her historical essays have appeared in *Rhetorica, College English*, and *African Journal of Rhetoric*.

Jeff Grabill serves Michigan State University as the Associate Provost for Teaching, Learning, and Technology, where he remains a Professor of Rhetoric and Professional Writing. Grabill is responsible for facilitating innovation in learning via his role as Director of the Hub for Innovation in Learning and Technology and educator professional development through the MSU's Academic Advancement Network.

Laurie Gries is an assistant professor at the University of Colorado-Boulder, where she has a joint appointment in the Program for Writing and Rhetoric and Communication. Her essays have appeared in several journals, and she received the 2016 CCCC Advancement of Knowledge and the 2016 CCCC Research Impact Award for her monograph *Still Life with Rhetoric*.

Byron Hawk is an associate professor of English at the University of South Carolina. He is the author of *Resounding the Rhetorical: Composition as a Quasi-Object* (University of Pittsburgh Press, 2018) and *A Counter-History of Composition: Toward Methodologies of Complexity* (University of Pittsburgh Press, 2007), which won *JAC*'s W. Ross Winterowd Award in 2007 and received honorable mention for MLA's Mina Shaughnessy Prize in 2008.

John Jones is an associate professor at The Ohio State University where he serves as the Director of Digital Media Studies in the Department of English. His essays have appeared in *Rhetoric Review, Written Communication*, and the *Journal of Business and Technical Communication*.

Nate Kreuter is an associate professor of rhetoric at Western Carolina University where he serves as the writing program administrator.

Devoney Looser is Foundation Professor of English at Arizona State University and the author or editor of seven books, including *The Making of Jane Austen* (Johns Hopkins UP, 2017), a *Publishers Weekly* Best Summer Book (Non-fiction). A 2018 Guggenheim Fellow in English Literature, Looser has published essays in *The New York Times*, the *TLS, The Atlantic*, and *Entertainment Weekly*.

Rudy McDaniel is a professor at the University of Central Florida where he serves as director of the School of Visual Arts and Design. He is co-author of *The Rhetorical Nature of XML* and has forthcoming books on digital ethics and digital badges.

Brian McNely is an associate professor of Writing, Rhetoric, & Digital Studies at the University of Kentucky. His essays have appeared in the *Journal of Business and Technical Communication, Technical Communication Quarterly, College Composition and Communication, Enculturation, Kairos*, and in several edited collections.

Derek Mueller is an associate professor at Virginia Tech, where he also serves as Director of Composition. His scholarship has appeared in *College Composition and Communication, Kairos, Present Tense,* and *Composition Forum.*

Liza Potts is an associate professor at Michigan State University, where she leads WIDE Research and is the Co-Founder of the Experience Architecture program. Her work has appeared in publications such as *Technical Communication Quarterly, Kairos, Present Tense,* and the ACM digital library; her books have been published by Routledge, Parlor Press, and Enculturation's Intermezzo.

Jeff Pruchnic is an associate professor and Director of Composition in the Department of English at Wayne State University. He is the author of *Rhetoric and Ethics in the Cybernetic Age: The Transhuman Condition* (Routledge 2014) and his writing on the intersections of rhetoric, science, and digital media have appeared in such journals as *JAC, Rhetoric Review,* and *Rhetoric Society Quarterly.*

Jeff Rice is chair and Martha B. Reynolds Professor of Writing, Rhetoric, & Digital Studies at the University of Kentucky. He is the author of several books, including, most recently, *Craft Obsession,* from SIU Press.

Jim Ridolfo is an associate professor at the University of Kentucky, where he serves as the writing program administrator. His work has appeared in *JAC, Enculturation, Kairos, Pedagogy,* and *Rhetoric Review.* He is the recipient of the 2014 Richard Ohmann Award for Outstanding Article in *College English.*

Nathaniel A. Rivers is an associate professor of English at Saint Louis University. His current research addresses topics such as environmentalism, locative media, and accessibility. He co-edited *Thinking with Bruno Latour in Rhetoric and Composition* (SIUP, 2015). His recent work has appeared in journals such as *Rhetoric Society Quarterly, Enculturation,* and *Quarterly Journal of Speech.*

Jillian Sayre is an assistant professor of English at Rutgers University-Camden where she teaches courses in American literature and literary theory. Her recent and forthcoming work includes pieces for *Early American Literature, Americanist Approaches to The Book of Mormon,* and *Inventing Place: Writing Lone Star Rhetorics.*

Lars Söderlund is an associate professor of English at Western Oregon University, where he directs the Professional and Technical Writing Program. He has published in the *Journal of Technical Writing and Communication*, *Pedagogy*, and *IEEE Transactions on Professional Communication*.

Clay Spinuzzi is a professor at the University of Texas at Austin, where he researches how people communicate, coordinate, and collaborate at work. He is the author of four books and several articles.

Kathleen Blake Yancey is Kellogg Hunt Professor and Distinguished Research Professor at Florida State University. She has authored or edited 14 scholarly books, and she received the 2018 Exemplar Award from the Conference on College Composition and Communication.

Index

www.ingramcontent.com/pod-product-compliance
Lightning Source LLC
Chambersburg PA
CBHW031124270326
41929CB00011B/1482